FOURTH EDITION

CONTEMPORARY MORAL PROBLEMS

War, Terrorism, Torture and Assassination

JAMES E. WHITE
St. Cloud State University

WADSWORTH
CENGAGE Learning

Australia • Brazil • Japan • Korea • Mexico • Singapore • Spain • United Kingdom • United States

WADSWORTH
CENGAGE Learning™

Contemporary Moral Problems:
War, Terrorism, Torture and Assassination
Fourth Edition
James E. White

Publisher: Clark Baxter

Senior Sponsoring Editor: Joann Kozyrev

Development Editor: Ian Lague

Assistant Editor: Nathan Gamache

Editorial Assistant: Michaela Henry

Marketing Manager: Mark T. Haynes

Marketing Coordinator: Josh Hendrick

Marketing Communications Manager:
Laura Localio

Content Project Manager: Alison Eigel Zade

Senior Art Director: Jennifer Wahi

Print Buyer: Linda Hsu

Senior Rights Acquisition Specialist-Text:
Katie Huha

Production Service:
    S4Carlisle Publishing Services

Cover Designer: Kate Scheible

Cover Image: iStockphotoImage #: 501340

Compositor: S4Carlisle Publishing Services

For product information and technology assistance,
contact us at
Cengage Learning Customer & Sales Support,
1-800-354-9706
For permission to use material from this text or product,
submit all requests online at
www.cengage.com/permissions
Further permissions questions can be emailed to
permissionrequest@cengage.com

ISBN-13: 978-1-111-52351-0
ISBN-10: 1-111-52351-7

Wadsworth
20 Channel Center Street
Boston, MA 02210
USA

Cengage Learning is a leading provider of customized learning solutions with office locations around the globe, including Singapore, the United Kingdom, Australia, Mexico, Brazil and Japan. Locate your local office at **international.cengage.com/region**

Cengage Learning products are represented in Canada by Nelson Education, Ltd.

For your course and learning solutions, visit
www.cengage.com

Purchase any of our products at your local college store or at our preferred online store **www.cengagebrain.com**

Printed in the United States of America
1 2 3 4 5 6 7 14 13 12 11 10

CONTENTS

PREFACE

Can war be morally justified? If so, can terrorism be justified too? Is it permissible to torture suspects to prevent a terrorist attack? Is the assassination of military or political leaders allowed in war? What about the targeted killing of suspected insurgents using pilotless drones? This text addresses these important and difficult moral problems.

The fourth edition has seven new readings and a new chapter on assassination. There are five new Problem Cases on current topics such as the ongoing war in Afghanistan and the mission to assassinate Osama bin Laden. The other Problem Cases have been updated as necessary.

The readings are by philosophers (except for the lawyer Alan Dershowitz). The emphasis is on critical reasoning based on theories and moral principles. The chapter on war and terrorism includes discussions of the classical theories of pacifism and just war theory, as well as the current view of war as preemptive or preventative. Thomas Nagel argues that terrorism is wrong, whereas Laurie Calhoun shows how terrorists can use just war theory to justify their attacks. David Luban discusses the effects of the so-called war on terrorism on human rights.

The chapter on torture has readings both defending and attacking the use of torture on suspected terrorists. Alan Dershowitz thinks that torturing a suspect to stop a nuclear attack is morally permitted. Uwe Steinhoff agrees that torture is permitted in the ticking-bomb case, but unlike Dershowitz he does not want to make it legal. David Luban is opposed to the use of torture in the hypothetical ticking-bomb case, and argues for an absolute prohibition of torture.

The chapter on assassination is mainly concerned with the use of assassination or targeted killing as a means of fighting a war or combating terrorists. Whitley Kaufman argues that assassination is generally prohibited under just war theory. Daniel Statman maintains that the targeted killing of military or terrorist leaders is preferable to conventional war. He also defends assassination as retribution.

The choice of readings involved various considerations. To ensure readings of high quality, only previously published articles were used. Contrasting views were found. The readings are intended for college students, but they should be of interest to anyone concerned about moral issues. For students having difficulty, several aids have been provided:

1. *Chapter introductions.* Each chapter introduction is divided into three sections: factual background, the readings, and philosophical issues. An attempt has been

made to provide accurate and up-to-date information, but this has not been easy. The people engaged in terrorism, torture, and assassinations often try to keep their activities secret. Next, there are brief summaries of the readings, showing how they respond to each other, and finally a short discussion of the main philosophical issues.

2. *Reading introductions.* An author biography and a short summary of the author's main points precede each reading.

3. *Study questions.* Two types of study questions follow each reading. First, there are rather detailed and pedestrian review questions that test the student's grasp of the main points in the reading. These are intended for students wanting or needing help in following the text. They can be read either before or after studying the reading, or both. Second, there are more difficult discussion questions that probe deeper into the reading. They are aimed at students who have understood the reading and are ready to discuss it critically.

4. *Problem Cases.* The Problem Cases at the end of each chapter require the student to apply the arguments and theories in the chapter to hard cases, either actual or hypothetical. This case study method, as it is called in law schools and business schools, can produce lively discussion and is a good way to get students to think about the issues. The Problem Cases can also be assigned as short paper topics or used for essay tests.

5. *Suggested Readings.* Instead of going to the library, I have come to rely on the Internet for information, using Google as my main search engine. For factual information, I include a few websites. Nevertheless, the Internet is not yet a substitute for printed books and articles, which still constitute most of the annotated suggestions for further reading.

In revising the book for the fourth edition of this text, I have benefited from the help and support of many people. I had weekly discussions on current affairs with Myron Anderson, George Yoos, Lee Davis, and Jim Lundquist. As always, Elena White provided invaluable support. I am grateful to the following reviewers for their thoughtful advice and criticisms:

Brian Barnes, University of Louisville; Donald L. Batz, Scott Community College; Michael Bollenbaugh, Northwest Christian University; Sarah Conrad, University of North Texas; Darci Doll, Central Michigan University; Kerry Edwards, Red Rocks Community College; Tammie Foltz, Des Moines Area Community College; Jonathan D. Gainor; Harrisburg Area Community College; Heimir Geirsson, Iowa State University; Benjamin Gorman, York College of Pennsylvania; Paul Greenberg, Tulane University School of Continuing Studies; John M. Gulley, Winston-Salem State University; Meredith Gunning, Northern Essex Community College; Jill Hernandez, University of Texas at San Antonio; Ramona Ilea, Pacific University; Shawn Kaplan, Adelphi University; Shin Kim, Central Michigan University; Gene Kleppinger, Eastern Kentucky University; Ernani Magalhaes, West Virginia University; Ron Martin, Lynchburg College; Robert Micallef, Madonna University; Caleb Miller, Messiah College; Shaun Miller, Weber State University; Eugene Mills, Virginia Commonwealth University; Mark T. Nelson, Westmont College; Ronald Novy, University of Central Arkansas; David Phillips, University of Houston; Gaile Pohlhaus, Miami University; George Schedler, Southern Illinois University; Barbara Solheim, William Rainey Harper College; Mary Lyn Stoll, University of Southern Indiana; Richard Sumpter, Baker University; Todd Thompson, Randolph Community College; Mary Whall, University of Alabama at Birmingham; Matt Zwolinski, University of San Diego.

C H A P T E R   O N E

War and Terrorism

INTRODUCTION

Factual Background

The history of humans is a sad chronicle of war and terrorism. Almost every year there has been a war or an act of terrorism somewhere in the world. Thus far there have been no nuclear or biological wars, but the weapons are there ready to be used. India and Pakistan have been fighting over a disputed area of Kashmir for more than fifty years, and continue to do so. Israel has fought several wars, and continues to fight the Palestinians on a daily basis. The Palestinians respond with suicide bombers. A war in Bosnia was generated by ethnic differences. Saddam Hussein invaded Kuwait and the result was the Gulf War. A short list of the major wars in the twentieth century includes World Wars I and II, the Korean War, the Vietnam War, and a bitter struggle in Afghanistan when Russian forces tried to invade. Iran and Iraq fought a bloody war, with Iraq being armed and supported by the United States.

Constant war continues in the twenty-first century. In 2001, U.S. and British forces invaded Afghanistan in order to capture Osama bin Laden and remove the Taliban regime, which had supported the al-Qaeda terrorist organization responsible for the 9/11 attacks. After nine years of fighting, U.S. troops were still looking for bin

Laden, and battling Taliban insurgents who remained in mountain strongholds. In 2003, U.S., British, and other troops invaded and occupied Iraq, claiming that Iraq had weapons of mass destruction and ties to al Qaeda. (In 2009, the United Kingdom ended combat operations and the U.S. began withdrawing its troops, though the conflict was far from over.) In 2006, Israel fought a short war in Lebanon that killed more than a thousand people, damaged Lebanese infrastructure, and displaced more than 900,000 Lebanese.

Terrorist attacks have dramatically increased in the twenty-first century. Suicide bombings, missile strikes, shootings, and other attacks have become frequent occurrences. Sometimes soldiers or police officers are killed, but many times it is civilians who die. In 2004, Israeli missiles killed Sheik Ahmed Yassin, the spiritual leader of the militant group Hamas, which Israel claimed was responsible for terrorist bombings in Israel. In 2004, ten bombs ripped through four commuter trains in Madrid during the morning rush hour, killing nearly 200 and wounding more than 1,400. This was the deadliest terrorist attack on a European target since World War II. On September 11, 2001, nineteen terrorists hijacked four airplanes. They crashed two of the planes into the World Trade Center in New York City, destroying the twin towers. It is estimated that 3,000 people were killed. A third plane hit the Pentagon, killing nearly 200 workers. The fourth plane crashed in rural southwest Pennsylvania after the passengers overpowered the terrorists. A total of 266 people were killed on the four planes. This was the most devastating terrorist attack in U.S. history. Some compared it to the Japanese attack on Pearl Harbor that resulted in war with Japan, a war that ended shortly after Hiroshima and Nagasaki were destroyed with nuclear bombs in August 1945.

The United States produced convincing evidence that Osama bin Laden and his al-Qaeda network of terrorists were responsible for the 9/11 attacks. On September 23, 2001, bin Laden issued a statement urging his followers to remain steadfast on the path of jihad against the infidels—that is, the United States and her allies. In 2010, bin Laden had still not been captured, and he continued to issue videos promoting war against the infidels.

The 9/11 attacks were only the latest and most shocking of a series of terrorist attacks on U.S. citizens and service members. On October 12, 2000, a terrorist bombing killed 17 U.S. sailors aboard the *U.S.S. Cole* as it refueled in Yemen's port of Aden. The United States said that bin Laden was the prime suspect. On August 7, 1998, there were car bombings of U.S. embassies in Nairobi, Kenya, and Dar es Salaam, Tanzania. More than 5,500 people were injured and 224 were killed. Once again the prime suspect was Osama bin Laden. In June 1996, a truck bomb exploded outside the Khobar Towers in Dharan, Saudi Arabia, killing 19 U.S. servicemen and wounding hundreds of other people. Members of a radical Lebanese terrorist group, Hezbollah, were indicted for the attack. On February 26, 1993, a bomb exploded in a parking garage below the World Trade Center, killing 6 people and wounding more than 1,000. Six radical Muslim terrorists were convicted and sentenced to life in prison. On April 19, 1995, a federal building in Oklahoma City was destroyed by a truck bomb. There were 168 deaths. Timothy J. McVeigh was executed for the attack and Terry L. Nichols was sentenced to life in prison. On December 21, 1998, Pam Am flight 103 exploded over Lockerbie, Scotland, killing 270 people onboard. Two Libyan intelligence officers were accused of planting a suitcase containing the bomb. One was convicted in February 2001 and the other was set free.

The Readings

A traditional and important position on war and terrorism is pacifism. Pacifism can take different forms, and Douglas P. Lackey distinguishes between four of them: (1) the view that all killing is wrong; (2) the view that all violence is wrong; (3) the view that personal violence is always wrong, but political violence is sometimes morally right; and (4) the view that personal violence is sometimes morally permissible, but war is always morally wrong. Albert Schweitzer's position is an example of the first type of pacifism; he held that all killing is wrong because all life is sacred. Mohandas Gandhi's pacifism is an example of the second type because he opposed all violence. According to Lackey, a problem with both of these views is that sometimes killing or violence is required to save lives. For example, shouldn't a terrorist airplane hijacker be killed or restrained to prevent the hijacker from crashing the plane and killing all the passengers? The third view that condemns personal violence but allows political violence is attributed to St. Augustine. But this view raises a problem with personal self-defense. Most people would agree that personal violence is justified in defense of one's life, as in the case of the terrorist airplane hijacker. The kind of pacifism that Lackey supports is the fourth view, which condemns all war as morally wrong but allows some personal violence. But this antiwar pacifism has a problem, too. Why can't some wars be justified by appealing to some great moral good, such as political freedom? Certainly the Revolutionary War in America (to use Lackey's own example) could be defended in this way.

After the 9/11 attacks, pacifism did not seem to be an option for most people. Now just war theory dominates discussions of war and terrorism. The theory was originally formulated by medieval Christian theologians called Scholastics, and it has been discussed ever since. The theory distinguishes between two questions about war. First, there is the question about the right to go to war, called *jus ad bellum*, or "right to war": What are the conditions that justify going to war? Second, there is the question about right conduct in war, called *jus in bello*, or "right in war": How should combatants conduct themselves while fighting a war?

Michael W. Brough, John W. Lango, and Harry van der Linden explain the basic principles of traditional just war theory in the second reading. They note that there are disagreements about how the principles are to be understood and applied. They list eight principles: six *jus ad bellum* principles (just cause, legitimate authority, right intention, last resort, reasonable chance of success, and proportionality) and two *jus in bello* principles (discrimination and proportionality). They also note that some just war theorists hold that the conclusion of the war should be guided by a third set of principles, which they call *jus post bellum* principles. One such principle is order, that is, the end of the war should produce a stable post-conflict environment. Another principle concerns punishment for crimes. For example, after World War II, the Nuremberg trials were conducted to try German leaders for war crimes and genocide.

Besides stating the basic principles of just war theory, Brough, Lango, and van der Linden mention some important controversies raised by each principle. Is humanitarian intervention or protecting citizens from human rights violations a just cause for war? Can insurgent or terrorists groups have the legitimate authority to engage in warfare? Can motives such as economic gain or access to resources be accepted as motivations for war? Is the killing of noncombatants allowed by the principle of discrimination? How can the use of nuclear weapons or landmines be justified when they indiscriminately kill innocent civilians?

Pacifism and just war theory developed in the tradition of Christianity. Another important doctrine about war comes from Islam, and is used to justify both war and terrorism: the Islamic doctrine of *jihad*. Although the term *jihad* is often translated as "holy war," this is not exactly what the term means. According to Michael G. Knapp (see the Suggested Readings), the jihad means struggle or striving in the path of God for a noble cause. The classic view of jihad allowed defensive war against the enemies of Islam, but it did not sanction the killing of all non-Muslims or even their conversion by force. Knapp quotes the Koran (2:256): "There is no compulsion in religion." Killing of other Muslims could be justified only by classifying them as non-Muslims (e.g., as apostates or rebels). He notes that the Islamic law tradition was very hostile toward terrorism and severely punished rebels who attacked innocent victims.

Osama bin Laden (see the Suggested Readings) has tried to justify attacks on the United States by appealing to the doctrine of jihad, which he interprets as allowing attacks on enemies of Islam. He says that he and his followers are attacking America "because you attacked us and continue to attack us." He gives a long list of places where the alleged U.S. attacks have occurred, including Palestine, Somalia, Chechnya, Lebanon, Iraq, and Afghanistan. He says that the Palestinians are fighting to regain the land taken away from them by Israel. American infidels are occupying holy places in Saudi Arabia, namely the cities of Mecca and Medina; and fighting a war of annihilation against Iraq, which for 500 years was the heart of an Islamic empire. He goes on to morally condemn American society as a cesspool of usury, sexual debauchery, drug addiction, gambling, prostitution, and so on. He concludes by arguing that the United States violates human rights while claiming to uphold them.

In response to the 9/11 attacks, the United States attacked Afghanistan and then Iraq. Many commentators have called these *preventive wars*, that is, wars justified by the possibility of a future attack by terrorists or rogue states. By contrast, a *preemptive war* is one justified by the imminent threat of attack, not just the chance of an attack in the future.

In the third reading, Neta C. Crawford argues that a slippery slope leads from defensive preemptive war to offensive preventive war. In her view, a morally legitimate preemptive attack must meet four necessary conditions. The "self" to be defended is lives, not other national interests such as a need for oil or world domination. War should be inevitable and likely in the near future, and not something that might happen in the distant future. The preemptive attack should be likely to succeed. Military force must be necessary, and no other measures available, to counter the threat. When an attack does not meet one or more of these necessary conditions, then the line between preemptive war and preventive war has been crossed. Crawford warns that aggressive preventive war has risks. It increases instability and insecurity. It makes states arm themselves defensively because of fear of attack. It increases resentment. At its worst, it is a recipe for constant conflict.

In the fourth reading, Laurie Calhoun applies just war theory to terrorism, focusing on political and moral/religious terrorists. She does not argue that terrorism is morally wrong. Rather, she wants to show how just war theory can be used by terrorists to defend their actions, at least to themselves and their followers, using the very same theory that democratic nations use to justify their military campaigns, which kill innocent civilians. To see how terrorists can do this, we need to look more closely at just war theory, and particularly the doctrine of double effect. How can a nation justify dropping bombs on another nation when this act results in the killing of innocent civilians? If the principle of discrimination is understood as absolutely forbidding the killing of innocents, then no modern war could be justified. Lackey and others make this point. To justify killing innocents, just war theorists appeal to the Catholic doctrine of double effect. This doctrine distinguishes between two effects of an action: an intended effect; and one that is foreseen but not intended, that is, a side effect. The doctrine says that as long as the intended consequence of an act is good (for example, winning a war or saving lives), then a bad foreseen consequence (for example, the death of innocents) is morally allowed, provided this bad consequence is not intended. Calhoun argues that terrorists can use this sort of reasoning to justify their actions, as Timothy McVeigh did when he characterized the deaths of innocent people in the Oklahoma City bombing as "collateral damage." In other words, she argues, "just war" rationalizations are available to everyone, bin Laden as well as President Obama. Terrorists can present themselves to their followers as warriors for justice, and not as mere murderers or vigilantes.

Unlike Calhoun, Louise Richardson (see the Suggested Readings) gives us a precise definition of *terrorism*. It simply means deliberately and violently targeting civilians for political purposes. The point of doing this is to send a political message to an audience that is not the same as the victims. To do this, the act and the victim usually have symbolic significance. To use her example, the Twin Towers and the Pentagon targeted in the 9/11 attacks were seen as icons of America's economic and military power, and this symbolism enhanced the shock value of the attacks. She denies that terrorists are irrational or insane. In fact, they attempt to justify their actions in various ways.

In the fifth reading, Thomas Nagel explains why terrorism is wrong. The condemnation of terrorism does not require rejecting the terrorists' ends. Rather, terrorism is wrong because of the means used by the terrorists. They *aim* directly at noncombatants and this violates the basic moral principle that aiming at (intending) the death of a harmless person is morally wrong. However, Nagel allows that killing innocent people in war does not violate this principle as long as the victims are killed as a side effect of an attack on a legitimate military target, and are not deliberately or intentionally killed.

Claudia Card (see the Suggested Readings) has no difficulty seeing the 9/11 attacks as terrorist and evil, but she doubts that the war on terrorism is the appropriate response. Terrorism is not an identifiable agent, and it is not clear what kinds of terrorists count as legitimate targets. For example, is a war on terrorism a justifiable response to domestic battering? If not, then similar objections may apply to the war on public terrorism. A more appropriate response, in her view, would be to hunt down those responsible for the planning and support of the attacks, and bring them to trial by international tribunals.

In the last reading for the chapter, David Luban discusses more problems with the war on terrorism. Luban agrees with Card that the current fight against terrorism does not fit the traditional model of a just war. Instead, the war on terrorism uses a new hybrid war-law model that combines features of the war model with the law model. The new war model allows the use of lethal force, the foreseen but unintended killing of innocents, and the capture and killing of suspected terrorists. These are features of war. But in traditional war, the enemy can legitimately fight back, other nations can opt for neutrality, and enemy soldiers have certain rights under the Geneva Convention. The war on terrorism rejects these features by appealing to a law model. Terrorists are criminals, so they cannot legitimately fight back. Other nations cannot be neutral when it comes to illegal murder; if they harbor or aid terrorists, they are against us. Finally, terrorists are treated as enemy combatants rather than as soldiers or ordinary criminals, and as such they have no rights, neither the rights of ordinary criminals nor the rights of soldiers under the Geneva Convention. There is no presumption of innocence, they have no right to a hearing, and they can be detained indefinitely. Even torture is allowable. So, according to Luban, the war on terrorism puts an end to international human rights because anyone identified as a terrorist has no rights. (For an example of the treatment of suspected terrorists, see the case of Jose Padilla in the Problem Cases.)

Philosophical Issues

The readings in the chapter raise some very important issues. Can war be justified? If so, how? Pacifists such as Schweitzer and Gandhi, who were opposed to all killing or all violence, hold that no war is ever justified. The problem with these absolutist views is that there seems to be an obvious exception, namely, killing or violence in the defense of one's life. Lackey's antiwar pacifism is not so easily dismissed. If one agrees that the killing of soldiers and civilians is a very great evil, one that cannot be balanced by goods such as political freedom, then it seems very difficult, if not impossible, to justify modern wars.

Just war theorists such as William V. O'Brien (see the Suggested Readings) try to justify modern wars such as World War II, but to do so they have to modify or interpret the principles of the theory. The most troublesome principle is the one about discrimination. As O'Brien says, if this principle is understood to forbid absolutely the killing of noncombatants, then it is hard to see how any modern war could have been justified, since they all involved killing noncombatants. Perhaps the most graphic example was the atomic bombing of Hiroshima and Nagasaki, which killed more than 200,000 innocent noncombatants.

There are various ways to get around the problem. One is to deny that there are any innocent noncombatants in war; everyone in an enemy nation is a legitimate target. (Some terrorists take this position, too.) The most common way of justifying the killing of innocents, as we have seen, is to appeal to the Catholic doctrine of double effect.

There is debate about how to formulate and apply the doctrine of double effect. O'Brien admits that the distinction between the two effects—one that is directly intended and the other an unintended side effect—is often difficult to accept. Consider President Harry Truman's decision to bomb Hiroshima and Nagasaki. At the time, he said that his decision was based on the fact that an invasion of Japan would cost the lives of thousands of American soldiers, and he wanted to save those lives. But he surely knew that using atomic bombs on these undefended cities would result in the deaths of thousands of innocent Japanese noncombatants. Did he directly intend the killing of innocents, or merely foresee this killing as an unintended consequence? Can we make the distinction in this case? If we do, then what is the basis for the distinction?

Are acts of terrorism ever justified? As we have seen, Calhoun argues that terrorists can and do appeal to the just war theory, the very theory that others use to demonstrate that terrorism is wrong. How can just war theory be used to defend terrorism? Calhoun argues that terrorists can appeal to the doctrine of double effect. To see how this might be done, let's take another look at the doctrine as stated by Father Richard McCormick and quoted by O'Brien. McCormick says, "It is immoral directly to take innocent human life except with divine authorization." Why is the killing of innocents allowed if there is divine authorization? One explanation is that just war theory was developed by Catholic theologians to defend the holy crusades against infidels, crusades that were believed to be commanded by God. But of course fundamentalist Muslim terrorists also believe they have divine authorization; they believe they are engaged in a holy war commanded by Allah against infidels. Thus, both Christians and Muslims claim divine authorization for war and terrorism.

Now let us turn to the distinction between direct and indirect killing, which is at the heart of the doctrine of double effect. As McCormick explains it, "Direct taking of human life implies that one performs a lethal action with the intention that death should result for himself or another. Death is therefore deliberately willed as the effect of one's action." But Muslim terrorists may sincerely believe that all things happen by Allah's will, and they do not will anything, much less the death of others. They are merely submitting to the will of Allah, and Allah commands them to jihad. Hence, they can claim that the deaths that result from their actions are not positively willed, but merely foreseen as a consequence of following Allah's commands. In other words, they are only indirectly killing innocents. It appears, then, that terrorists can attempt to justify their actions by appealing to the Catholic doctrine of double effect, at least as it is stated by McCormick.

How do we define terrorism? This is another issue discussed in the readings. Calhoun argues that there is no satisfactory definition of terrorism. The moral definition, which defines terrorism as killing or threatening to kill innocent people, is unsatisfactory because it seems to apply to every nation that has engaged in bombing campaigns resulting in the deaths of innocent children. The legal definition, which defines terrorism as illegal acts of killing or harming people, is defective because it would not apply to the reign of terror imposed by the Third Reich in Nazi Germany.

Richardson asserts that *terrorism* simply means deliberately and violently targeting civilians for political purposes. She admits that this simple definition applies to some actions of democratic states. She mentions the Allied bombing campaign in World War II, which targeted cities in Germany, and the nuclear bombing of Hiroshima and Nagasaki. Current examples are not hard to find. In the Lebanon War, Israel used unguided cluster bombs to attack civilian targets. In 1986, the United States tried to kill Colonel Gaddafi, the Libyan leader, and succeeded in killing his fifteen-month-old daughter and fifteen other civilians. Richardson's solution to the problem of state terrorism is to stipulate, for the sake of "analytic clarity," that terrorism is the act of substate groups, not states. She adds, however, that when states deliberately target civilian populations, as they did in World War II, this is the moral equivalent of terrorism.

Card adopts Carl Wellman's definition of terrorism as political violence with two targets: a direct but secondary target that suffers the harm and an indirect but primary target that gets a political message. By this definition, the 9/11 attacks were clearly terrorist attacks. They were also evil, indeed paradigmatically evil, because the harms were intolerable, planned, and foreseeable.

Finally, how should we deal with terrorists? Do we treat them as enemy soldiers who have rights under the Geneva Convention, such as the right not to be tortured and the right to be fed, clothed, given medical treatment, and released when hostilities are over? In Card's view, terrorists should be treated as criminals, not soldiers. We should hunt down those responsible for the terrorist attacks like 9/11, including those who planned and supported the attacks. When captured, they should be charged with crimes against humanity and given an international trial. But if they are criminals, do they have the legal rights accorded to ordinary criminals in the United States, such as the presumption of innocence, the right to a fair trial, the right to be defended by a lawyer, the right not to testify against themselves, and the right not to be held without charges? Luban argues that the war on terrorism treats suspected terrorists as neither soldiers nor criminals but as enemy combatants with no rights at all, and this amounts to the end of international human rights.

Pacifism

DOUGLAS P. LACKEY

Douglas P. Lackey is professor of philosophy at Baruch College and the Graduate Center of the City University of New York. He is the author of *Moral Principles and Nuclear Weapons* (1984); *The Ethics of War and Peace* (1989); *God, Immortality, Ethics* (1990); and *Ethics and Strategic Defense* (1990). Our reading is taken from *The Ethics of War and Peace* (1989).

Lackey distinguishes between four types of pacifism. There is the universal pacifist view that all killing is wrong, the universal pacifist view that all violence is wrong, private pacifism that condemns personal violence but not political violence, and antiwar pacifism that allows personal violence but condemns all wars. Lackey discusses objections to all of these views, but he seems to defend antiwar pacifism. At least, he answers every objection to antiwar pacifism, leaving the reader with the impression that he supports this view.

1. VARIETIES OF PACIFISM

Everyone has a vague idea of what a pacifist is, but few realize that there are many kinds of pacifists. (Sometimes the different kinds quarrel with each other!) One task for the student of international ethics is to distinguish the different types of pacifism and to identify which types represent genuine moral theories.

Most of us at some time or other have run into the "live and let live" pacifist, the person who says, "I am absolutely opposed to killing and violence—but I don't seek to impose my own code on anyone else. If other people want to use violence, so be it. They have their values and I have mine." For such a person, pacifism is one life-style among others, a life-style committed to gentleness and care, and opposed to belligerence and militarism. Doubtless, many people who express such commitments are sincere and are prepared to live by their beliefs. At the same time, it is important to see why "live and let live" pacifism does not constitute a moral point of view.

When someone judges that a certain action, A, is morally wrong, that judgment entails that no one should do A. Thus, there is no way to have moral values without believing that these values apply to other people. If a person says that A is morally wrong but that it doesn't matter if other people do A, than that person either is being inconsistent or doesn't know what the word "moral" means. If a person believes that killing, in certain circumstances, is morally wrong, that belief implies that no one should kill, at least in those circumstances. If a pacifist claims that killing is wrong in *all* circumstances, but that it is permissible for other people to kill on occasion, then he has not understood the universal character of genuine moral principles. If pacifism is to be a moral theory, it must be prescribed for all or prescribed for none.

Once one recognizes this "universalizing" character of genuine moral beliefs, one will take moral commitments more seriously than those who treat a moral code as a personal life-style. Since moral principles apply to everyone, we must take care that our moral principles are correct, checking that they are not inconsistent with each other, developing and adjusting them so that they are detailed and subtle enough to deal with a variety of circumstances, and making sure that they are defensible against the objections of those who do not accept them. Of course many pacifists do take the business of morality seriously and advance pacifism as a genuine moral position, not as a mere life-style. All such serious pacifists believe that *everyone* ought to be a pacifist, and that those who reject pacifism are deluded or wicked. Moreover, they do not simply endorse pacifism; they offer arguments in its defense.

We will consider four types of pacifist moral theory. First, there are pacifists who maintain that the central idea of pacifism is the immorality of killing. Second, there are pacifists who maintain that the essence of pacifism is the immorality of violence, whether this be violence in personal relations or violence in relations between nation-states. Third, there are pacifists who argue that personal violence is always morally wrong but that political violence is sometimes morally right: for example, that it is sometimes morally permissible for a nation to go to war. Fourth and finally, there are pacifists who believe that personal violence is sometimes permissible but that war is always morally wrong.

Albert Schweitzer, who opposed all killing on the grounds that life is sacred, was the first sort of pacifist. Mohandas Gandhi and Leo Tolstoy, who opposed not only killing but every kind of coercion and violence, were pacifists of the second sort: I will call such pacifists "universal pacifists." St. Augustine, who condemned self-defense but endorsed wars against heretics, was a pacifist of the third sort. Let us call him a "private pacifist," since he condemned only violence in the private sphere. Pacifists of the fourth sort, increasingly common in the modern era of nuclear and total war, I will call "antiwar pacifists."

2. THE PROHIBITION AGAINST KILLING

(a) The Biblical Prohibition

One simple and common argument for pacifism is the argument that the Bible, God's revealed word, says to all people "Thou shalt not kill" (Exod. 20:13). Some pacifists interpret this sentence as implying that no one should kill under any circumstances, unless God indicates that this command is suspended, as He did when He commanded Abraham to slay Isaac. The justification for this interpretation is the words themselves, "Thou shalt not kill," which are presented in the Bible bluntly and without qualification, not only in Exodus but also in Deuteronomy (5:17).

This argument, however, is subject to a great many criticisms. The original language of Exodus and Deuteronomy is Hebrew, and the consensus of scholarship says that the Hebrew sentence at Exodus 20:23, "Lo Tirzach," is best translated as "Thou shalt do no murder," not as "Thou shalt not kill." If this translation is correct, then Exodus 20:13 does not forbid all killing but only those killings that happen to be murders. Furthermore, there are many places in the Bible where God commands human beings to kill in specified circumstances. God announces 613 commandments in all, and these include "Thou shalt not suffer a witch to live" (Exod. 22:18); "He that blasphemeth the name of the Lord . . . shall surely be put to death, and all the congregation shall stone him" (Lev. 24:16); "He that killeth any man shall surely be put to death" (Lev. 24:17); and so forth. It is difficult to argue that these instructions are like God's specific instructions to Abraham to slay Isaac: these are general commandments to be applied by many people, to many people, day in and day out. They are at least as general and as divinely sanctioned as the commandment translated "Thou shalt not kill."

There are other difficulties for pacifists who pin their hopes on prohibitions in the Hebrew Bible. Even if the commandment "Thou shalt not kill," properly interpreted, did prohibit all types of killing, the skeptics can ask whether this, by itself, proves that all killing is immoral. First, how do we know that statements in the Hebrew Bible really are God's word, and not just the guesses of ancient scribes? Second, even if the commandments in the Bible do express God's views, why are we morally bound to obey divine commands? (To say that we will be punished if we do not obey is to appeal to fear and self-interest, not to moral sentiments.) Third, are the commandments in the Old Testament laws for all people, or just laws for the children of Israel? If they are laws for all people, then all people who do not eat unleavened bread for Passover are either deluded or wicked. If they are laws only for the children of Israel, they are religious laws and not moral laws, since they lack the universality that all moral laws must have.

Finally, the argument assumes the existence of God, and philosophers report that the existence of God is not easy to demonstrate. Even many religious believers are more confident of the truth of basic moral judgments, such as "Small children should not be tortured to death for purposes of amusement," than they are confident of the existence of God. For such people, it would seem odd to try to justify moral principles by appeals to religious principles, since the evidence for those religious principles is weaker than the evidence for the moral principles they are supposed to justify.

(b) The Sacredness of Life

There are, however, people who oppose all killing but do not seek justification in divine revelation. Many of these defend pacifism by appeal to the sacredness of life. Almost everyone is struck with wonder when watching the movements and reactions of a newborn baby, and almost everyone can be provoked to awe by the study of living things, great and small. The complexity of the mechanisms found in living bodies, combined with the efficiency with which they fulfill their functions, is not matched by any of the processes in nonliving matter. People who are particularly awestruck by the beauty of living things infer [from] these feelings that life is sacred, that all killing is wrong.

Different versions of pacifism have been derived from beliefs about the sacredness of life. The most extreme version forbids the killing of any living thing. This view was allegedly held by Pythagoras, and presently held by members of the Jain religion in India. (Those who think that such pacifists must soon starve to death should note that a life-sustaining diet can easily be constructed from milk, honey, fallen fruit and vegetables, and other items that are consumable without prior killing.) A less extreme view sanctions the killing of plants but forbids the killing of animals. The most moderate view prohibits only the killing of fellow beings.

There is deep appeal in an argument that connects the sacredness of life with the wrongfulness of taking life. Even people who are not pacifists are often revolted by the spectacle of killing, and most Americans would be unable to eat meat if they had to watch how the animals whose flesh they consume had been slaughtered, or if they had to do the slaughtering themselves. Most people sense that they do not own the world they inhabit and recognize that they are not free to do with the world as they will, that the things in it, most especially living things, are worthy of respect and care. Seemingly nothing could violate the respect living things deserve more than killing, especially since much of the taking of human and nonhuman life is so obviously unnecessary.

But with the introduction of the word "unnecessary" a paradox arises. Sometimes—less often than we think, but sometimes—the taking of some lives will save other lives. Does the principle that life is sacred and ought to be preserved imply that nothing should ever be killed, or does it imply that as much life should be preserved as possible? Obviously pacifists take the former view; nonpacifists, the latter.

The view that killing is wrong because it destroys what is sacred seems to imply that killing is wrong because killing diminishes the amount of good in the world. It seems to follow that if a person can save more lives by killing than by refusing to kill, arguments about the sacredness of life would not show that killing in these circumstances is wrong. (It might be wrong for other reasons.) The more lives saved, the greater the quantity of good in the world.

The difficulty that some killing might, on balance, save lives, is not the only problem for pacifism based on the sacredness of life. If preserving life is the highest value, a value not comparable with other, non-life-preserving goods, it follows that any acts which place life at risk are immoral. But many admirable actions have been undertaken in the face of death, and many less heroic but morally impeccable actions—driving on a road at moderate speed, authorizing a commercial flight to take off, and so forth—place life at risk. In cases of martyrdom in which people choose death over religious conversion, life is just as much destroyed as it is in a common murder. Yet, on the whole, automobile drivers, air traffic controllers, and religious martyrs are not thought to be wicked. Likewise, people on life-sustaining machinery sometimes request that the machines be turned off, on the grounds that quality of life matters more than quantity of life. We may consider such people mistaken, but we hardly think that they are morally depraved.

In answering this objection, the pacifist may wish to distinguish between *killing other people* and *getting oneself killed*, arguing that only the former is immoral. But although there is a genuine distinction between killing and getting killed, the distinction does not entail that killing other people destroys life but getting oneself killed does not. If life is sacred, life, including one's own life, must be preserved at all cost. In many cases, people consider the price of preserving their own lives simply too high.

(c) The Right to Life

Some pacifists may try to avoid the difficulties of the "sacredness of life" view by arguing that the essential immorality of killing is that it violates the *right to life* that every human being possesses. If people have a right to life, then it is never morally permissible to kill some people in order to save others, since according to the usual interpretation of rights, it is never permissible to violate a right in order to secure some good.

A discussion of the logic of rights in general and the right to life in particular is beyond the scope of this book. But a number of students of this subject are prepared to argue that the possession of any right implies the permissibility of defending that right against aggression: if this were not so, what would be the point of asserting the existence of rights? But if the possession of a right to life implies the permissibility of defending that right against aggression—a defense that may require killing the aggressor—then the existence of a right to life cannot by itself imply the impermissibility of killing. On this view, the right to life implies the right to self-defense, including violent self-defense. It does not imply pacifism.

3. UNIVERSAL PACIFISM

(a) Christian Pacifism

Universal pacifists are morally opposed to all violence, not just to killing. Many universal pacifists derive their views from the Christian Gospels. In the Sermon on the Mount, Christ taught:

> Ye have heard that it hath been said, An eye for an eye, a tooth for a tooth:
>> But I say unto you, that ye resist not evil: but whosoever shall smite thee on the right cheek, turn to him the other also. . . .
>> Ye have heard it said, thou shalt love thy neighbor, and hate thine enemy. But I say unto you, Love your enemies, bless them that curse you, do good to them that hate you . . . . that ye may be the children of your father which is in heaven: for he maketh the sun to rise on the evil and on the good, and sendeth the rain on the just and the unjust. (Matt. 5:38–45)

In the early centuries of the Christian era, it was widely assumed that to follow Christ and to obey His teaching meant that one should reject violence and refuse service in the Roman army. But by the fifth century, after the Roman Empire had become Christian and after barbarian Goths in 410 sacked Rome itself, Church Fathers debated whether Christ really intended that the Empire and its Church should remain undefended. The Church Fathers noticed passages in the Gospels that seem to contradict pacifism:

> Think not that I am come to send peace on earth: I came not to send peace, but a sword.
>
> For I am come to set a man at variance against his father, and the daughter against her mother, and the daughter-in-law against her mother-in-law. (Matt. 10:34–35)

And there are several instances in the Gospels (for instance, Matt. 8:5–10) in which Jesus encounters soldiers and does not rebuke them for engaging in an occupation that is essentially committed to violence. Rather, he argues, "Render unto Caesar the things which are Caesar's; and unto God the things that are God's" (Matt. 22:21). This would seem to include military service, or at least taxes to pay for the army.

A thorough analysis of whether the Gospels command pacifism is beyond the scope of this book. The passages in the Sermon on the Mount seem to be clearly pacifist; yet many eminent scholars have denied the pacifist message. A more interesting question, for philosophy, if not for biblical scholarship, is this: If Jesus did preach pacifism in the Sermon on the Mount, did He preach it as a *moral* doctrine?

Jesus did not view his teaching as replacing the moral law as he knew it:

> Think not that I am come to destroy the law, or the prophets: I am come not to destroy, but to fulfill. . . .
>
> Till heaven and earth pass, one jot or one tittle shall in no wise pass from the law, till all be fulfilled. (Matt. 5:17–18)

Perhaps, then, the prescriptions of the Sermon on the Mount should be interpreted as rules that one must obey in order to follow Christ, or rules that one must follow in order to obtain salvation. But it does not follow from this alone that everyone has an obligation to follow Christ, and it does not follow from this alone that everyone has an obligation to seek salvation. Even Christians will admit that some people have refused to become Christians and have led morally admirable lives nonetheless; and if salvation is a good, one can nevertheless choose to reject it, just as a citizen can neglect to hand in a winning lottery ticket without breaking the law. If so, the prescriptions of the Sermon on the Mount apply only to Christians seeking a Christian salvation. They are not universally binding rules and do not qualify as moral principles.

(b) The Moral Exemplar Argument

Many people and at least one illustrious philosopher, Immanuel Kant, believe that morally proper action consists in choosing to act in such a way that your conduct could serve as an example for all mankind. (It was Kant's genius to recognize that moral conduct is *essentially* exemplary.) Some universal pacifists appeal to this idea, arguing that if everyone were a pacifist, the world would be a much better place than it is now. This is an argument that Leo Tolstoy (1828–1910) used to support the Gospel prescription not to resist evil:

> [Christ] put the proposition of non-resistance to evil in such a way that, according to his teaching, it was to be the foundation of the joint life of men and was to free humanity from the evil that is inflicted on itself. (*My Religion*, Ch. 4) Instead of having the whole life based on violence and every joy obtained and guarded through violence; instead of seeing each one of us punished or inflicting punishment from childhood to old age, I imagined that we were all impressed in word and deed by the idea that vengeance is a very low, animal feeling; that violence is not only a disgraceful act, but also one that deprives man of true happiness. . . .
>
> I imagined that instead of those national hatreds which are impressed on us under the form of patriotism, instead of those glorifications of murder, called wars . . . that we were impressed with the idea that the recognition of any countries, special laws, borders, lands, is a sign of grossest ignorance. . . .
>
> Through the fulfillment of these commandments, the life of men will be what every human

heart seeks and desires. All men will be brothers and everybody will always be at peace with others, enjoying all the benefits of the world. (*My Religion*, Ch. 6)

Few would deny that if everyone were a pacifist, the world would be a better place, perhaps even a paradise. Furthermore, since the argument is essentially hypothetical, it cannot be refuted (as many nonpacifists believe) by pointing out that not everyone will become a pacifist. The problem is whether this argument can establish pacifism as a moral imperative.

One difficulty with the argument is that it seems to rely on a premise the truth of which is purely verbal. In what way would the world be a better place if people gave up fighting? The most obvious way is that the world would be better because there would be no war. But the statement "If everyone gave up fighting, there would be no war" is true by definition, since "war" implies "fighting." It is difficult to see how a statement that simply relates the meanings of words could tell us something about our moral obligations.

A deeper problem with Tolstoy's argument is that "resist not evil" is not the only rule that would yield paradise if everyone obeyed it. Suppose that everyone in the world subscribed to the principle "Use violence, but only in self-defense." If everyone used violence only in self-defense, the same consequences would follow as would arise from universal acceptance of the rule "Never use violence." Consequently, pacifism cannot be shown to be superior to nonpacifism by noting the good consequences that would undeniably ensue if everyone were a pacifist.

(c) Gandhian Pacifism

Certainly the most interesting and effective pacifist of the twentieth century was Mohandas Gandhi (1869–1948). Though a devout Hindu, Gandhi developed his doctrine of nonviolence from elementary metaphysical concepts that are by no means special to Hinduism:

Man as an animal is violent, but as spirit, nonviolent. The moment he awakes to the spirit he cannot remain violent. Either he progresses towards *ahimsa* [nonviolence] or rushes to his doom. (*Nonviolence in Peace and War*, I, p. 311)

The requirement not to be violent seems wholly negative; sleeping people achieve it with ease. But for Gandhi the essential moral task is not merely to be nonviolent but to use the force of the soul (*satyagraha*, "truth grasping") in a continual struggle for justice. The methods of applied *satyagraha* developed by Gandhi— the weaponless marches, the sit-downs and sit-ins, strikes and boycotts, fasts and prayers— captured the admiration of the world and have been widely copied, most notably by Martin Luther King, Jr., in his campaigns against racial discrimination. According to Gandhi, each person, by engaging in *satyagraha* and experiencing suffering on behalf of justice, purifies the soul from pollution emanating from man's animal nature:

A *satyagrahi* is dead to his body even before his enemy attempts to kill him, i.e. he is free from the attachments of his body and lives only in the victory of his soul. (*Nonviolence in Peace and War*, I, p. 318) Nonviolence implies as complete self-purification as is humanly possible. (*Nonviolence in Peace and War*, I, p. 111)

By acting nonviolently, pacifists not only purify their own souls but also transform the souls of their opponents: "A nonviolent revolution is not a program of seizure of power. It is a program of transformation of relationships, ending in peaceful transfer of power." (*Nonviolence in Peace and War*, II, p. 8)

Though in most places Gandhi emphasizes the personal redemption that is possible only through nonviolent resistance to evil, the spiritually positive effect of nonviolence on evil opponents is perhaps equally important, since "The soul of the *satyagrahi* is love." (*Nonviolence in Peace and War*, II, p. 59)

Gandhi, then, is far from preaching the sacredness of biological life. What matters is not biological life but the condition of the soul, the natural and proper state of which is *ahimsa*. The evil of violence is that it distorts and disrupts this natural condition of the soul. The basic moral law (*dharma*) for all people is to seek the restoration of their souls to the harmony of *ahimsa*. This spiritual restoration cannot be achieved by violence, but only by the application of *satyagraha*.

Disharmony cannot produce harmony; violence cannot produce spiritual peace.

The "sacredness of life" defense of pacifism ran into difficulties analyzing situations in which taking one life could save many lives. For Gandhi, this is no problem at all: taking one life may save many biological lives, but it will not save souls. On the contrary, the soul of the killer will be perverted by the act, and that perversion—not the loss of life—is what matters morally.

The system of values professed by Gandhi—that the highest human good is a harmonious condition of soul—must be kept in mind when considering the frequent accusation that Gandhi's method of nonviolent resistance "does not work," that nonviolence alone did not and could not force the British to leave India, and that nonviolent resistance to murderous tyrants like Hitler will only provoke the mass murder of the innocent. Perhaps the practice of nonviolence could not "defeat" the British or "defeat" Hitler, but by Gandhi's standard the use of military force would only produce a greater defeat, perverting the souls of thousands engaged in war and intensifying the will to violence on the opposing side. On the other hand, the soul of the *satyagrahi* will be strengthened and purified by nonviolent struggle against British imperialism or German Nazism, and in this purification the Gandhian pacifist can obtain spiritual victory even in the face of political defeat.

India did not adopt the creed of nonviolence after the British left in 1948, and it is hardly likely that any modern nation-state will organize its international affairs along Gandhian lines. But none of this affects the validity of Gandhi's arguments, which indicate how things ought to be, not how they are. We have seen that Gandhi's principles do not falter in the face of situations in which taking one life can save lives on balance. But what of situations in which the sacrifice of spiritual purity by one will prevent the corruption of many souls? Suppose, for example, that a Gandhian believes (on good evidence) that a well-timed commando raid will prevent a nation from embarking on an aggressive war, a war that would inflame whole populations with hatred for the enemy. Wouldn't a concern with one's own spiritual purity in such a situation show an immoral lack of concern for the souls of one's fellow men?

Another problem for Gandhi concerns the relationship between violence and coercion. To coerce people is to make them act against their will, for fear of the consequences they will suffer if they do not obey. Coercion, then, is a kind of spiritual violence, directed against the imagination and will of the victim. The "violence" most conspicuously rejected by Gandhi—pushing, shoving, striking with hands, the use of weapons, the placing of bombs and explosives—is essentially physical violence, directed against the bodies of opponents. But if physical violence against bodies is spiritually corrupting, psychological violence directed at the will of opponents must be even more corrupting.

In his writings Gandhi condemned coercion. Yet in practice he can hardly be said to have renounced *psychological* coercion. Obviously he would have preferred to have the British depart from India of their own free will, deciding that it was in their own best interest, or at least morally necessary, to leave. But if the British had decided, in the absence of coercion, to stay, Gandhi was prepared to exert every kind of nonviolent pressure to make them go. And when Gandhi on occasion attempted to achieve political objectives by a "fast unto death," his threat of self-starvation brought enormous psychological pressure on the authorities, who, among other things, feared [that] riots would ensue should Gandhi die.

The Gandhian pacifist, then, must explain why psychological pressure is permissible if physical pressure is forbidden. One possible answer is that physical pressure cannot transform the soul of the opponents, but psychological pressure, since it operates on the mind, can effect a spiritual transformation. Indeed, Gandhi characterized his terrifying fasts as acts of education, not coercion. But the claim that these fasts were not coercive confuses the noncoercive intention behind the act with its predictable coercive effects; and if education is the name of the game, the nonpacifists will remark that violence has been known to teach a few good lessons in its day. In many spiritual traditions, what matters essentially is not the kind of pressure but that the right pressure be applied at the right time and in the right way. Zen masters have brought students to enlightenment by clouting them on the ears, and God helped St. Paul to see the light by knocking him off his horse.

In addition to these technical problems, many people will be inclined to reject the system of values from which Gandhi's deductions flow. Many will concede that good character is important and that helping others to develop moral virtues is an important task. But few agree with Gandhi that the development of moral purity is the supreme human good, and that other goods, like the preservation of human life, or progress in the arts and sciences, have little or no value in comparison. If even a little value is conceded to these other things, then on occasion it will be necessary to put aside the project of developing spiritual purity in order to preserve other values. These acts of preservation may require physical violence, and those who use violence to defend life or beauty or liberty may indeed be corrupting their souls. But it is hard to believe that an occasional and necessary act of violence on behalf of these values will totally and permanently corrupt the soul, and those who use violence judiciously may be right in thinking that the saving of life or beauty or liberty may be worth a small or temporary spiritual loss.

4. PRIVATE PACIFISM

Perhaps the rarest form of pacifist is the pacifist who renounces violence in personal relations but condones the use of force in the political sphere. Such a pacifist will not use violence for self-defense but believes that it is permissible for the state to use judicial force against criminals and military force against foreign enemies. A private pacifist renounces self-defense but supports national defense.

(a) Augustine's Limited Pacifism

Historically, private pacifism developed as an attempt to reconcile the demands of the Sermon on the Mount with the Christian duty to charity. The Sermon on the Mount requires Christians to "resist not evil"; the duty of charity requires

pity for the weak who suffer the injustice of the strong. For St. Augustine (354–430), one essential message of the Gospels is the good news that this present life is as nothing compared with the life to come. The person who tries to hold on to earthly possessions is deluded as to what is truly valuable: "If any man will sue thee at the law, and take away thy coat, let him have thy cloak also" (Matt. 5:40). What goes for earthly coats should go for earthly life as well, so if any man seeks to take a Christian life, the Christian should let him have it. On this view, the doctrine "resist no evil" is just an expression of contempt for earthly possessions.

But according to Augustine there are some things in this world that do have value: justice, for example, the relief of suffering, and the preservation of the Church, which Augustine equated with civilization itself. To defend these things with necessary force is not to fall prey to delusions about the good. For Augustine, then, service in the armed forces is not inconsistent with Christian values.

One difficulty for theories like Augustine's is that they seem to justify military service only when military force is used in a just cause. Unfortunately, once in the service, the man in the ranks is not in a position to evaluate the justice of his nation's cause; indeed, in many modern nations, the principle of military subordination to civilian rule prevents even generals from evaluating the purposes of war declared by political leaders. But Augustine argues that the cause of justice cannot be served without armies, and armies cannot function unless subordinates follow orders without questioning the purposes of the conflict. The necessary conditions for justice and charity require that some men put themselves in positions in which they might be required to fight for injustice.

(b) The Problem of Self-Defense

Many will agree with Augustine that most violence at the personal level—the violence of crime, vendetta, and domestic brutality, for example—goes contrary to moral principles. But most are prepared to draw the line at personal and collective self-defense. Can the obligation to be charitable justify participation in military service but stop short of justifying the use of force by private citizens, if that force is exercised to protect the weak from the oppression of the strong? Furthermore, the obligation to be charitable does not exclude acts of charity toward oneself. For Augustine, violence was a dangerous tool, best kept out of the hands of the citizens and best left strictly at the disposal of the state. Beset with fears of crime in the streets, the contemporary American is less inclined to worry about the anarchic effects of private uses of defensive force and more inclined to worry about the protection the police seem unable to provide.

For these worried people, the existence of a right to self-defense is self-evident. But the existence of this right is not self-evident to universal or private pacifists; and it was not self-evident to St. Augustine. In the Christian tradition, no right to self-defense was recognized until its existence was certified by Thomas Aquinas in the thirteenth century. Aquinas derived the right to self-defense from the universal tendency to self-preservation, assuming (contrary to Augustine) that a natural tendency must be morally right. As for the Christian duty to love one's enemy, Aquinas argued that acts of self-defense have two effects— the saving of life and the taking of life—and that self-defensive uses of force intend primarily the saving of life. This makes the use of force in self-defense a morally permissible act of charity. The right to self-defense is now generally recognized in Catholic moral theology and in Western legal systems. But it can hardly be said that Aquinas's arguments, which rely heavily on assumptions from Greek philosophy, succeed in reconciling the claims of self-defense with the prescriptions of the Sermon on the Mount.

5. ANTIWAR PACIFISM

Most people who believe in the right to personal self-defense also believe that some wars are morally justified. In fact, the notion of self-defense and the notion of just war are commonly linked; just wars are said to be defensive wars, and the justice of defensive war is inferred from the right of personal self-defense, projected from the individual to the national level. But some people reject this projection: they endorse the validity of personal self-defense, but they deny that war can be justified by appeal to self-defense or any other right. On the contrary, they argue that war always involves an inexcusable violation of rights. For such anti-war pacifists, all participation in war is morally wrong.

(a) The Killing of Soldiers

One universal and necessary feature of wars is that soldiers get killed in them. Most people accept such killings as a necessary evil, and judge the killing of soldiers in war to be morally acceptable. If the war is fought for the just cause, the killing of enemy soldiers is justified as necessary to the triumph of right. If the war is fought for an unjust cause, the killing of enemy soldiers is acceptable because it is considered an honorable thing to fight for one's country, right or wrong, provided that one fights well and cleanly. But the antiwar pacifist does not take the killing of soldiers for granted. Everyone has a right to life, and the killing of soldiers in war is intentional killing, a deliberate violation of the right to life. According to the standard interpretation of basic rights, it is never morally justifiable to violate a basic right in order to produce some good; the end, in such cases, does not justify the means. How, then, can the killing of soldiers in war be morally justified—or even excused?

Perhaps the commonest reply to the challenge of antiwar pacifism is that killing in war is a matter of self-defense, *personal* self-defense, the right to which is freely acknowledged by the antiwar pacifist. In war, the argument goes, it is either kill or be killed—and that type of killing is killing in self-defense. But though the appeal to self-defense is natural, antiwar pacifists believe that it is not successful. First of all, on the usual understanding of "self-defense," those who kill can claim the justification of self-defense only if (a) they had no other way to save their lives or preserve themselves from physical harm except by killing, and (b) they did nothing to provoke the attack to which they are subjected. Antiwar pacifists point out that soldiers on the battlefield do have a way of saving themselves from death or harm without killing anyone: they can surrender. Furthermore, for soldiers fighting for an unjust cause—for example, German soldiers fighting in the invasion of Russia in 1941—it is difficult to argue that they "did nothing to provoke" the deadly force directed at them. But if the German army provoked the Russians to stand and fight on Russian soil, German soldiers cannot legitimately claim self-defense as a moral justification for killing Russian soldiers.

To the nonpacifist, these points might seem like legalistic quibbles. But the antiwar pacifist has an even stronger argument against killing soldiers in war. The vast majority of soldiers who die in war do not die in "kill or be killed" situations. They are killed by bullets, shells, or bombs directed from safe launching points—"safe" in the sense that those who shoot the bullets or fire the shells or drop the bombs are in no immediate danger of death. Since those who kill are not in immediate danger of death, they cannot invoke "self-defense" to justify the deaths they cause.

Some other argument besides self-defense, then, must explain why the killing of soldiers in war should not be classified as murder. Frequently, nonpacifists argue that the explanation is found in the doctrine of "assumption of risk," the idea, common in civil law, that persons who freely assume a risk have only themselves to blame if the risk is realized. When a soldier goes to war, he is well aware that one risk of his trade is getting killed on the battlefield. If he dies on the field, the responsibility for his death lies with himself, not with the man who shot him. By assuming the risk—so the argument goes—he waived his right to life, at least on the battlefield.

One does not have to be a pacifist to see difficulties in this argument. First of all, in all substantial modern wars, most of the men on the line are not volunteers, but draftees. Only a wealthy nation like the United States can afford an all-volunteer army, and most experts believe that the American volunteer ranks will have to be supplemented by draftees should the United States become involved in another conflict on the scale of Korea or Vietnam. Second, in many cases in which a risk is realized, responsibility for the bad outcome lies not with the person who assumed

the risk but with the person who created it. If an arsonist sets fire to a house and a parent rushes in to save the children, dying in the rescue attempt, responsibility for the parent's death lies not with the parent who assumed the risk, but with the arsonist who created it. So if German armies invade Russia, posing the risk of death in battle, and if Russian soldiers assume this risk and fight back, the deaths of Russians are the fault of German invaders, not the fault of the defenders who assumed the risk.

These criticisms of German foot soldiers will irritate many who served in the armed forces and who know how little political and military decision making is left to the men on the front lines, who seem to be the special target of these pacifist arguments. But antiwar pacifists will deny that their aim is to condemn the men on the battlefield. Most antiwar pacifists feel that soldiers in war act under considerable compulsion and are excused for that reason from responsibility for the killing they do. But to say that battlefield killings are *excusable* is not to say that they are morally *justified*. On the contrary, if such killings are excusable, it must be that there is some immorality to be excused.

(b) The Killing of Civilians

In the chronicles of ancient wars, conflict was total and loss in battle was frequently followed by general slaughter of men, women, and children on the losing side. It has always been considered part of the trend toward civilization to confine the destruction of war to the personnel and instruments of war, sparing civilians and their property as much as possible. This civilizing trend was conspicuously reversed in World War II, in which the ratio of civilian deaths to total war deaths was perhaps the highest it had been since the wars of religion in the seventeenth century. A very high ratio of civilian deaths to total deaths was also characteristic of the war in Vietnam. Given the immense firepower of modern weapons and the great distances between the discharges of weapons and the explosions of bullets or shells near the targets, substantial civilian casualties are an inevitable part of modern land war. But it is immoral to kill civilians, the antiwar pacifist argues, and from this it follows that modern land warfare is necessarily immoral.

Few nonpacifists will argue that killing enemy civilians is justifiable when such killings are avoidable. Few will argue that killing enemy civilians is justifiable when such killings are the *primary* objective of a military operation. But what about the deaths of civilians that are the unavoidable results of military operations directed to some *other* result? The pacifist classifies such killings as immoral, whereas most nonpacifists call them regrettable but unavoidable deaths, not murders. But why are they not murder, if the civilians are innocent, and if it is known in advance that some civilians will be killed? Isn't this an intentional killing of the innocent, which is the traditional definition of murder?

The sophisticated nonpacifist may try to parry this thrust with analogies to policies outside the arena of war. There are, after all, many morally acceptable policies that, when adopted, have the effect of killing innocent persons. If the Congress decides to set a speed limit of 55 miles per hour on federal highways, more people will die than if Congress sets the speed limit at 45 miles per hour. Since many people who die on the highway are innocent, the Congress has chosen a policy that knowingly brings death to the innocent, but no one calls it murder. Or suppose, for example, that a public health officer is considering a national vaccination program to forestall a flu epidemic. He knows that if he does not implement the vaccination program, many people will die from the flu. On the other hand, if the program is implemented, a certain number of people will die of allergic reactions to the vaccine. Most of the people who die from allergic reactions will be people who would not have died of the flu if the vaccination program had not been implemented. So the vaccination program will kill innocent people who would otherwise be saved if the program were abandoned. If the public health officer implements such a program, we do *not* think that he is a murderer.

Nonpacifists argue that what makes the action of Congress and the action of the public health officer morally permissible in these cases

is that the deaths of the innocent, although foreseen, are not the intended goal of these policies. Congress does not want people to die on the highways; every highway death is a regrettable death. The purpose of setting the speed limit at 55 miles per hour is not to kill people but to provide a reasonable balance between safety and convenience. Likewise, it is not the purpose of the public health officer to kill people by giving them vaccine. His goal is to save lives on balance, and every death from the vaccine is a regrettable death. Likewise, in war, when civilians are killed as a result of necessary military operations, the deaths of the civilians are not the intended goal of the military operation. They are foreseen, but they are always regretted. If we do not accuse Congress of murder and the Public Health Service of murder in these cases, consistency requires that we not accuse military forces of murder when they cause civilian deaths in war, especially if every attempt is made to keep civilian deaths to a minimum.

Antiwar pacifists do not condemn the Congress and the Public Health Service in cases like these. But they assert that the case of war is different in a morally relevant way. To demonstrate the difference, antiwar pacifists provide an entirely different analysis of the moral justification for speed limits and vaccination programs. In their opinion, the facts that highway deaths and vaccination deaths are "unintended" and "regretted" is morally irrelevant. The real justification lies in the factor of consent. In the case of federal highway regulations, the rules are decided by Congress, which is elected by the people, the same people who use the highways. If Congress decides on a 55-mile-an-hour limit, this is a regulation that, in some sense, highway drivers have imposed upon themselves. Those people who die on the highway because of a higher speed limit have, in a double sense, assumed the risks generated by that speed limit: they have, through the Congress, created the risk, and by venturing onto the highway, have freely exposed themselves to the risk. The responsibility for these highway deaths, then, lies either on the drivers themselves or on the people who crashed into them—not on the Congress.

Likewise, in the case of the vaccination program, if people are warned in advance of the risks of vaccination, and if they nevertheless choose to be vaccinated, they are responsible for their own deaths should the risks be realized. According to the antiwar pacifist, it is this consent given by drivers and vaccination volunteers that justifies these policies, and it is precisely this element of consent that is absent in the case of the risks inflicted on enemy civilians in time of war.

Consider the standard textbook example of allegedly justifiable killing of civilians in time of war. Suppose that the destruction of a certain bridge is an important military objective, but if the bridge is bombed, it is very likely that civilians living close by will be killed. (The civilians cannot be warned without alerting the enemy to reinforce the bridge.) If the bridge is bombed and some civilians are killed, the bombing victims are not in the same moral category as highway victims or victims of vaccination. The bombing victims did not order the bombing of themselves through some set of elected representatives. Nor did the bombing victims freely consent to the bombing of their bridge. Nor was the bombing in any way undertaken as a calculated risk in the interest of the victims. For all these reasons, the moral conclusions regarding highway legislation and vaccination programs do not carry over to bombing of the bridge.

Nonpacifists who recognize that it will be very difficult to fight wars without bombing bridges may argue that the victims of this bombing in some sense assumed the risks of bombardment by choosing to live close to a potential military target. Indeed, it is occasionally claimed that all the civilians in a nation at war have assumed the risks of war, since they could avoid the risks of war simply by moving to a neutral country. But such arguments are strained and uncharitable, even for those rare warring nations that permit freedom of emigration. Most people consider it a major sacrifice to give up their homes, and an option that requires such a sacrifice cannot be considered an option open for free choice. The analogy between the unintended victims of vaccination and the unintended civilian victims of war seems to have broken down.

(c) The Balance of Good and Evil in War

It is left to the nonpacifist to argue that the killing of soldiers and civilians in war is in the end justifiable in order to obtain great moral goods that can be obtained only by fighting for them. Civilians have rights to life, but those rights can be outweighed by the national objectives, provided those objectives are morally acceptable and overwhelmingly important. Admittedly, this argument for killing civilians is available only to the just side in a war, but if the argument is valid, it proves that there can *be* a just side, contrary to the arguments of antiwar pacifism.

Antiwar pacifists have two lines of defense. First, they can continue to maintain that the end does not justify the means, if the means be murderous. Second, they can, and will, go on to argue that it is a tragic mistake to believe that there are great moral goods that can be obtained only by war. According to antiwar pacifists, the amount of moral good produced by war is greatly exaggerated. The Mexican War, for example, resulted in half of Mexico being transferred to American rule. This was a great good for the United States, but not a great moral good, since the United States had little claim to the ceded territory, and no great injustice would have persisted if the war had not been fought at all.

The Revolutionary War in America is widely viewed as a war that produced a great moral good; but if the war had not been fought, the history of the United States would be similar to the history of Canada (which remained loyal)—and no one feels that the Canadians have suffered or are suffering great injustices that the American colonies avoided by war. Likewise, it is difficult to establish the goods produced by World War I or the moral losses that would have ensued if the winning side, "our side," had lost. Bertrand Russell imagined the results of a British loss in World War I as follows:

> The greatest sum that foreigners could possibly exact would be the total economic rent of the land and natural resources of England. [But] the working classes, the shopkeepers, manufacturers, and merchants, the literary men and men

of science—all the people that make England of any account in the world—have at most an infinitesimal and accidental share in the rental of England. The men who have a share use their rents in luxury, political corruption, taking the lives of birds, and depopulating and enslaving the rural districts. It is this life of the idle rich that would be curtailed if the Germans exacted tribute from England. (*Justice in War Time*, pp. 48–49)

But multiplying examples of wars that did little moral good will not establish the pacifist case. The pacifist must show that *no* war has done enough good to justify the killing of soldiers and the killing of civilians that occurred in the war. A single war that produces moral goods sufficient to justify its killings will refute the pacifist claim that *all* wars are morally unjustifiable. Obviously this brings the antiwar pacifist head to head with World War II.

It is commonly estimated that 35 million people died as a result of World War II. It is difficult to imagine that any cause could justify so much death, but fortunately the Allies need only justify their share of these killings. Between 1939 and 1945 Allied forces killed about 5.5 million Axis soldiers and about 1 million civilians in Axis countries. Suppose that Britain and the United States had chosen to stay out of World War II and suppose Stalin had, like Lenin, surrendered to Germany shortly after the invasion. Does avoiding the world that would have resulted from these decisions justify killing 6.5 million people?

If Hitler and Tojo had won the war, doubtless they would have killed a great many people both before and after victory, but it is quite likely that the total of *additional* victims, beyond those they killed in the war that *was* fought, would have been less than 6.5 million and, at any rate, the responsibility for those deaths would fall on Hitler and Tojo, not on Allied nations. If Hitler and Tojo had won the war, large portions of the world would have fallen under foreign domination, perhaps for a very long time. But the antiwar pacifist will point out that the main areas of Axis foreign domination—China and Russia—were not places in which the citizens enjoyed a high level of

freedom *before the war began*. Perhaps the majority of people in the conquered areas would have worked out a *modus vivendi* with their new rulers, as did the majority of French citizens during the German occupation. Nor can it be argued that World War II was necessary to save six million Jews from annihilation in the Holocaust, since in fact the war did *not* save them.

The ultimate aims of Axis leaders are a matter for historical debate. Clearly the Japanese had no intention of conquering the United States, and some historians suggest that Hitler hoped to avoid war with England and America, declaring war with England reluctantly, and only after the English declared it against him. Nevertheless, popular opinion holds that Hitler intended to conquer the world, and if preventing the conquest of Russia and China could not justify six and one-half million killings, most Americans are quite confident that preventing the conquest of England and the United States does justify killing on this scale.

The antiwar pacifist disagrees. Certainly German rule of England and the United States would have been a very bad thing. At the same time, hatred of such German rule would be particularly fueled by hatred of foreigners, and hatred of foreigners, as such, is an irrational and morally unjustifiable passion. After all, if rule by foreigners were, by itself, a great moral wrong, the British, with their great colonial empire, could hardly consider themselves the morally superior side in World War II.

No one denies that a Nazi victory in World War II would have had morally frightful results. But, according to antiwar pacifism, killing six and one-half million people is also morally frightful, and preventing one moral wrong does not obviously outweigh committing the other. Very few people today share the pacifists' condemnation of World War II, but perhaps that is because the dead killed by the Allies cannot speak up and make sure that their losses are properly counted on the moral scales. Antiwar pacifists speak on behalf of the enemy dead, and on behalf of all those millions who would have lived if the war had not been fought. On this silent constituency they rest their moral case.

⚜ REVIEW QUESTIONS

1. Characterize universal pacifists (there are two types), private pacifists, and antiwar pacifists.
2. Why doesn't Lackey accept the appeal to the Bible, or the sacredness of life, or the right to life as a good reason for accepting pacifism?
3. What is Christian pacifism and Tolstoy's argument used to defend it? Why doesn't Lackey accept Tolstoy's argument?
4. Explain Gandhi's pacifism, including *satyagraha*. What problems does Lackey raise for this view?
5. Explain Augustine's so-called limited pacifism. What problems does this view have according to Lackey?
6. State the position of antiwar pacifism. Why do antiwar pacifists believe that all wars are wrong? According to Lackey, what are the objections to antiwar pacifism, and how can antiwar pacifists reply?

⚜ DISCUSSION QUESTIONS

1. Is Gandhi's view a defensible one? Why or why not?
2. Does the antiwar pacifist have a good reply to all the objections Lackey discusses? Are there any good objections that Lackey does not discuss?
3. Many people think that World War II was morally justified. What does the antiwar pacifist say? What do you think?
4. According to Lackey, no great moral good was produced by the Revolutionary War in America. If America had lost this war and remained under British rule, then its history would be like that of Canada—and Canada has not suffered, he says. Do you agree? Explain your answer.

Just War Principles

MICHAEL W. BROUGH, JOHN W. LANGO, HARRY VAN DER LINDEN

Michael W. Brough is a major in the U.S. Army, and was an assistant professor of philosophy at the U.S. Military Academy at West Point before being deployed to Iraq.

John W. Lango is professor of philosophy at Hunter College of the City University of New York. He is the author of *Whitehead's Ontology* (1972), and articles on war, ethics, and metaphysics.

Harry van der Linden is professor of philosophy at Butler University. He is the author of *Kantian Ethics and Socialism* (1988) and other writings on Kant and Marx. His most recent articles are on global poverty, economic migration, humanitarian intervention, and preventive war.

Brough, Lango, and van der Linden state and explain the basic principles of traditional just war theory. The first set of principles concern what justifies going to war. They are called *jus ad bellum* (justice in the resort to war) principles. These principles include the just cause for war, legitimate authority for war, and the right intention for war. Also, the war must be a last resort with a reasonable chance of success, and the anticipated goods must be commensurate with the expected evils. These principles are seen as the responsibility of the political leaders of a state. The second set of principles, called *jus in bello* (justice in the conduct of war) principles, is thought to be the responsibility of the military. They are concerned with how the war is fought. They say that soldiers should target combatants and not civilians, and that force should be used in proportion to the end pursued, and not beyond what is necessary.

Source: Appendix, Just War Principles: An Introduction with Further Reading from Rethinking the Just War Tradition by Michael W. Brough, John W. Lango and Harry Van Der Linden. Copyright © 2007. NY: State University of New York Press.

JUST WAR PRINCIPLES

The just war tradition is based on two highly contested ideas: that there are norms on the basis of which one can conclude that in some situations the resort to war is just, and that there are norms that enable war to be conducted in a just manner. What makes the first idea controversial, and especially disconcerting to pacifists, is the claim that the massive and systematic killing and maiming of human beings can sometimes be just. What makes the second idea controversial—and naive or unacceptable to the realist who holds that only self-preservation, national interest, and seeking power motivate conduct between states—is the belief that wars with all their horrors and unanticipated consequences can be fought in a morally constrained manner. Traditionally, the first set of norms, the *jus ad bellum* (justice in the resort to war) principles, is thought to be the responsibility mainly of the political leadership of a country, while the second set of norms, the *jus in bello* (justice in the conduct of war) principles, is viewed as the primary responsibility of military commanders and soldiers. This traditional understanding is not without controversy. It may be questioned, for example, whether soldiers in a war of aggression can be honored for killing in accordance with *jus in bello* principles. And, it may be argued that, since citizens in a democratic society are to some degree responsible for the wars fought in their name, just war thinking is their civic duty.

Not all contemporary just war theorists offer the same list of just war principles, and instead of the term *principles* some authors use other terms, such as *criteria* or *norms*. More importantly, there is disagreement about how the various principles are to be articulated or comprehended. And there are other disagreements—for example, concerning how (and even whether) *jus ad bellum* principles are to be weighed in the resort to war decision. Our view is that much philosophical work remains to be done in terms of clarifying the individual principles and elucidating their rationale, their relative weight, and their connection to international law. This task—which is central to the project of rethinking the just war tradition—is an ongoing one, since (among other reasons) just

war thinking should evolve with the changing nature of warfare caused by broader economic, cultural, technological, and political developments.

The list of just war principles stated here is widely accepted. The accounts of the different principles include some controversies about their interpretation and significance, which illustrate the need to rethink the principles. It should be noted that some recent just war theorists have argued that the conclusion of war must be guided by a third set of just war norms, *jus post bellum* principles. These principles are not included here. . . .

We have added an annotated list of writings pertinent to the theme of this book. It is not a comprehensive bibliography but rather a list of suggestions for further reading, especially for readers less familiar with the just war tradition. For lack of space, we had to leave out equally valuable writings. We have not included writings by our contributors. Joan T. Philips of Air University Library, Maxwell Air Force Base, Alabama, maintains a detailed online bibliography of current publications on just war theory at http://www.au.af.mil/au/aul/bibs/just/justwar.htm.

JUS AD BELLUM PRINCIPLES

1. Just cause. A war is justified only if waged for one or more just causes. Just war theorists generally agree that defense against an unjust attack is a just cause. Similarly, although this might be contested, assisting an ally against an unjust attack is a just cause. More controversial just causes include protecting civilians from massive basic human rights violations committed by their own government or by other parties in a civil war (humanitarian intervention), the imminent threat of aggression (preemptive war), and, especially, future threats—notably, as posed by the possible use of weapons of mass destruction by terrorists or "rogue" states (preventive war).

2. Legitimate authority. The use of military force is permissible only if it is authorized by a political body that is widely recognized as having this power. This principle is also referred to as the *proper, right*, or *competent authority principle*. It is matter of some controversy whether governments irrespective of their moral status or credibility have legitimate authority. There is also disagreement about whether non-state actors, such as guerrilla, insurgent groups, or terrorist groups, can have legitimate authority. And there is dispute about whether an international body—in particular, the United Nations, but also regional organizations, such as NATO or the African Union—can have legitimate authority and what the scope of this authority might be vis-à-vis states.

3. Right intention. A war must be waged with the pursuit of its just cause as its sole (or primary) motive. For instance, if the just cause is stopping genocide, then the sole (or primary) motive guiding the armed humanitarian intervention must be to stop the genocide. As signaled by the parenthetical word *primary*, it is controversial whether there may be other motives. Thus it is controversial whether armed intervention with a primary humanitarian motive may also be secondarily motivated by national self-interest. Clearly, some secondary motives, such as access to resources, economic gain, territorial expansion, increased international influence and power, or ethnic hatred, may weaken or undermine the moral legitimacy of a war.

4. Last resort. Nonmilitary alternatives, including diplomacy, negotiations, sanctions, and legal adjudication, must be pursued—within reasonable limits—prior to resorting to military force. Delaying the use of military force, or threat thereof, too long may be morally objectionable in that it may stimulate aggression or allow for the escalation of a humanitarian disaster. Crucial to a correct explication of this principle is determining what is meant by *within reasonable limits*.

5. Reasonable chance (hope) of success. A war should be fought only if there is a reasonable hope that the goals embedded in its just cause will be realized. It is objectionable to demand great sacrifices of combatants—or inflict serious harms on noncombatants—if military victory seems a very remote possibility. On a broader and more controversial account, a just war entails a possibility of creating an enduring peace.

6. Proportionality. The anticipated goods of waging a war must be proportionate or commensurate to its expected evils. On the common interpretation, this means that the anticipated benefits of war must outweigh its harms, but on a less demanding account it requires only that the expected harms do not greatly exceed the benefits. The principle of proportionality is also referred to as the *principle of macro-proportionality*, so as to distinguish it from the *jus in bello* proportionality principle, which is then referred to as the principle of micro-proportionality. The benefits and costs for one's own people of resorting to war should definitely be counted, but how much weight should be given to the goods and evils that the war imposes upon the enemy or non-warring countries is a matter of debate. Whether goods should be counted resulting from war but not related to its just cause is also a matter of dispute. In light of the history of controversies about how to measure utility, it is not surprising that some just war theorists have contested whether the proportionality principle provides significant moral guidance.

JUS IN BELLO PRINCIPLES

7. Discrimination. Soldiers should discriminate between combatants and noncombatants and target only the former. This principle is also called the *principle of noncombatant immunity*. Just war theorists offer differing accounts of who is to be counted as noncombatants and why. Harm to noncombatants is typically seen as an acceptable result of a military action if it is not intentionally inflicted and is proportionate to the importance of the goals of the military action. A more stringent—and contested—view of how much "collateral damage" is morally acceptable is to demand of soldiers that they seek to minimize noncombatant casualties even at the risk of greater costs to themselves. It is morally impermissible to destroy targets that have primarily civilian purposes. It is a matter of controversy whether structures with both weighty military and civilian significance may be directly targeted. Some weapons, such as nuclear weapons, biological weapons, and (more controversially) landmines, are morally objectionable due to their indiscriminate impact.

8. Proportionality. Force should be used in proportion to the end pursued, and destruction beyond what is necessary to reach a military objective is morally suspect. It might be claimed that the laws of war allow the killing of enemy soldiers without limit, but such a claim is objectionable in terms of the principle of proportionality. Weapons that cause injuries to people long after they have ceased to be combatants, such as nuclear and biological weapons, are disproportionate. Additionally, as with the *jus ad bellum* proportionality principle, there are disputes about which benefits and costs are to be counted, and how they are to be weighted.

⚜ FURTHER READING

Chatterjee, Deen K., and Scheid, Don E., eds. *Ethics and Foreign Intervention*. Cambridge: Cambridge University Press, 2003.

A collection of essays exploring the ethics and legality of secession and humanitarian intervention. A few essays offer qualified support for humanitarian intervention on the basis of the just war tradition. Several contributions articulate a normative and pragmatic "critique of interventionism," concluding that "altruistic wars" are seldom, if ever, justified.

Childress, James F. "Just War Theories: The Bases, Interrelations, Priorities, and Functions of Their Criteria." *Theological Studies* 39 (1978). Revised as chapter 3 in his *Moral Responsibility in Conflicts: Essays on Nonviolence, War, and Conscience*. Baton Rouge: Louisiana State University Press, 1982.

Instead of simply presupposing just war principles, the author attempts to ground them in W. D. Ross's conception of prima facie duties, especially the duty of nonmaleficence. In terms of such a grounding, he discusses the order, strength, and function of the principles.

Coates, A. J. *The Ethics of War*. Manchester: Manchester University Press, 1997.

The book offers chapter-length discussions of just war principles, paying attention to their historical roots but focusing on their contemporary significance and interpretative controversies. Many historical illustrations are provided.

Coppieters, Bruno, and Fotion, Nick, eds. *Moral Constraints on War: Principles and Cases*. Lanham, MD: Lexington Books, 2002.

Scholars from Belgium, China, Russia, and the United States analyze each of the just war principles in a separate chapter with a wide range of historical examples. The book also offers five case studies, all involving American resort to war except for a study of the First Chechen War.

Evans, Mark, ed. *Just War Theory: A Reappraisal*. Edinburgh: Edinburgh University Press, 2005.

A collection of essays, mainly by political scientists, that are distributed among parts entitled "Just Cause," "Justice in the Conduct of War," and "Justice and the End of War." The essays are on such topics as preventive war, proportionality, supreme emergency, and *jus post bellum*.

Held, Virginia. "Legitimate Authority in Non-State Groups Using Violence." *Journal of Social Philosophy* 36 (2005): 175–193.

The author argues that non-state groups using violence and even terrorism may represent their people and meet the requirement of legitimate authority.

Hurka, Thomas. "Proportionality in the Morality of War." *Philosophy and Public Affairs* 33 (2005): 34–66.

With respect to both the *jus ad bellum* and *jus in bello* principles of proportionality, this article discusses which goods and evils fall within their scope and how they should be weighted against one another. Hurka argues that only goods included in the sufficient and contributing just causes of a war should be counted in macroproportionality.

Johnson, James Turner. *Morality and Contemporary Warfare*. New Haven: Yale University Press, 1999.

This book offers an introduction to the just war tradition and covers such topics as humanitarian intervention, noncombatant immunity and modern war, and reconciliation after war. Johnson draws from his influential historical studies of the just war tradition.

Luban, David. "Just War and Human Rights." *Philosophy and Public Affairs* 9 (1980): 160–181.

The author argues that only wars in defense of "socially basic human rights" are just, so that self-defensive wars by corrupt regimes may be unjust and an attack on such regimes may be just.

Lucas, George R., Jr., *Perspectives on Humanitarian Military Intervention*. Berkeley: Berkeley Public Policy Press, 2001.

On analogy with just war theory's *jus ad bellum* and *jus in bello* principles, the author advocates principles for just humanitarian military intervention, which are termed *jus ad interventionem* and *jus in interventione* criteria.

———. "The Role of the 'International Community' in Just War Tradition—Confronting the Challenges of Humanitarian Intervention and Preemptive War." *Journal of Military Ethics* 2 (2003): 122–144.

The author describes important similarities between preemptive war and humanitarian intervention, including that both in their justification appeal to a poorly defined notion of the "international community." Criteria for just resort to force in both cases are proposed with special attention to the issue of international authorization.

McMahan, Jeff. "The Ethics of Killing in War." *Ethics* 114 (2004): 693–733.

The author challenges the principle of noncombatant immunity and the common view that soldiers in an unjust war do not act wrongly as long as they uphold the *jus in bello* principles.

Orend, Brian. *War and International Justice: A Kantian Perspective*. Waterloo: Wilfrid Laurier University Press, 2000.

Orend makes the controversial claim that Kant had a just war theory and was the first thinker to maintain that just war theory should be completed by a category of *jus post bellum*. The book articulates a list of Kantian principles of justice after war. See also Orend, "Justice after War," *Ethics and International Affairs* 16 (2002): 43–56.

Rodin, David. *War and Self-Defense*. Oxford: Oxford University Press, 2002.

This book contests the commonly accepted idea that war is justified in case of national self-defense and carefully argues that the domestic analogy of individual self-defense fails. Rodin proposes that the use of armed force may be justified as a police action against enemy soldiers involved in an aggressive war. His view is commented upon in "Symposium: War and Self-Defense," *Ethics and International Affairs* 18 (Winter 2004).

Sterba, James P., ed. *Terrorism and International Justice*. Oxford: Oxford University Press, 2003.

A collection of essays focused on 9/11 and its aftermath. Several contributors argue that 9/11 was a criminal act, requiring a legal response. The U.S. war against the Taliban is also assessed on the basis of "just war pacifism" and more traditional just war criteria. Attention is also paid to whether weaker parties in asymmetric conflict may rightfully loosen *jus in bello* criteria.

Walzer, Michael. *Just and Unjust Wars: A Moral Argument with Historical Illustrations*, third edition with a new preface by the author. New York: Basic Books, 2000. First edition appeared in 1977.

Even almost three decades after its publication it remains a reference point for much current just war thinking. At the occasion of its twentieth year of publication, *Ethics and International Affairs* 11 (1997) published a handful of critical essays with a response by Walzer.

———. *Arguing About War*. New Haven: Yale University Press, 2004.

A collection of Walzer's essays written after his classic *Just and Unjust War* (1977). Topics include military responsibility, humanitarian intervention, and terrorism. The very recent essays are all applications of just war criteria, covering Kosovo, the Israel-Palestine conflict, 9/11, and the Iraq war, with the exception of an essay that proclaims the triumph of just war theory and poses the question of what is still left to be done for just war theorists.

Zupan, Daniel S. *War, Morality, and Autonomy: An Investigation in Just War Theory*. Burlington, VT: Ashgate, 2003.

The author argues that autonomy, based on a Kantian notion of humanity, provides a better theoretical underpinning for the war convention or *jus in bello* principles than consequentialist or rights-based theories. The analysis is applied to the supreme emergency doctrine and the war on terrorism.

✿ REVIEW QUESTIONS

1. According to Brough, Lango, and van der Lin-den, the just war tradition is based on two contro-versial ideas. What are they and why are they con-troversial?

2. State and explain the *jus ad bellum* principles.
3. State and explain the *jus in bello* principles.

✿ DISCUSSION QUESTIONS

1. Do the wars in Iraq and Afghanistan satisfy the just war principles? Defend your answer.
2. Can insurgents or rebels have the legitimate au-thority to fight a war? For example, did the I.R.A. have the legitimate authority to fight the British

rule of Ireland? What about the American revolu-tionaries who fought the British to achieve inde-pendence?
3. Do nuclear weapons violate the discrimination principle? Why or why not?

The Slippery Slope to Preventive War

NETA C. CRAWFORD

Neta C. Crawford is professor of political science and African American studies at Boston Uni-versity. She is the author of *Argument and Change in World Politics* (2002), and articles on intervention, prevention, and U.S. military strategy.

Crawford argues that the preemption doctrine of the Bush administration is flawed and can slide into a morally unacceptable practice of preventive war. The problem with the preemptive doctrine is that it makes no distinction between terrorists who want to harm us and rogue states that do not want to harm us and pose no imminent threat. Preemption is legitimate only if lives are threatened, war is inevitable in the immediate future, the preemption is likely to succeed, and military force is necessary. Preemption is not legitimate to protect other national interests, such as economic well-being, or because of fear of future attack. In such cases, defensive preemption becomes offensive preventive war that makes things worse by producing more war and increasing resentment.

The Bush administration's arguments in favor of a preemptive doctrine rest on the view that war-fare has been transformed. As Colin Powell ar-gues, "It's a different world . . . it's a new kind of threat."[1] And in several important respects, war has changed along the lines the administra-tion suggests, although that transformation has been under way for at least the last ten to fif-teen years. Unconventional adversaries prepared to wage unconventional war can conceal their movements, weapons, and immediate intentions and conduct devastating surprise attacks.[2] Nu-clear, chemical, and biological weapons, though not widely dispersed, are more readily available

Source: The Slippery Slope to Preventive War by Neta C. Crawford from Ethics & International Affairs, Volume 17, No 1, Spring 2003. NY: Carnegie Council for Ethics in International Affairs.

than they were in the recent past. And the everyday infrastructure of the United States can be turned against it as were the planes the terrorists hijacked on September 11, 2001. Further, the administration argues that we face enemies who "reject basic human values and hate the United States and everything for which it stands."[3] Although vulnerability could certainly be reduced in many ways, it is impossible to achieve complete invulnerability.

Such vulnerability and fear, the argument goes, means the United States must take the offensive. Indeed, soon after the September 11, 2001, attacks, members of the Bush administration began equating self-defense with preemption:

> There is no question but that the United States of America has every right, as every country does, of self-defense, and the problem with terrorism is that there is no way to defend against the terrorists at every place and every time against every conceivable technique. Therefore, the only way to deal with the terrorist network is to take the battle to them. That is in fact what we're doing. That is in effect self-defense of a preemptive nature.[4]

The character of potential threats becomes extremely important in evaluating the legitimacy of the new preemption doctrine, and thus the assertion that the United States faces rogue enemies who oppose everything about the United States must be carefully evaluated. There is certainly robust evidence to believe that al-Qaeda members desire to harm the United States and American citizens. The National Security Strategy makes a questionable leap, however, when it assumes that "rogue states" also desire to harm the United States and pose an imminent military threat. Further, the administration blurs the distinction between "rogue states" and terrorists, essentially erasing the difference between terrorists and those states in which they reside: "We make no distinction between terrorists and those who knowingly harbor or provide aid to them."[5] But these distinctions do indeed make a difference.

Legitimate preemption could occur if four necessary conditions were met. First, the party contemplating preemption would have a narrow conception of the "self" to be defended in circumstances of self-defense. Preemption is not justified to protect imperial interests or assets taken in a war of aggression. Second, there would have to be strong evidence that war was inevitable and likely in the immediate future. Immediate threats are those which can be made manifest within days or weeks unless action is taken to thwart them. This requires clear intelligence showing that a potential aggressor has both the capability and the intention to do harm in the near future. Capability alone is not a justification. Third, preemption should be likely to succeed in reducing the threat. Specifically, there should be a high likelihood that the source of the military threat can be found and the damage that it was about to do can be greatly reduced or eliminated by a preemptive attack. If preemption is likely to fail, it should not be undertaken. Fourth, military force must be necessary; no other measures can have time to work or be likely to work.

A DEFENSIBLE SELF

On the face of it, the self-defense criteria seem clear. When our lives are threatened, we must be able to defend ourselves using force if necessary. But self-defense may have another meaning, that in which our "self" is expressed not only by mere existence, but also by a free and prosperous life. For example, even if a tyrant would allow us to live, but not under institutions of our own choosing, we may justly fight to free ourselves from political oppression. But how far do the rights of the self extend? If someone threatens our access to food, or fuel, or shelter, can we legitimately use force? Or if they allow us access to the material goods necessary for our existence, but charge such a high price that we must make a terrible choice between food and health care, or between mere existence and growth, are we justified in using force to secure access to a good that would enhance the self? When economic interests and vulnerabilities are understood to be global, and when the moral and political community of democracy and human rights are defined more broadly than ever before, the self-conception of great powers tends to enlarge. But a broad conception of self is not necessarily legitimate and neither are the values to be defended completely obvious.

For example, the U.S. definition of the self to be defended has become very broad. The administration, in its most recent Quadrennial Defense Review, defines "enduring national interests" as including "contributing to economic well-being," which entails maintaining "vitality and productivity of the global economy" and "access to key markets and strategic resources." Further, the goal of U.S. strategy, according to this document, is to maintain "preeminence."[6] The National Security Strategy also fuses ambitious political and economic goals with security: "The U.S. national security strategy will be based on a distinctly American internationalism that reflects the fusion of our values and our national interests. The aim of this strategy is to help make the world not just safer but better." And "today the distinction between domestic and foreign affairs is diminishing."[7]

If the self is defined so broadly and threats to this greater "self" are met with military force, at what point does self-defense begin to look like aggression? As Richard Betts has argued, "When security is defined in terms broader than protecting the near-term integrity of national sovereignty and borders, the distinction between offense and defense blurs hopelessly. . . . Security can be as insatiable an appetite as acquisitiveness—there may never be enough buffers."[8] The large self-conception of the United States could lead to a tendency to intervene everywhere that this greater self might conceivably be at risk of, for example, losing access to markets. Thus, a conception of the self that justifies legitimate preemption in self-defense must be narrowly confined to immediate risks to life and health within borders or to the life and health of citizens abroad.

THRESHOLD AND CONDUCT OF JUSTIFIED PREEMPTION

The Bush administration is correct to emphasize the United States' vulnerability to terrorist attack. The administration also argues that the United States cannot wait for a smoking gun if it comes in the form of a mushroom cloud. There may be little or no evidence in advance of a terrorist attack using nuclear, chemical, or biological weapons. Yet, under this view, the requirement for evidence is reduced to a fear that the other has, or might someday acquire, the means for an assault. But the bar for preemption seems to be set too low in the Bush administration's National Security Strategy. How much and what kind of evidence is necessary to justify preemption? What is a credible fear that justifies preemption?

As Michael Walzer has argued persuasively in *Just and Unjust Wars*, simple fear cannot be the only criterion. Fear is omnipresent in the context of a terrorist campaign. And if fear was once clearly justified, when and how will we know that a threat has been significantly reduced or eliminated? The nature of fear may be that once a group has suffered a terrible surprise attack, a government and people will, justifiably, be vigilant. Indeed they may, out of fear, be aware of threats to the point of hypervigilance—seeing small threats as large, and squashing all potential threats with enormous brutality.

The threshold for credible fear is necessarily lower in the context of contemporary counterterrorism war, but the consequences of lowering the threshold may be increased instability and the premature use of force. If this is the case, if fear justifies assault, then the occasions for attack will potentially be limitless since, according to the Bush administration's own arguments, we cannot always know with certainty what the other side has, where it might be located, or when it might be used. If one attacks on the basis of fear, or suspicion that a potential adversary may someday have the intention and capacity to harm you, then the line between preemptive and preventive war has been crossed. Again, the problem is knowing the capabilities and intentions of potential adversaries.

There is thus a fine balance to be struck. The threshold of evidence and warning cannot be too low, where simple apprehension that a potential adversary might be out there somewhere and may be acquiring the means to do the United States harm triggers the offensive use of force.

This is not preemption, but paranoid aggression. We must, as stressful as this is psychologically, accept some vulnerability and uncertainty. We must also avoid the tendency to exaggerate the threat and inadvertently to heighten our own fear. For example, although nuclear weapons are more widely available than in the past, as are delivery vehicles of medium and long range, these forces are not yet in the hands of dozens of terrorists. A policy that assumes such a dangerous world is, at this historical juncture, paranoid. We must, rather than assume this is the present case or will be in the future, work to make this outcome less likely.

On the other hand, the threshold of evidence and warning for justified fear cannot be so high that those who might be about to do harm get so advanced in their preparations that they cannot be stopped or the damage limited. What is required, assuming a substantial investment in intelligence gathering, assessment, and understanding of potential advisories, is a policy that both maximizes our understanding of the capabilities and intentions of potential adversaries and minimizes our physical vulnerability. While uncertainty about intentions, capabilities, and risk can never be eliminated, it can be reduced.

Fear of possible future attack is not enough to justify preemption. Rather, aggressive intent, coupled with a capacity and plans to do immediate harm, is the threshold that may trigger justified preemptive attacks. We may judge aggressive intent if the answer to these two questions is yes: First, have potential aggressors said they want to harm us in the near future or have they harmed us in the recent past? Second, are potential adversaries moving their forces into a position to do significant harm?

While it might be tempting to assume that secrecy on the part of a potential adversary is a sure sign of aggressive intentions, secrecy may simply be a desire to prepare a deterrent force. After all, potential adversaries may feel the need to look after their own defense against their neighbors or even the United States. We cannot assume that all forces in the world are aimed offensively at the United States and that all want to broadcast their defensive preparations—especially if that means

they might become the target of a preventive offensive strike by the United States.

The conduct of preemptive actions must be limited in purpose to reducing or eliminating the immediate threat. Preemptive strikes that go beyond this purpose will, reasonably, be considered aggression by the targets of such strikes. Those conducting preemptive strikes should also obey the *jus in bello* limits of just war theory, specifically avoiding injury to noncombatants and avoiding disproportionate damage. For example, in the case of the plans for the September 11, 2001, attacks, on these criteria—and assuming intelligence warning of preparations and clear evidence of aggressive intent—a justifiable preemptive action would have been the arrest of the hijackers of the four aircraft that were to be used as weapons. But, prior to the attacks, taking the war to Afghanistan to attack al-Qaeda camps or the Taliban could not have been justified preemption.

THE RISKS OF PREVENTIVE WAR

Foreign policies must not only be judged on grounds of legality and morality, but also on grounds of prudence. Preemption is only prudent if it is limited to clear and immediate dangers and if there are limits to its conduct—proportionality, discrimination, and limited aims. If preemption becomes a regular practice or if it becomes the cover for a preventive offensive war doctrine, the strategy then may become self-defeating as it increases instability and insecurity.

Specifically, a legitimate preemptive war requires that states identify that potential aggressors have both the capability and the intention of doing great harm to you in the immediate future. However, while capability may not be in dispute, the motives and intentions of a potential adversary may be misinterpreted. Specifically, states may mobilize in what appear to be aggressive ways because they are fearful or because they are aggressive. A preemptive doctrine which has, because of great fear and a desire to control the international environment, become a preventive war doctrine of eliminating potential threats that may materialize at some point in the future is likely to create more of both fearful and aggressive states. Some states may defensively arm because they are afraid of the preemptive-preventive state; others may arm offensively because they resent the preventive war aggressor who may have killed many innocents in its quest for total security.

In either case, whether states and groups armed because they were afraid or because they have aggressive intentions, instability is likely to grow as a preventive war doctrine creates the mutual fear of surprise attack. In the case of the U.S. preemptive-preventive war doctrine, instability is likely to increase because the doctrine is coupled with the U.S. goal of maintaining global preeminence and a military force "beyond challenge."[9]

Further, a preventive offensive war doctrine undermines international law and diplomacy, both of which can be useful, even to hegemonic powers. Preventive war short-circuits nonmilitary means of solving problems. If all states reacted to potential adversaries as if they faced a clear and present danger of imminent attack, security would be destabilized as tensions escalated along already tense borders and regions. Article 51 of the UN Charter would lose much of its force. In sum, a preemptive-preventive doctrine moves us closer to a state of nature than a state of international law. Moreover, while preventive war doctrines assume that today's potential rival will become tomorrow's adversary, diplomacy or some other factor could work to change the relationship from antagonism to accommodation. As Otto von Bismarck said to Wilhelm I in 1875, "I would . . . never advise Your Majesty to declare war forthwith, simply because it appeared that our opponent would begin hostilities in the near future. One can never anticipate the ways of divine providence securely enough for that."[10]

One can understand why any administration would favor preemption and why some would be attracted to preventive wars if they think a preventive war could guarantee security from future attack. But the psychological reassurance promised by a preventive offensive war doctrine is at best illusory, and at worst, preventive war is a recipe for conflict. Preventive wars are imprudent because they bring wars that might not happen and increase resentment. They are also unjust because they assume perfect knowledge of an adversary's ill intentions when such a presumption of guilt may be premature or unwarranted. Preemption can be justified, on the other hand, if it is undertaken due to an immediate threat, where there is no time for diplomacy to be attempted, and where the action is limited to reducing that threat. There is a great temptation, however, to step over the line from preemptive to preventive war, because that line is vague and because the stress of living under the threat of war is great. But that temptation should be avoided, and the stress of living in fear should be assuaged by true prevention—arms control, disarmament, negotiations, confidence-building measures, and the development of international law.

NOTES

1. Colin Powell, "Perspectives: Powell Defends a First Strike as Iraq Option," interview, *New York Times*, September 8, 2002, sec. 1, p. 18.
2. For more on the nature of this transformation, see Neta C. Crawford, "Just War Theory and the U.S. Counterterror War," *Perspectives on Politics* 1 (March 2003), forthcoming.
3. "The National Security Strategy of the United States of America September 2002," p. 14; available at www.whitehouse.gov/nsc/nss.pdf.
4. Donald H. Rumsfeld, "Remarks at Stakeout Outside ABC TV Studio," October 28, 2001; available at www.defenselink.mil/news/Oct2001/t10292001_t1028sd3.html.
5. "National Security Strategy," p. 5.
6. Department of Defense, "Quadrennial Defense Review" (Washington, D.C.: U.S. Government Printing Office, September 30, 2001), pp. 2, 30, 62.
7. "National Security Strategy," pp. 1, 31.
8. Richard K. Betts, *Surprise Attack: Lessons for Defense Planning* (Washington, D.C.: Brookings Institution, 1982), pp. 14–43.
9. Department of Defense, "Quadrennial Defense Review," pp. 30, 62; and "Remarks by President George W. Bush at Graduation Exercise of the

United States Military Academy, West Point, New York," June 1, 2002; available at www.whitehouse.gov/news/releases/2002/06/20020601-3.html.

10. Quoted in Gordon A. Craig, *The Politics of the Prussian Army, 1640–1945* (Oxford: Oxford University Press, 1955), p. 255.

⚜ REVIEW QUESTIONS

1. How has war changed, according to Crawford?
2. What is the new preemption doctrine? How does Crawford criticize it?
3. Crawford claims that legitimate preemption requires four conditions. What are they?
4. Why does Crawford think that the Bush administration set the bar too low for preemption?
5. When does preemption turn into paranoid aggression, in Crawford's view?

⚜ DISCUSSION QUESTIONS

1. What does Crawford mean by a broad conception of self, as distinguished from a narrow conception? Should this broad self be defended? Why or why not?
2. Suppose Iran is developing nuclear weapons in secret. Does that justify a preventive attack? What is Crawford's view? What do you think?

The Terrorist's Tacit Message[*]

LAURIE CALHOUN

Laurie Calhoun is the author of *Philosophy Unmasked: A Skeptic's Critique* (1997) and many essays on ethics, rhetoric, and war.

    Calhoun applies just war theory to terrorism. Terrorism is condemned by the governments of democratic nations, who continue to engage in "just wars." But when the assumptions involved in the "just war" approach to group conflict are examined, it emerges that terrorists merely follow these assumptions to their logical conclusion. They see themselves fighting "just wars," as "warriors for justice." That is their tacit message. Accordingly, unless the stance toward war embraced by most governments of the world transforms radically, terrorism can be expected to continue over time. As groups proliferate, so will conflicts, and some groups will resort to deadly force, reasoning along "just war" lines. Because terrorists are innovative strategists, it is doubtful that measures based upon conventional military operations will effectively counter terrorism.

Source: Reprinted from *The Peace Review*, vol. 14, no. 1 (2002). Reprinted with permission from Taylor & Francis Ltd.

[*] Editor's Note: This article was written before 9/11.

The refusal to "negotiate with terrorists" is a common refrain in political parlance. It is often accepted as self-evident that terrorists are so far beyond the pale that it would be morally reprehensible even to engage in discourse with them. But the term "terrorist" remains elusive, defined in various ways by various parties, albeit always derogatorily. Judging from the use of the term by the government officials of disparate nations, it would seem to be analytically true that, whoever the speakers may be, they are not terrorists. "Terrorists" refers exclusively to *them*, a lesser or greater set of political actors, depending ultimately upon the sympathies of the speaker.

Government leaders often speak as though terrorists are beyond the reach of reason, but particular terrorists in particular places believe that they are transmitting to the populace a message with concrete content. The message invariably takes the following general form: *There is something seriously wrong with the world in which we live, and this must be changed.* Terrorists sometimes claim to have as their aim to rouse the populace to consciousness so that they might at last see what the terrorists take themselves to have seen. However, the members of various terrorist groups together transmit (unwittingly) a more global message. The lesson that we ought to glean from terrorists is not the specific, context-dependent message that they hope through their use of violence to convey. Terrorists are right that there is something seriously wrong with the world in which we and they live, but they are no less a party to the problem than are the governments against which they inveigh.

That the annihilation of human life is sometimes morally permissible or even obligatory is embodied in two social practices: the execution of criminals and the maintenance of military institutions. This suggests that there are two distinct ways of understanding terrorists' interpretations of their own actions. Either they are attempting to effect "vigilante justice," or else they are fighting "just wars." Because their victims are typically non-combatants, terrorist actions more closely resemble acts of war than vigilante killings. There are of course killers who do not conceive of their own crimes along these lines, having themselves no political agenda or moral mission. Unfortunately, the tendency of governments to conflate terrorists with ordinary murderers (without political agendas) shrouds the similarity between the violent activities of factional groups and those of formal nations.

Attempts to identify "terrorists" by appeal to what these people do give rise to what some might find to be embarrassing implications. For example, to specify "terrorism" as necessarily *illegal* leads to problems in interpreting the reign of terror imposed by the Third Reich in Nazi Germany and other governmental regimes of ill repute. One might, then, propose a moral rather than a legal basis, for example, by delineating "terrorists" as *ideologically or politically motivated actors who kill or threaten to kill innocent people bearing no responsibility for the grievances of the killers.* This would imply that every nation that has engaged in bombing campaigns resulting in the deaths of innocent children has committed acts of terrorism. Faced with this proposed assimilation of nations and factions that deploy deadly force, most people will simply back away, insisting that, though a precise definition is not possible, certain obvious examples of terrorists can be enumerated, and so "terrorist" can be defined by ostension.

The governments of democratic nations harshly condemn "terrorists," but when the assumptions involved in any view according to which war is sometimes just are carefully examined, it emerges that terrorists merely follow these assumptions to their logical conclusion, given the situations in which they find themselves. While nations prohibit the use of deadly force by individuals and sub-national factions, in fact, violent attacks upon strategic targets can be understood straightforwardly as permitted by "just war" rationales, at least as interpreted by the killers. Small terrorist groups could not, with any chance of success, attack a formal military institution, so instead they select targets for their shock appeal.

While secrecy is often thought to be of the very essence of terrorism, the covert practices of terrorist groups are due in part to their illegality. The members of such groups often hide their identities (or at least their own involvement in particular acts of terrorism), not because they believe that their actions are wrong, but because it would be imprudent to expose themselves. Clearly, if one is subject to arrest for publicly committing an act, then one's efficacy as a soldier for the cause in question will be short-lived. Committing illegal acts in the open renders an actor immediately vulnerable to arrest and incarceration, but it is precisely because factional groups reject the legitimacy of the reigning regime that they undertake secretive initiatives best understood as militarily strategic. "Intelligence agencies" are an important part of modern military institutions, and secrecy has long been regarded as integral to martial excellence. Sun Tzu, author of the ancient Chinese classic *The Art of War*, observed nearly three thousand years ago that "All warfare is based on deception."

It is perhaps often simply terrorists' fervent commitment to their cause that leads them to maximize the efficacy of their campaigns by sheltering themselves from vulnerability to the laws of the land, as any prudent transgressor of the law would do. At the other extreme, suicide missions, in which agents openly act in ways that lead to their personal demise, are undertaken only when such martyrdom appears to be the most effective means of drawing attention to the cause. Far from being beyond rational comprehension, the actions of terrorists are dictated by military strategy deployed in the name of what the actors believe to be justice. The extreme lengths to which terrorists are willing to go, the sacrifices that they will make in their efforts to effect a change in the *status quo*, evidence their ardent commitment to their cause.

The common construal of war as a sometimes "necessary evil" implies that war may be waged when the alternative (not waging war) would be worse. If the military could have achieved its objectives without killing innocent people, then it would have done so. Military spokesmen have often maintained that unintended civilian deaths, even when foreseen, are permissible, provided the situation is sufficiently grave. In the just war tradition, what matters, morally speaking, is whether such "collateral damage" is intended by the actors. Equally integral to defenses of the moral permissibility of collateral damage is the principle of last resort, according to which nonbelligerent means must have been attempted and failed. If war is not a last resort, then collateral damage is avoidable and therefore morally impermissible. Few would deny that, if there exist ways to resolve a conflict without destroying innocent persons in the process, then those methods must, morally speaking, be pursued. But disputes arise, in specific contexts, regarding whether in fact nonbelligerent means to conflict resolution exist. To say that during wartime people *resort* to deadly force is to say that they have a reason, for it is of the very nature of justification to advert to reasons. Defenders of the recourse by nations to deadly force as a means of conflict resolution are willing to condone the killing of innocent people under certain circumstances. The question becomes: When have nonbelligerent means been exhausted?

Perhaps the most important (though seldom acknowledged) problem with just war theory is its inextricable dependence upon the interpretation of the very people considering recourse to deadly force. Human fallibility is a given, so in owning that war is justified in some cases, one must acknowledge that the "facts" upon which a given interpretation is based may prove to be false. And anyone who affirms the right (or obligation) to wage war when *they believe* the tenets of just war theory to be satisfied, must, in consistency, also affirm this right (or obligation) for all those who find themselves in analogous situations. But throughout human history wars have been characterized by their instigators as "just," including those retrospectively denounced as grossly unjust, for example, Hitler's campaign. People tend to ascribe good intentions to their own leaders and comrades while ascribing evil intentions to those stigmatized by officials as "the enemy."

The simplicity of its intuitive principles accounts for the widespread appeal of the "just war" paradigm. Throughout human history appeals to principles of "just cause" and "last resort" have been made by both sides to virtually every violent conflict. "Just war" rationalizations are available to everyone, Hussein as well as Bush, Milosevic as well as Clinton. To take a recent example, we find Timothy McVeigh characterizing the deaths of innocent people in the Oklahoma City bombing as "collateral damage." The public response to McVeigh's "preposterous" appropriation of just war theory suggests how difficult it is for military supporters to admit that they are not so very different from the political killers whose actions they condemn.

The received view is that the intention of planting bombs in public places such as the Federal Building in Oklahoma City or the World Trade Center in New York City is to terrorize, and the people who do such things are terrorists. According to the received view, though some innocent people may have been traumatized and killed during the Vietnam War, the Gulf War, and NATO's 1999 bombing campaign in Kosovo, whatever the intentions behind those actions may have been, they certainly were not to *terrorize* people. Nations excuse as regrettable though unavoidable the deaths of children such as occurred during the Gulf War, the Vietnam War, and in Kosovo during NATO's bombing campaign against the regime of Slobodan Milosevic. "Terrorists" are the people who threaten or deploy deadly force for causes of which we do not approve.

Political organizations have often engaged in actions intended to instill fear in the populace and thus draw attention to their cause. But the groups that engage in what is typically labeled "terrorism" are motivated by grievances no less than are nations engaged in war. Were their grievances somehow alleviated, dissenting political groups would no longer feel the need to engage in what they interpret to be "just wars." In appropriating military rationales and tactics, terrorists underscore the obvious, that nations are conventionally assembled groups of people who appoint their leaders just as do sub-national factions. The

problem with the received view is that it exercises maximal interpretive charity when it comes to nations (most often, the interpreter's own), while minimal interpretive charity when it comes to sub-national groups. The intention of a terrorist act, *as understood by the terrorist*, is not the immediate act of terrorism, but to air some grave concern, which the terrorist is attempting to bring to the public's attention. In reality, the requirement of "last resort" seems far simpler to fulfill in the cases of smaller, informal factional groups than in those involving a first-world super power such as the United States, the economic policies of which can, with only minor modifications, spell catastrophe for an offending regime. According to the just war tradition, the permissible use of deadly force is a last resort, deployed only after all pacific means have proven infeasible, and the terrorist most likely reasons along precisely these lines. Indeed, the urgency of the terrorist's situation (to his own mind) makes his own claims regarding last resort all the more compelling. A terrorist, no less than the military spokesmen of established nations, may regret the deaths of the innocent people to which his activities give rise. But, applying the "just war" approach to "collateral damage," terrorists may emerge beyond moral reproach, since were their claims adequately addressed by the powers that be, they would presumably cease their violent activities. It is because they believe that their rights have been denied that groups engage in the activities identified as "terrorism" and thought by most people to be morally distinct from the military actions of states.

Once one grants the possibility of a "just war," it seems to follow straightforwardly that political dissidents convinced of the unjust practices of the government in power ought to engage in violent acts of subversion. Factions lack the advantage of currently enshrined institutions that naturally perpetuate the very *status quo* claimed by dissidents to be unjust. Accordingly, so long as nations continue to wage wars in the name of "justice," it seems plausible that smaller groups and factions will do so as well. Many terrorist groups insist that their claims have been squelched or ignored by the regime in power. But if formal nations may wage war to defend their own integrity and sovereignty, then why not separatist groups? And if such a group lacks a nationally funded and sanctioned army, then must not the group assemble its own?

The terrorist is not a peculiar type of creature who nefariously resorts to deadly force in opposition to the demands of morality upheld by all civilized nations. Rather, the terrorist merely embraces the widely held view that deadly military action is morally permissible, while delimiting "nations" differently than do those who uncritically accept the conventions which they have been raised to believe. The nations in existence are historically contingent, not a part of the very essence of things. The terrorist recognizes that current nations came into being and transformed as a result of warfare. Accordingly, agents who, in the name of justice, wield deadly force against the society in which they live conceive of themselves as civil warriors. Terrorist groups are smaller armies than those of established nations funded by taxpayers and sanctioned by the law, but for this very reason they may feel compelled to avail themselves of particularly drastic methods. No less than the military leaders of most countries throughout history, terrorists maintain that the situations which call for war are so desperate as to require the extremest of measures.

That a terrorist is not *sui generis* can be illustrated as follows: Imagine the commander-in-chief of any established nation being, instead, the leader of a group dissenting from the currently reigning regime. The very same person's acts of deadly violence (or his ordering his comrades to commit such acts) do not differ in his own mind merely because he has been formally designated the commander-in-chief in one case but not in the other. Both parties to every conflict maintain that they are right and their adversaries wrong, and terrorist factions are not exceptional in this respect. When we look carefully at the situation of terrorists, it becomes difficult to identify any morally significant distinction between what they do and what formal nations do in flying planes over enemy nations and dropping bombs,

knowing full well that innocent people will die as a result of their actions.

Most advanced nations with standing armies not only produce but also export the types of deadly weapons used by factions in terrorist actions. If we restrict the use of the term "terrorist" to those groups that deploy deadly violence "beyond the pale" of any established legal system, then it follows that terrorists derive their weapons from more formal (and legal) military institutions and industries. The conventional weapons trade has proven all but impossible to control, given the ease with which stockpiled arms are transferred from regime to regime and provided by some countries to smaller groups that they deem to be politically correct. And even when scandals such as Iran-Contra are brought to light, seldom are the culpable agents held more than nominally accountable for their actions. Leniency toward military personnel and political leaders who engage in or facilitate patriotic though illegal weapons commerce results from the basic assumption on the part of most people, that they and their comrades are good, while those who disagree are not.

In some cases, terrorists develop innovative weapons through the use of materials with nonmilitary applications, for example, sulfuric acid or ammonium nitrate. Given the possibility for innovative destruction by terrorist groups, it would seem that even more instrumental to the perpetuation of terrorism than the ongoing exportation of deadly weapons is the support by national leaders of *the idea* that killing human beings can be a mandate of justice. Bombing campaigns serve as graphic illustrations of the approbation by governments of the use of deadly force. It is simple indeed to understand what must be a common refrain among members of dissenting groups who adopt violent means: "If they can do it, then why cannot we?"

Political groups have agendas, and some of these groups deploy violence strategically in attempting to effect their aims. Terrorists are not "beyond the pale," intellectually and morally speaking, for their actions are best understood through appeal to the very just war theory invoked by nations in defending their own military campaigns. Terrorists interpret their own wars as just, while holding culpable all those who benefit from the policies of the government with which they disagree. The groups commonly identified as "terrorists" disagree with governments about not whether there can be a just war, nor whether morality is of such paramount importance as sometimes to require the killing of innocent people. Terrorist groups and the military institutions of nations embrace the very same "just war" schema, disagreeing only about facts.

Thus we find that the terrorist conveys two distinct messages. First, and this is usually the only claim to truth recognized by outsiders, the terrorist alleges injustices within the framework of society. In many cases there may be some truth to the specific charges made by terrorist groups, and this would be enough to turn against them all those who benefit from the regime in power. But a second and more important type of truth is highlighted by the very conduct of the terrorist. Perhaps there is something profoundly misguided about not only some of the specific policies within our societies, but also the manner in which we conceptualize the institutionalized use of deadly force, the activity of war, as an acceptable route to dispute resolution.

The connotations associated with "terrorist" are strongly pejorative and, although terrorists clearly operate from within what they take to be a moral framework, they are often subject to much more powerful condemnation than nonpolitical killers. But murderers who reject the very idea of morality would seem to be worse enemies of society than are political terrorists, who are motivated primarily by moral considerations. Why is it, then, that people fear and loathe terrorists so intensely? Perhaps they recognize, on some level, that terrorists are operating along lines that society in fact implicitly condones and even encourages. Perhaps people see shadows of themselves and their own activities in those of terrorists.

If it is true that terrorists view themselves as warriors for justice, then unless the stance toward war embraced by most governments of the world transforms radically, terrorism should be expected to continue over time. To the extent to which groups proliferate, conflicts will as well, and some subset of the parties to conflict will resort to deadly force, buoyed by what they, along with most of the populace, take to be the respectability of "just war." Military solutions are no longer used even by stable nations merely as "last resorts." Tragically, the ready availability of deadly weapons and the widespread assumption that the use of such weapons is often morally acceptable, if not obligatory, has brought about a world in which leaders often think first, not last, of military solutions to conflict. This readiness to deploy deadly means has arguably contributed to the escalation of violence in the contemporary world on many different levels, the most frightening of which being to many people those involving the unpredictable actions of factional groups, "the terrorists." But the leaders of established nations delude themselves in thinking that they will quell terrorism through threats and weapons proliferation. Terrorists "innovate" by re-defining what are commonly thought of as non-military targets as military. There is no reason for believing that terrorists' capacity for innovation will be frustrated by the construction of an anti-ballistic missile system or the implementation of other initiatives premised upon conventional military practices and strategies.

🏵 RECOMMENDED READINGS

Arendt, Hannah. 1979. *The Origins of Totalitarianism*. New York: Harcourt Brace.

Calhoun, Laurie. 2002. "How Violence Breeds Violence: Some Utilitarian Considerations," *Politics*, vol. 22, no. 2, pp. 95–108.

Calhoun, Laurie. 2001. "Killing, Letting Die, and the Alleged Necessity of Military Intervention," *Peace and Conflict Studies*, vol. 8, no. 2, pp. 5–22.

Calhoun, Laurie. 2001. "The Metaethical Paradox of Just War Theory," *Ethical Theory and Moral Practice*, vol. 4, no. 1, pp. 41–58.

Calhoun, Laurie. 2002. "The Phenomenology of Paid Killing," *International Journal of Human Rights*, vol. 6, no. 1, pp. 1–18.

Calhoun, Laurie. 2001. "Violence and Hypocrisy," and "Laurie Calhoun replies [to Michael Walzer]," *Dissent*, (winter) vol. 48, no. 1, pp. 79–87. Reprinted in *Just War: A Casebook in Argumentation*, eds. Walsh & Asch, Heinle/Thomson, 2004.

Cerovic, Stanko. 2001. *Dans les griffes des humanistes*, trans. Mireille Robin. Paris: Éditions Climats.

Colson, Bruno. 1999. *L'art de la guerre de Machiavel à Clausewitz*. Namur: Bibliothèque Universitaire Moretus Plantin.

Cooper, H. H. A. 2001. "Terrorism: The Problem of Definition Revisited," *American Behavioral Scientist*, vol. 44, no. 6, pp. 881–893.

Gibbs, Jack P. 1989. "Conceptualization of Terrorism," *American Sociological Review*, vol. 54, no. 3, pp. 329–340.

Grossman, Lt. Colonel Dave. 1995. *On Killing: The Psychological Cost of Learning to Kill in War and Society*. Boston: Little Brown.

Harman, Gilbert. 2000. *Explaining Value*. Oxford: Oxford University Press.

Harman, Gilbert. 1977. *The Nature of Morality*. New York: Oxford University Press.

Holmes, Robert L. 1989. *On War and Morality*. Princeton: Princeton University Press.

Le Borgne, Claude. 1986. *La Guerre est Morte . . . mais on ne le sait pas encore*. Paris: Bernard Grasset.

Rapoport, David C. 1984. "Fear and Trembling: Terrorism in Three Religious Traditions," *The American Political Science Review*, vol. 78, no. 3, pp.

REVIEW QUESTIONS

1. According to Calhoun, what is the concrete message of terrorists? What is the more global message, the "tacit message"?
2. What problems does Calhoun see with the legal and moral definitions of the term *terrorists*?
3. How do terrorists view their actions, according to Calhoun?
4. How do military justify "collateral damage," or the killing of innocent people, according to Calhoun?
5. What role does interpretation play in just war theory, in Calhoun's view? Why does she think that "just war" rationalizations are available to everyone, from Hussein to Bush?
6. According to Calhoun, what is the intention of the terrorist act, as understood by the terrorist?
7. Why does Calhoun believe that terrorism is best understood by appealing to the very just war theory invoked by nations defending their wars?

DISCUSSION QUESTIONS

1. Calhoun argues that anyone can rationalize war or terrorism by appealing to just war theory. Is this true? Why or why not?
2. Calhoun says, "Terrorists are people who threaten or deploy deadly force for causes of which we do not approve." Do you agree? Why or why not?
3. Calhoun claims that there is hardly any moral difference between what the terrorists do and what nations such as the United States do when they drop bombs on enemy nations knowing full well that innocent people will die. Do you agree? Why or why not?

What Is Wrong with Terrorism?

THOMAS NAGEL

Thomas Nagel is university professor, professor of law, and professor of philosophy at New York University. He is the author of *The Possibility of Altruism* (1970), *Mortal Questions* (1979), *The View from Nowhere* (1986), *What Does It All Mean* (1987), *Equality and Partiality* (1991), *Other Minds* (1995), *The Last Word* (1997), *The Myth of Ownership*: *Taxes and Justice* (with Liam Murphy, 2002), and *Concealment and Exposure* (2002).

To explain what is wrong with terrorism, Nagel makes a distinction between means and ends. It is not the ends or goals of the terrorist that make terrorism wrong, but the means used, namely the deliberate killing of harmless persons. This violates the basic moral principle that aiming at the death of a harmless person is morally wrong. In his view, killing in self-defense does not violate this moral prohibition. Also, killing harmless persons in warfare is morally allowed as long this occurs as an unintended side effect of an attack on a legitimate military target.

People all over the world react with visceral horror to attacks on civilians by Al Qaeda, by Palestinian suicide bombers, by Basque or Chechen separatists, or by IRA militants. As there now seems to be a pause in the spate of suicide bombings and other terrorist acts—if only momentary—perhaps now is a moment to grapple with a fundamental question: What makes *terrorist* killings any more worthy of condemnation than other forms of murder?

The special opprobrium associated with the word "terrorism" must be understood as a condemnation of means, not ends. Of course, those who condemn terrorist attacks on civilians often also reject the ends that the attackers are trying to achieve. They think that a separate Basque state, or the withdrawal of US forces from the Middle East, for example, are not aims that anyone should be pursuing, let alone by violent means.

But the condemnation does not depend on rejecting the aims of the terrorists. The reaction to the attacks of September 11, 2001 on New York and Washington and their like underscores that such means are outrageous whatever the end; they should not be used to achieve even a good end—indeed, even if there is no other way to achieve it. The normal balancing of costs against benefits is not allowable here.

This claim is not as simple as it appears because it does not depend on a general moral principle forbidding all killing of non-combatants. Similarly, those who condemn terrorism as beyond the pale are usually not pacifists. They believe not only that it is all right to kill soldiers and bomb munitions depots in times of war, but that inflicting "collateral damage" on non-combatants is sometimes unavoidable—and morally permissible.

But if that is permissible, why is it wrong to aim *directly* at non-combatants if killing them will have a good chance of inducing the enemy to cease hostilities, withdraw from occupied territory, or grant independence? Dying is bad, however one is killed. So why should a civilian death be acceptable if it occurs as a side effect of combat that serves a worthy end, whereas a civilian death that is inflicted deliberately as a means to the *same* end is a terrorist outrage?

The distinction is not universally accepted—certainly not by the major belligerents in World

Source: What's Wrong with Terrorism by Thomas Nagel from Project-Syndicate.org, 2002.

War II. Hiroshima is the most famous example of terror bombing, but the Germans, the Japanese, and the British as well as the Americans deliberately slaughtered civilian non-combatants in large numbers. Today, however, terrorism inspires widespread revulsion, which in turn helps to justify military action against it. So it is essential that the reason for that revulsion become better understood.

The core moral idea is a prohibition against *aiming* at the death of a harmless person. Everyone is presumed to be inviolable in this way until he himself becomes a danger to others; so we are permitted to kill in self-defense, and to attack enemy combatants in war. But this is an exception to a general and strict requirement of respect for human life. So long as we are not doing any harm, no one may kill us just because it would be useful to do so. This minimal basic respect is owed to *every* individual, and it may not be violated even to achieve valuable long-term goals.

However, there are some activities, including legitimate self-defense or warfare, that create an unavoidable risk of harm to innocent parties. This is true not only of violent military or police actions but also of peaceful projects like major construction in densely populated cities. In those cases, if the aim is important enough, the activity is not morally prohibited provided due care is taken to minimize the risk of harm to innocent parties, consistent with the achievement of the aim.

The moral point is that we are obliged to do our best to avoid or minimize civilian casualties in warfare, even if we know that we cannot avoid them completely. Those deaths do not violate the strictest protection of human life—that we may not *aim* to kill a harmless person. On the contrary, our aim is if possible to avoid such collateral deaths.

Of course, the victim ends up dead whether killed deliberately by a terrorist or regrettably as the side effect of an attack on a legitimate military target. But in our sense of what we are owed morally by our fellow human beings, there is a huge difference between these two acts, and the attitudes they express toward human life.

So long as it remains an effective means for weak parties to exert pressure on their more powerful enemies, terrorism cannot be expected to disappear. But we should hope nonetheless that the recognition of its special form of contempt for humanity will spread, rather than being lost as a result of its recent successes.

REVIEW QUESTIONS

1. What is it about terrorist killing that makes it worse than other forms of murder, according to Nagel?

2. What exactly makes terrorism wrong in Nagel's view?

DISCUSSION QUESTIONS

1. Is terrorism always wrong? What if it produces a good result such as the elimination of apartheid in South Africa or the overthrow of an oppressive government?
2. Nagel says that the atomic bombing of Hiroshima is an example of morally prohibited "terror bombing" rather than an attack on a legitimate military target. Do you agree? Why or why not?

3. Nagel thinks there is a "huge difference" between being deliberately killed by a terrorist and being killed as the side effect of an attack on a military target. But in both cases a harmless person is killed. Is there really such a huge difference? What is your view?

The War on Terrorism and the End of Human Rights

DAVID LUBAN

David Luban is the Frederick J. Hass Professor of Law and Philosophy at the Georgetown University Law Center. He is the author of *Lawyers and Justice* (1988), *Legal Modernism* (1994), *Legal Ethics and Human Dignity* (2007), and numerous journal articles and book chapters.

Luban argues that the current War on Terrorism combines a war model with a law model to produce a new model of state action, a hybrid war-law model. This hybrid model selectively picks out elements of the war and law models to maximize the use of lethal force while eliminating the rights of both adversaries and innocent bystanders. The result is that the War on Terrorism means the end of human rights.

In the immediate aftermath of September 11, President Bush stated that the perpetrators of the deed would be brought to justice. Soon afterwards, the President announced that the United States would engage in a war on terrorism. The first of these statements adopts the familiar language of criminal law and criminal justice. It treats the September 11 attacks as horrific crimes—mass murders—and the government's mission as apprehending and punishing the surviving planners and conspirators for their roles in the crimes. The War on Terrorism is a different proposition, however, and a different model of governmental action—not law but war. Most obviously, it dramatically broadens the scope of action, because now terrorists who knew nothing about September 11 have been earmarked as enemies. But that is only the beginning.

THE HYBRID WAR-LAW APPROACH

The model of war offers much freer rein than that of law, and therein lies its appeal in the wake of 9/11. First, in war but not in law it is permissible to use lethal force on enemy troops regardless of their degree of personal involvement with the adversary. The conscripted cook is as legitimate a target as the enemy general. Second, in war but not in law "collateral damage," that is, foreseen but unintended killing of noncombatants, is permissible. (Police cannot blow up an apartment building full of people because a murderer is inside, but an air force can bomb the building if it contains a military target.) Third, the requirements of evidence and proof are drastically weaker in war than in criminal justice. Soldiers do not need proof beyond a reasonable doubt, or even proof by a preponderance of evidence, that someone is an enemy soldier before firing on him or capturing and imprisoning him. They don't need proof at all, merely plausible intelligence. Thus, the U.S. military remains regretful but unapologetic about its January 2002 attack on the Afghani town of Uruzgan, in which 21 innocent civilians were killed, based on faulty intelligence that they were al Qaeda fighters. Fourth, in war one can attack an enemy without concern over whether he has done anything. Legitimate targets are those who in the course of combat *might* harm us, not those who *have* harmed us. No doubt there are other significant differences as well. But the basic point should be clear: Given Washington's mandate to eliminate the danger of future 9/11s, so far as humanly possible, the model of war offers important advantages over the model of law.

There are disadvantages as well. Most obviously, in war but not in law, fighting back is a *legitimate* response of the enemy. Second, when nations fight a war, other nations may opt for neutrality. Third, because fighting back is legitimate, in war the enemy soldier deserves special regard once he is rendered harmless through injury or surrender. It is impermissible to punish him for his role in fighting the war. Nor can he be harshly interrogated after he is captured. The Third Geneva Convention provides: "Prisoners of war who refuse to answer [questions] may not be threatened, insulted, or exposed to unpleasant or disadvantageous treatment of any kind." And, when the war concludes, the enemy soldier must be repatriated.

Here, however, Washington has different ideas, designed to eliminate these tactical disadvantages in the traditional war model. Washington regards international terrorism not only as a military adversary, but also as a criminal activity and criminal conspiracy. In the law model, criminals don't get to shoot back, and their acts of violence subject them to legitimate punishment. That is what we see in Washington's prosecution of the War on Terrorism. Captured terrorists may be tried before military or civilian tribunals, and shooting back at Americans, including American troops, is a federal crime (for a statute under which John Walker Lindh was indicted criminalizes anyone regardless of nationality, who "outside the United States attempts to kill, or engages in a conspiracy to kill, a national of the United States" or "engages in physical violence with intent to cause serious bodily injury to a national of the United States; or with the result that serious bodily injury is caused to a national of the United States"). Furthermore, the U.S. may rightly demand that other countries not be neutral about murder and terrorism. Unlike the war model, a nation may insist that those who are not with us in fighting murder and terror are against us, because by not joining our operations they are providing a safe haven for terrorists or their bank accounts. By selectively combining elements of the war model and elements of the law model, Washington is able to maximize its own ability to mobilize lethal force against terrorists while eliminating most traditional rights of a military adversary, as well as the rights of innocent bystanders caught in the crossfire.

A LIMBO OF RIGHTLESSNESS

The legal status of al Qaeda suspects imprisoned at the Guantanamo Bay Naval Base in Cuba is emblematic of this hybrid war-law approach to the threat of terrorism. In line with the war model, they lack the usual rights of criminal suspects—the presumption of innocence, the right to a hearing to determine guilt, the opportunity to prove that the authorities have grabbed the wrong man. But, in line with the law model, they are considered *unlawful* combatants. Because they are not uniformed forces, they lack the rights of prisoners of war and are liable to criminal punishment. Initially, the American government declared that the Guantanamo Bay prisoners have no rights under the Geneva Conventions. In the face of international protests, Washington quickly backpedaled and announced that the Guantanamo Bay prisoners would indeed be treated as decently as POWs—but it also made clear that the prisoners have no right to such treatment. Neither criminal suspects nor POWs, neither fish nor fowl, they inhabit a limbo of rightlessness. Secretary of Defense Rumsfeld's assertion that the U.S. may continue to detain them even if they are acquitted by a military tribunal dramatizes the point.

To understand how extraordinary their status is, consider an analogy. Suppose that Washington declares a War on Organized Crime. Troops are dispatched to Sicily, and a number of Mafiosi are seized, brought to Guantanamo Bay, and imprisoned without a hearing for the indefinite future, maybe the rest of their lives. They are accused of no crimes, because their capture is based not on what they have done but on what they might do. After all, to become "made" they took oaths of obedience to the bad guys. Seizing them accords with the war model: they are enemy foot soldiers. But they are foot soldiers out of uniform; they lack a "fixed distinctive emblem," in the words of The Hague Convention. That makes them unlawful combatants, so they lack the rights of POWs. They may object that it is only a unilateral declaration by the American President that has turned them into combatants in the first place—he called it a war, they didn't—and that, since they do not regard themselves as literal foot soldiers it never occurred to them to wear a fixed distinctive emblem. They have a point. It seems too easy for the President to divest anyone in the world of rights and liberty simply by announcing that the U.S. is at war with them and then declaring them unlawful combatants if they resist. But, in the hybrid war-law model, they protest in vain.

Consider another example. In January 2002, U.S. forces in Bosnia seized five Algerians and a Yemeni suspected of al Qaeda connections and took them to Guantanamo Bay. The six had been jailed in Bosnia, but a Bosnian court released them for lack of evidence, and the Bosnian Human Rights Chamber issued an injunction that four of them be allowed to remain in the country pending further legal proceedings. The Human Rights Chamber, ironically, was created under U.S. auspices in the Dayton peace accords, and it was designed specifically to protect against treatment like this. Ruth Wedgwood, a well-known international law scholar at Yale and a member of the Council on Foreign Relations, defended the Bosnian seizure in war-model terms. "I think we would simply argue this was a matter of self-defense. One of the fundamental rules of military law is that you have a right ultimately to act in self-defense. And if these folks were actively plotting to blow up the U.S. embassy, they should be considered combatants and captured as combatants in a war." Notice that Professor Wedgwood argues in terms of what the men seized in Bosnia were *planning to do*, not what they *did*; notice as well that the decision of the Bosnian court that there was insufficient evidence does not matter. These are characteristics of the war model.

More recently, two American citizens alleged to be al Qaeda operatives (Jose Padilla, a.k.a.

Abdullah al Muhajir, and Yasser Esam Hamdi) have been held in American military prisons, with no crimes charged, no opportunity to consult counsel, and no hearing. The President described Padilla as "a bad man" who aimed to build a nuclear "dirty" bomb and use it against America; and the Justice Department has classified both men as "enemy combatants" who may be held indefinitely. Yet, as military law expert Gary Solis points out, "Until now, as used by the attorney general, the term 'enemy combatant' appeared nowhere in U.S. criminal law, international law or in the law of war." The phrase comes from the 1942 Supreme Court case *Ex parte Quirin*, but all the Court says there is that "an enemy combatant who without uniform comes secretly through the lines for the purpose of waging war by destruction of life or property" would "not . . . be entitled to the status of prisoner of war, but . . . [they would] be offenders against the law of war subject to trial and punishment by military tribunals." For the Court, in other words, the status of a person as a non-uniformed enemy combatant makes him a criminal rather than a warrior, and determines *where* he is tried (in a military, rather than a civilian, tribunal) but not *whether* he is tried. Far from authorizing open-ended confinement, *Ex parte Quirin* presupposes that criminals are entitled to hearings: without a hearing how can suspects prove that the government made a mistake? *Quirin* embeds the concept of "enemy combatant" firmly in the law model. In the war model, by contrast, POWs may be detained without a hearing until hostilities are over. But POWs were captured in uniform, and only their undoubted identity as enemy soldiers justifies such openended custody. Apparently, Hamdi and Padilla will get the worst of both models—open-ended custody with no trial, like POWs, but no certainty beyond the U.S. government's say-so that they really are "bad men." This is the hybrid war-law model. It combines the *Quirin* category of "enemy combatant without uniform," used in the law model to justify a military trial, with the war model's practice of indefinite confinement with no trial at all.

THE CASE FOR THE HYBRID APPROACH

Is there any justification for the hybrid war-law model, which so drastically diminishes the rights of the enemy? An argument can be offered along the following lines. In ordinary cases of war among states, enemy soldiers may well be morally and politically innocent. Many of them are conscripts, and those who aren't do not necessarily endorse the state policies they are fighting to defend. But enemy soldiers in the War on Terrorism are, by definition, those who have embarked on a path of terrorism. They are neither morally nor politically innocent. Their sworn aim—"Death to America!"—is to create more 9/11s. In this respect, they are much more akin to criminal conspirators than to conscript soldiers. Terrorists will fight as soldiers when they must, and metamorphose into mass murderers when they can.

Furthermore, suicide terrorists pose a special, unique danger. Ordinary criminals do not target innocent bystanders. They may be willing to kill them if necessary, but bystanders enjoy at least some measure of security because they are not primary targets. Not so with terrorists, who aim to kill as many innocent people as possible. Likewise, innocent bystanders are protected from ordinary criminals by whatever deterrent force the threat of punishment and the risk of getting killed in the act of committing a crime offer. For a suicide bomber, neither of these threats is a deterrent at all—after all, for the suicide bomber one of the hallmarks of a *successful* operation is that he winds up dead at day's end. Given the unique and heightened danger that suicide terrorists pose, a stronger response that grants potential terrorists fewer rights may be justified. Add to this the danger that terrorists may come to possess weapons of mass destruction, including nuclear devices in suitcases. Under circumstances of such dire menace, it is appropriate to treat terrorists as though they embody the most dangerous aspects of both warriors and criminals. That is the basis of the hybrid war-law model.

THE CASE AGAINST EXPEDIENCY

The argument against the hybrid war-law model is equally clear. The U.S. has simply chosen the bits of the law model and the bits of the war model that are most convenient for American interests, and ignored the rest. The model abolishes the rights of potential enemies (and their innocent shields) by fiat—not for reasons of moral or legal principle, but solely because the U.S. does not want them to have rights. The more rights they have, the more risk they pose. But Americans' urgent desire to minimize our risks doesn't make other people's rights disappear. Calling our policy a War on Terrorism obscures this point.

The theoretical basis of the objection is that the law model and the war model each comes as a package, with a kind of intellectual integrity. The law model grows out of relationships within states, while the war model arises from relationships between states. The law model imputes a ground-level community of values to those subject to the law—paradigmatically, citizens of a state, but also visitors and foreigners who choose to engage in conduct that affects a state. Only because law imputes shared basic values to the community can a state condemn the conduct of criminals and inflict punishment on them. Criminals deserve condemnation and punishment because their conduct violates norms that we are entitled to count on their sharing. But, for the same reason—the imputed community of values—those subject to the law ordinarily enjoy a presumption of innocence and an expectation of safety. The government cannot simply grab them and confine them without making sure they have broken the law, nor can it condemn them without due process for ensuring that it has the right person, nor can it knowingly place bystanders in mortal peril in the course of fighting crime. They are our fellows, and the community should protect them just as it protects us. The same imputed community of values that justifies condemnation and punishment creates rights to due care and due process.

War is different. War is the ultimate acknowledgment that human beings do not live in a single community with shared norms. If their norms conflict enough, communities pose a physical danger to each other, and nothing can safeguard a community against its enemies except force of arms. That makes enemy soldiers legitimate targets; but it makes our soldiers legitimate targets as well, and, once the enemy no longer poses a danger, he should be immune from punishment, because if he has fought cleanly he has violated no norms that we are entitled to presume he honors. Our norms are, after all, our norms, not his.

Because the law model and war model come as conceptual packages, it is unprincipled to wrench them apart and recombine them simply because it is in America's interest to do so. To declare that Americans can fight enemies with the latitude of warriors, but if the enemies fight back they are not warriors but criminals, amounts to a kind of heads-I-win-tails-you-lose international morality in which whatever it takes to reduce American risk, no matter what the cost to others, turns out to be justified. This, in brief, is the criticism of the hybrid war-law model.

To be sure, the law model could be made to incorporate the war model merely by rewriting a handful of statutes. Congress could enact laws permitting imprisonment or execution of persons who pose a significant threat of terrorism whether or not they have already done anything wrong. The standard of evidence could be set low and the requirement of a hearing eliminated. Finally, Congress could authorize the use of lethal force against terrorists regardless of the danger to innocent bystanders, and it could immunize officials from lawsuits or prosecution by victims of collateral damage. Such statutes would violate the Constitution, but the Constitution could be amended to incorporate antiterrorist exceptions to the Fourth, Fifth, and Sixth Amendments. In the end, we would have a system of law that includes all the essential features of the war model.

It would, however, be a system that imprisons people for their intentions rather than their actions, and that offers the innocent few protections against mistaken detention or inadvertent

death through collateral damage. Gone are the principles that people should never be punished for their thoughts, only for their deeds, and that innocent people must be protected rather than injured by their own government. In that sense, at any rate, repackaging war as law seems merely cosmetic, because it replaces the ideal of law as a protector of rights with the more problematic goal of protecting some innocent people by sacrificing others. The hypothetical legislation incorporates war into law only by making law as partisan and ruthless as war. It no longer resembles law as Americans generally understand it.

THE THREAT TO INTERNATIONAL HUMAN RIGHTS

In the War on Terrorism, what becomes of international human rights? It seems beyond dispute that the war model poses a threat to international human rights, because honoring human rights is neither practically possible nor theoretically required during war. Combatants are legitimate targets; noncombatants maimed by accident or mistake are regarded as collateral damage rather than victims of atrocities; cases of mistaken identity get killed or confined without a hearing because combat conditions preclude due process. To be sure, the laws of war specify minimum human rights, but these are far less robust than rights in peacetime—and the hybrid war-law model reduces this schedule of rights even further by classifying the enemy as unlawful combatants.

One striking example of the erosion of human rights is tolerance of torture. It should be recalled that a 1995 al Qaeda plot to bomb eleven U.S. airliners was thwarted by information tortured out of a Pakistani suspect by the Philippine police—an eerie real-life version of the familiar philosophical thought-experiment. The *Washington Post* reports that since September 11 the U.S. has engaged in the summary transfer of dozens of terrorism suspects to countries where they will be interrogated under torture. But it isn't just the

United States that has proven willing to tolerate torture for security reasons. Last December, the Swedish government snatched a suspected Islamic extremist to whom it had previously granted political asylum, and the same day had him transferred to Egypt, where Amnesty International reports that he has been tortured to the point where he walks only with difficulty. Sweden is not, to say the least, a traditionally hard-line nation on human rights issues. None of this international transportation is lawful—indeed, it violates international treaty obligations under the Convention against Torture that in the U.S. have constitutional status as "supreme Law of the Land"—but that may not matter under the war model, in which even constitutional rights may be abrogated.

It is natural to suggest that this suspension of human rights is an exceptional emergency measure to deal with an unprecedented threat. This raises the question of how long human rights will remain suspended. When will the war be over?

Here, the chief problem is that the War on Terrorism is not like any other kind of war. The enemy, Terrorism, is not a territorial state or nation or government. There is no opposite number to negotiate with. There is no one on the other side to call a truce or declare a ceasefire, no one among the enemy authorized to surrender. In traditional wars among states, the war aim is, as Clausewitz argued, to impose one state's political will on another's. The *aim* of the war is not to kill the enemy—killing the enemy is the *means* used to achieve the real end, which is to force capitulation. In the War on Terrorism, no capitulation is possible. That means that the real aim of the war is, quite simply, to kill or capture all of the terrorists—to keep on killing and killing, capturing and capturing, until they are all gone.

Of course, no one expects that terrorism will ever disappear completely. Everyone understands that new anti-American extremists, new terrorists, will always arise and always be available for recruitment and deployment. Everyone understands that even if al Qaeda is destroyed

or decapitated, other groups, with other leaders, will arise in its place. It follows, then, that the War on Terrorism will be a war that can only be abandoned, never concluded. The War has no natural resting point, no moment of victory or finality. It requires a mission of killing and capturing, in territories all over the globe, that will go on in perpetuity. It follows as well that the suspension of human rights implicit in the hybrid war-law model is not temporary but permanent.

Perhaps with this fear in mind, Congressional authorization of President Bush's military campaign limits its scope to those responsible for September 11 and their sponsors. But the War on Terrorism has taken on a life of its own that makes the Congressional authorization little more than a technicality. Because of the threat of nuclear terror, the American leadership actively debates a war on Iraq regardless of whether Iraq was implicated in September 11; and the President's yoking of Iraq, Iran, and North Korea into a single axis of evil because they back terror suggests that the War on Terrorism might eventually encompass all these nations. If the U.S. ever unearths tangible evidence that any of these countries is harboring or abetting terrorists with weapons of mass destruction, there can be little doubt that Congress will support military action. So too, Russia invokes the American War on Terrorism to justify its attacks on Chechen rebels, China uses it to deflect criticisms of its campaign against Uighur separatists, and Israeli Prime Minister Sharon explicitly links military actions against Palestinian insurgents to the American War on Terrorism. No doubt there is political opportunism at work in some or all of these efforts to piggy-back onto America's campaign, but the opportunity would not exist if "War on Terrorism" were merely the code-name of a discrete, neatly-boxed American operation. Instead, the War on Terrorism has become a model of politics, a world-view with its own distinctive premises and consequences. As I have argued, it includes a new model of state action, the hybrid war-law model, which depresses human rights from their peace-time standard to the war-time standard, and indeed even further. So long as it continues, the War on Terrorism means the end of human rights, at least for those near enough to be touched by the fire of battle.

Sources: On the January 2002 attack on the Afghani town of Uruzgan, see: John Ward Anderson, "Afghans Falsely Held by U.S. Tried to Explain; Fighters Recount Unanswered Pleas, Beatings—and an Apology on Their Release," *Washington Post* (March 26, 2002); see also Susan B. Glasser, "Afghans Live and Die With U.S. Mistakes; Villagers Tell of Over 100 Casualties," *Washington Post* (Feb. 20, 2002). On the Third Geneva Convention, see: Geneva Convention (III) Relative to the Treatment of Prisoners of War, 6 U.S.T. 3317, signed on August 12, 1949, at Geneva, Article 17. Although the U.S. has not ratified the Geneva Convention, it has become part of customary international law, and certainly belongs to the war model. Count One of the Lindh indictment charges him with violating 18 U.S.C. 2332(b), "Whoever outside the United States attempts to kill, or engages in a conspiracy to kill, a national of the United States" may be sentenced to 20 years (for attempts) or life imprisonment (for conspiracies). Subsection (c) likewise criminalizes "engag[ing] in physical violence with intent to cause serious bodily injury to a national of the United States; or with the result that serious bodily injury is caused to a national of the United States." Lawful combatants are defined in the Hague Convention (IV) Respecting the Laws and Customs of War on Land, Annex to the Convention, 1 Bevans 631, signed on October 18, 1907, at The Hague, Article 1. The definition requires that combatants "have a fixed distinctive emblem recognizable at a distance." Protocol I Additional to the Geneva Conventions of 1949, 1125 U.N.T.S. 3, adopted on June 8, 1977, at Geneva, Article 44(3) makes an important change in the Hague Convention, expanding the definition of combatants to include non-uniformed irregulars. However, the United States has not agreed to Protocol I. The source of Ruth Wedgwood's remarks: Interview with Melissa Block, National Public Radio program, "All Things Considered" (January 18, 2002); Gary Solis, "Even a 'Bad Man' Has Rights," *Washington Post* (June 25, 2002); *Ex parte Quirin*, 317 U.S. 1, 31 (1942). On the torture of the Pakistani militant by Philippine police: Doug Struck et al., "Borderless Network of Terror; Bin Laden Followers Reach Across Globe," *Washington Post* (September 23, 2001): "'For weeks, agents hit him with a chair and a long piece of wood, forced water into his mouth, and crushed lighted cigarettes into his private parts,' wrote journalists Marites Vitug and Glenda Gloria in 'Under the Crescent Moon,' an acclaimed book on Abu Sayyaf. 'His ribs were almost totally broken and his captors were surprised he survived.'" On U.S. and Swedish transfers of Isamic militants to countries employing torture: Rajiv Chandrasakaran and Peter Finn, "U.S. Behind Secret Transfer of Terror Suspects," *Washington Post* (March 11, 2002); Peter Finn, "Europeans Tossing Terror Suspects Out the Door," *Washington Post* (January 29, 2002); Anthony Shadid, "Fighting Terror/Atmosphere in Europe, Military Campaign/Asylum Bids; in Shift, Sweden Extradites Militants to Egypt," *Boston Globe* (December 31, 2001). Article 3(1) of the Convention against Torture provides that "No State Party shall expel, return ('refouler') or extradite a person to another State where there are substantial grounds for believing that he would be in danger of being subjected to torture." Article 2(2) cautions that "No exceptional circumstances whatsoever, whether a state of war or a threat of war, internal political instability or any other public emergency, may be invoked as a justification of torture." But no parallel caution is incorporated into Article 3(1)'s non-*refoulement* rule, and a lawyer might well argue that its absence implies that the rule may be abrogated during war or similar public emergency. *Convention against Torture and Other Cruel, Inhuman or Degrading Treatment or Punishment*, 1465 U.N.T.S. 85. Ratified by the United States, Oct. 2, 1994. Entered into force for the United States, Nov. 20, 1994. (Article VI of the U.S. Constitution provides that treaties are the "supreme Law of the Land.")

⚜ REVIEW QUESTIONS

1. According to Luban, what is the traditional model of war? What are its four main features? What are its disadvantages?
2. How does Luban describe the law model? How is it combined with the war model to produce a hybrid war-law approach to terrorism?
3. In Luban's view, what is the legal status of al-Qaeda suspects? Do they have any rights?
4. Describe the case of the al-Qaeda suspects seized in Bosnia.
5. How does Luban explain the concept of enemy combatant? How is this concept applied to Jose Padilla and Yasser Esam Harudi?
6. According to Luban, what is the case for the hybrid war-law model? What is the case against it?
7. In Luban's view, what becomes of human rights in the War on Terrorism?

⚜ DISCUSSION QUESTIONS

1. In January 2002, the U.S. military killed twenty-one innocent civilians in an attack on the Afghani town of Uruzgan. Was this attack justified? Why or why not?
2. Should the Guantánamo prisoners have rights? If so, what are they? If not, why not?
3. Is it acceptable to confine suspected terrorists indefinitely with no trial?

4. Is the hybrid war-law model of the War on Terrorism acceptable? Why or why not?
5. Should torture be used to fight terrorism? Why or why not?

PROBLEM CASES

1. The Draft

According to the U.S. Selective Service System (www.sss.gov), if you are a man aged eighteen to twenty-five, you are legally required to register with the Selective Service System. You can register online or at any U.S. post office.

Congress passed the law requiring registration in 1980, but currently it is not being enforced. Since 1986, no one has been prosecuted for failure to register, but this could change if the Selective Service starts drafting men—that is, calling men up for mandatory military service. (No one has been drafted since 1973, when conscription ended.) The mission of the Selective Service System is to "serve the emergency manpower needs of the Military by conscripting untrained manpower, or personnel with professional health care skills, if directed by Congress and the President in a national crisis." The national crisis could be the ongoing wars in Iraq and Afghanistan, a war with Iran, or some other conflict.

During the Vietnam War, many young men were drafted to fight in this unpopular war. There were many ways to avoid the draft. One way was to get a college deferment. This was how Dick Cheney and Paul Wolfowitz, the advocates of the Iraq war, avoided military service. President Bill Clinton also had a college deferment. President George W. Bush used his family connections to get into the National Guard, which involved low-risk duty in the United States. Another avoidance tactic was to get a medical rejection by claiming to be suicidal or a homosexual. Men with criminal records were rejected, as well as those saying they were

communists. As a last resort, some men went to Canada, which did not support the Vietnam War.

Perhaps the most famous draft resister was boxer Muhammad Ali. In 1967, he refused induction into the armed forces. He maintained that fighting in the Vietnam War was against his Muslim religion and famously said, "I ain't got no quarrel with those Vietcong." He was convicted of refusing induction, sentenced to five years in prison, and not allowed to box professionally for more than three years. In late 1971, the Supreme Court reversed his conviction.

The Iraq war and the war in Afghanistan have produced enormous strain in the U.S. voluntary army. Soldiers are suffering from extended and repeated tours of duty. Many soldiers and officers are not reenlisting. As a result, some leaders are calling for a reinstatement of the draft. U.S. Representative Charles Rangel (D-N.Y.) has argued that poor men and women are far more likely to enlist for military service, and that this is unfair. The draft would ensure that the rich and the poor equally share military service in Iraq and other wars. Also, he argues that a country with conscription would be less likely to engage in military adventures like the one in Iraq.

In December 2006, President Bush announced that he was sending more troops to Iraq, and the next day the Selective Service System announced that it was getting ready to test the system's operations. Should the draft be reinstated? Under what circumstances, if any, would you be willing to be drafted? The question applies to women as well as men.

If we draft men for military service, why not draft women too? Other countries such as Israel draft women. Women now serve in the U.S. military with distinction; they fly jets and command troops in combat. There are plenty of young women who are just as capable as young men. Why shouldn't women be drafted?

As we have seen, during the Vietnam War many men avoided the draft by getting a college deferment. The Selective Service System has since modified this rule. Now a deferment lasts only to the end of the semester, although if a man is a senior, he can defer until the end of the academic year. Should there be college deferments? Is this fair?

During the Vietnam War, a man who claimed to be homosexual was not drafted. Currently, the armed forces discharge any person who is openly gay or lesbian. Should gay men or lesbians be drafted? Why or why not?

Why limit the draft to citizens aged eighteen to twenty-five? Why not draft older and younger people too? Is this a good idea? Why or why not?

2. War in Afghanistan

(For information and opinions on the war, see the Institute for the Study of War (www.understandingwar.org), the Center for a New American Security (www.cnas.org), and Peace Direct (www.peacedirect.org). The war began in 2001 as a response to the 9/11 attacks. The United States launched an invasion (called Operation Enduring Freedom) together with British forces. The United Nations did not approve the invasion. The initial goal was to find Osama bin Laden and other al-Qaeda members responsible for planning the 9/11 attacks and to remove the Taliban regime, which had provided a safe haven for bin Laden and the al-Qaeda organization.

In 2010, after nine years of fighting and some initial success, the U.S. and coalition forces had failed to find bin Laden and had not defeated the Taliban, who continued to fight with suicide bombers and improvised explosive devices. Bin Laden continued to issue statements from his hideout in Pakistan.

The Afghan President Hamid Karzai requested more U.S. troops in 2009, and President Obama responded by sending 30,000 additional troops in 2010, bringing the total to nearly 100,000. U.S. General Stanley A. McChrystal said that the defeat of the Taliban would require 500,000 troops and at least 5 more years of fighting, but President Obama was committed to withdrawing troops after a year or so.

According to the website www.causalities.org, there have been a total of 1,713 coalition military fatalities, including 1,034 American deaths. It is estimated that about 3,000 U.S. troops have been seriously injured in the war, and about 2,000 coalition troops seriously injured. No official estimates have been given for Afghan casualties and injuries, but a conservative estimate is that more than 8,000 Afghan troops have been killed, and about 25,000 seriously injured. It is estimated that at least 10,000 Afghan civilians have died in the fighting, and 15,000 have been seriously injured.

So far the war in Afghanistan has cost U.S. taxpayers more than $200 billion, and it is projected to cost at least half a trillion dollars when future occupation and veterans' benefits are taken into account. It is likely that U.S. troops will be based in the country for years, perhaps indefinitely. By comparison, Britain has spent about $6 billion and Canada $7 billion on the war.

Afghanistan is the world's leading producer of opium. The country makes about 90 percent of the world's opium, which is processed into heroin and sold in Europe and Russia. Heroin is one of the main sources of income in this poor country, and U.S. efforts to stop the drug trade have repeatedly failed. It is suspected that many of the top officials in the Karzai government are in the drug business. The Karzai government is widely perceived as corrupt and illegitimate. Apparently there was widespread fraud in Karzai's election. Furthermore, Karzai himself seems to be mentally unstable, having recently suggested that he was going to join the Taliban.

Should the United States continue to support the Karzai government? If not, what is the alternative?

Critics of the war point out that the Soviets also committed 100,000 troops in Afghanistan and were defeated after suffering huge loses. Does the same fate await the U.S. campaign? What do you think?

The international community has offered a billion dollars to support negotiations with the Taliban, including the leadership in Pakistan. Is this a good idea? Why or why not?

It was the al-Qaeda organization that attacked the United States, not the Taliban. The Taliban never posed a threat to the security of the United States. Now that

al-Qaeda has shifted its operations to Pakistan, defeating the Taliban will not shut down al-Qaeda. If this is true, then is continuing to fight in Afghanistan justified? Explain your position.

3. The Iraq War

For information, books, and articles on the Iraq war, see the Suggested Readings.) After a long buildup, U.S. and British troops invaded Iraq in March 2003. The war continued for at least seven years. On February 27, 2009, President Obama announced that the U.S. combat mission would end by August 31, 2010, but he also said that 50,000 troops would remain until the end of 2011. It seems likely that U.S. troops will be in Iraq for a long time.

At least two goals were accomplished by the war: First, Saddam Hussein, the brutal dictator of Iraq, was captured, given a trial, found guilty, and executed. Second, a democratically elected government, led by Prime Minister Nouri al-Maliki, took power in 2006. In an election in 2010, Maliki was defeated by Ayad Allawi, a former interim prime minister. During the election, 37 people were killed in 136 attacks using bombs, rockets, and small-arms fire. The attacks continued after the election, with nearly 60 people killed and more than 200 injured. Iraqi political experts predict a long period of political uncertainty and violence.

The war produced casualties and it was expensive. More than 4,300 U.S. troops were killed, and more than 30,000 injured. More than half of those injured returned to duty, but about 15,000 have serious injuries such as spinal cord injury or brain damage that will require life-long treatment. It is estimated that more than 300,000 troops have some level of brain damage caused by explosions from roadside bombs and other explosions. No reliable data exists for Iraqi casualties. One estimate is that the total number of deaths for all Iraqi civilians, military personnel, and insurgents is at least 70,000 and may be as high as 655,000. Another estimate is that 753,209 Iraqi civilians have been killed, and 1,355,776 have been seriously injured. About 2 million people, including many professional people, have left Iraq, and another 2 million have been displaced inside Iraq's borders. By 2010, only 15 percent of those who left Iraq had returned.

From 2003 to 2010, the war cost the United States more than $700 billion. It is estimated that the total cost to the U.S. economy will be about $3 trillion. The massive spending was conducive to bribes, fraud, and theft. For example, the U.S. Congress appropriated about $53 billion for reconstruction projects, and another $100 billion for rebuilding came from Iraqi assets. The use of cash payments and weak oversight allowed people to take bribes and steal cash. By 2010, there had been fifty-eight convictions for fraud and theft in various forms. In some cases, people simply mailed themselves money or carried it out of the country in duffel bags or suitcases. Millions of dollars were moved by wire transfer. There were about 16 million reports of suspicious financial activity involving cash deposits of more than $10,000.

What was the justification for this war? First, there was the prevention argument. In its most basic form, this is the argument that if one nation threatens another, or might be able to threaten another, then the threatened nation is justified in attacking the nation that poses the actual or possible threat. The Bush administration claimed that Iraq was possibly a threat to the United States and its allies, and that was the reason for attacking. In the words of President Bush's National Security Statement, the United States must "stop rogue states and their terrorist clients before they are able to threaten or use weapons of mass destruction against the United States and our allies and friends."

One problem with this statement is that Iraq did not have the weapons of mass destruction it was alleged to have, nor the programs to develop them. According to Hans Blix, the head of the UN inspection team, the UN inspections had been effective in eliminating the weapons or the programs to develop them. The Iraq Study Group came to similar conclusions. There was no solid evidence of the existence of the weapons or programs.

Another problem with President Bush's statement is that there was no credible evidence that Saddam Hussein was connected to either the 9/11 attacks or to the al-Qaeda organization. Richard A. Clark, the counterterrorism czar in both the Clinton and Bush administrations, claimed that President Bush was eager to attack Iraq from the beginning of his administration, and used the 9/11 attacks as an excuse to link Hussein and al Qaeda in the war on terrorism. Furthermore, it has been claimed that the Muslim terrorists hated the secular government of Saddam Hussein and welcomed its demise. The al-Qaeda organization was happy to see Hussein executed; it encouraged the violence in Iraq because it created more militants to fight the United States and its allies.

The main problem with the prevention argument is that it makes it too easy to justify war. Iraq was not an actual threat, but might have been "able to threaten," and that was enough justification for war, at least according to President Bush's statement. But, according to just war theory, war should be the last resort, not the first thing considered. Even Henry Kissinger, surely no peacenik, acknowledged this problem when he warned against using the appeal to prevention as a universal principle available to every nation. For example, during the Cold War, the USSR was actually threatened by the United States, which had thousands of missiles with nuclear warheads targeting Russian cities and military bases. Even today the United States has at least 15,000 nuclear warheads, which could be launched in a crisis or because of an accident; also, the United States reserves the right to strike first. The United States is a certainly an actual threat to Russia. Does that justify a Russian first strike?

North Korea is a rogue state that actually has nuclear weapons, and may be selling them to other countries. Are we justified in attacking North Korea? (The fact that we have not makes a good case for having nuclear weapons; they are an effective deterrent.) Iran is probably developing nuclear weapons. Should we attack Iran before it is able to produce them? This is not merely a hypothetical question. In 2010, war plans were being made to attack Iran in the event that it developed nuclear weapon capability.

A second argument used to justify the Iraq war was the humanitarian argument that Saddam Hussein was a brutal dictator—comparable to Hitler, no less— and needed to be removed from power. No doubt Hussein was an evil man, having launched aggressive wars against Iran and Kuwait; gassed thousands of Kurds; killed numerous rivals; and at least attempted to develop chemical, biological, and nuclear weapons before this was stopped by the UN inspections. These facts, however, constitute an argument for assassination, not war. The CIA tried to kill Fidel Castro several times because he was perceived to be evil, but the United States has not launched a massive invasion of Cuba. Why not? (The Bay of Pigs operation was not an all-out military operation with "shock and awe" like the Iraq war.) Besides, like the prevention argument, the humanitarian argument makes it too easy to justify war. Should we go to war against any and all countries ruled by evil persons?

A third argument used to justify the war is the legalistic argument that war with Iraq was necessary to enforce the United Nations resolutions in the face of Iraqi defiance. But France, Germany, and other member nations of the UN argued that more inspections would do the job, since Iraq was allowing them. They also contended that in the event war was necessary, it should have been undertaken by a genuine coalition of member nations, and not just by the United States and Britain with token forces contributed by other nations.

As the occupation continued through 2009, with civilian and military casualties continuing every day, pundits, analysts, and journalists offered various other justifications for war and permanent occupation by U.S. forces. One was the nation-building argument: the view that turning despotic regimes in the Middle East into secular democracies would be a good thing. This view was attributed to Bush former administration officials such as Paul Wolfowitz. However, there was the possibility that Iraq would end up being a fundamentalist Islamic state like Iran. Critics of the war maintained that the real reason for the war was President Bush getting back at his father's enemy. European critics thought the war was really about oil— America wanted to control one of the world's largest oil reserves. They pointed to President Bush's connection to the oil industry, and to the fact that Halliburton, the company run by Dick Cheney before he became vice president, was immediately given the contract to rebuild Iraq's oil industry.

All things considered, was the Iraq war justified or not? Can it be justified using just war theory? Can it be justified in some other way? Explain your position.

4. Jose Padilla

Mr. Padilla, age thirty-six, was born in Brooklyn and raised in Chicago. He served prison time for a juvenile murder in Illinois and for gun possession in Florida. He converted to Islam in prison and took the name Abdullah al Muhijir when he lived in Egypt. According to the U.S. government, he also spent time in Saudi Arabia, Pakistan, and Afghanistan.

The FBI arrested Mr. Padilla in May 2002 when he arrived from overseas at Chicago's O'Hare International Airport. Then he was held incommunicado at a Navy brig in Charleston, South Carolina, for three and one-half years, during which time he was denied counsel. No formal charges were brought against Mr. Padilla during this time, but not long after his arrest, Attorney General John Ashcroft claimed that Mr. Padilla was part of a plot by al Qaeda to explode a radiological dirty bomb.

On December 18, 2003, a federal appeals court in Manhattan ruled (2 to 1) that the president does not have the executive authority to hold American citizens indefinitely without access to lawyers simply by declaring them to be enemy combatants. The decision said that the president does not have the constitutional authority as Commander-in-Chief to detain as enemy combatants American citizens seized on American soil, away from the zone of combat. Furthermore, the ruling said, citing a 1971 statute, that Congress did not authorize detention of an American citizen under the circumstances of Mr. Padilla's case. The court ordered the government to release Mr. Padilla from military custody.

On the same day as the court's decision, the Department of Justice issued a statement on the case. The government's statement said that Mr. Padilla was associated with senior al-Qaeda leaders, including Osama bin Laden, and that he had received training from al-Qaeda operatives on wiring explosive devices and on the construction of a uranium-enhanced explosive device. The statement concluded that Mr. Padilla "is an enemy combatant who poses a serious and continuing threat to the American people and our national security."

Mr. Padilla appealed his case to the U.S. Supreme Court, but the court declined to take the case because it was moot. In November 2005, as the court challenge to his status was pending, the Bush administration suddenly announced that criminal charges had been filed against Padilla in Miami. He was moved out of military custody in Miami, where he was held without bail. Instead of being charged as an enemy combatant, he was accused of being part of a cell of Islamic terrorists. His lawyers moved to have the charges against him dismissed on the ground that the psychological damage he suffered during his long confinement from abuse and isolation left him incompetent to stand trial. The motion was denied and the trial went ahead. On August 16, 2007, he was found guilty of conspiring to kill people and supporting terrorism. Six months later, he was sentenced to 17 years and 4 months in prison.

This case raises some troubling questions. Does the government have the legal power to imprison American citizens indefinitely without bringing any charges and denying access to counsel? Is this constitutional? Do citizens charged with a crime have a right to a speedy trial?

In addition to Mr. Padilla, some 600 men of varying nationalities are being held at the Guantánamo Bay naval base in Cuba. These men were captured in Afghanistan and Pakistan during the operations against the Taliban. Like Mr. Padilla, they are deemed by the U.S. government to be enemy combatants having no legal rights. They are not being allowed to contest their detention through petitions for habeas corpus, the ancient writ which for centuries has been used in the English-speaking world to challenge the legality of confinement.

The basic issue is whether or not the president should have the power to deny basic rights in the name of fighting terrorism. What is your view of this?

5. Fighting Terrorism

What can the United States do to prevent terrorist attacks like the September 11 assault on the World Trade Center and the Pentagon? One proposal is national identity cards, discussed by Daniel J. Wakin in *The New York Times*, October 7, 2001. According to polls taken after the attacks, about 70 percent of

Americans favor such cards, which are used in other countries. French citizens are required to carry national ID cards, and they may be stopped by the police for card inspection at any time. Such cards are also required in Belgium, Greece, Luxembourg, Portugal, and Spain. Privacy International, a watchdog group in London, estimates that about one hundred countries have compulsory national IDs. Some, like Denmark, issue ID numbers at birth, around which a lifetime of personal information accumulates.

It is not clear if required ID cards would violate the U.S. Constitution. One objection is that a police demand to see the card would constitute a "seizure" forbidden by the Fourth Amendment. Another objection is that illegal immigrants would be targeted rather than terrorists. In contrast, proponents of the cards argue that they could be used to identify terrorists and protect travelers. Larry Ellison, the chief executive of the software maker Oracle, claims that people's fingerprints could be embedded on the cards and police or airport guards could scan the cards and check the fingerprints against a database of terrorists. The cards could protect airline travelers at check-in and guard against identity theft. Advocates of the cards argue that a great deal of personal information is already gathered by private industry, so any invasion of privacy occasioned by the ID cards would not matter much. What do you think? Are national ID cards a good way to fight against terrorism?

Another proposal is to allow suspicionless searches. In Israel, the police can search citizens and their belongings at any time without any particular cause or suspicion. These searches are conducted at shopping centers, airports, stadiums, and other public places. Citizens are also required to pass through metal detectors before entering public places. The U.S. Constitution requires police to have an objective suspicion or "probable cause" to search you, your belongings, or your car, but the Supreme Court has granted exceptions such as border searches and drunk-driving checkpoints. Why not allow suspicionless searches at public places like shopping centers, airports, and football stadiums?

Even more controversial is racial profiling. Israeli authorities single out travelers and citizens for questioning and searches based on racial profiling. Experts cite vigorous racial profiling as one of the reasons Israeli airplanes are not hijacked. The U.S. Supreme Court has not ruled on whether racial profiling violates the equal protection clause of the U.S. Constitution and has declined to hear cases on the practice. Opinions differ on what counts as racial profiling and when or if it is unconstitutional. Advocates of the practice claim that police already practice racial profiling and that it is effective in preventing crime. Critics object that it is nothing more than racism. Is racial profiling justified in the fight against terrorism?

In Canada, police are allowed to arrest and hold suspected terrorists without charges and without bail for up to ninety days. In France, suspects can be held for questioning for nearly five days without being charged and without having any contact with an attorney. Britain's antiterrorist legislation allows suspicious individuals to be detained for up to seven days without a court appearance. The new antiterrorist legislation proposed by the U.S. Congress would allow authorities to hold foreigners suspected of terrorist activity for up to a week without charges. Is this indefinite holding without charges and without bail acceptable?

Finally, in the fight against terrorism Israel has condoned assassinations or "judicially sanctioned executions," that is, killing of terrorist leaders such as Osama bin Laden. The United States does not currently permit assassination, but this prohibition stems from an executive order (which could be repealed), not because it is forbidden by the Constitution. Should the United States reconsider its position on assassination?

In general, are these methods of fighting terrorism acceptable to you? Why or why not?

6. National Missile Defense

National Missile Defense (NMD) is the controversial $8.3-billion missile defense shield championed by President George W. Bush and his Secretary of Defense, Donald Rumsfeld. It is an updated version of President Reagan's Strategic Defense Initiative. More than $60 billion has already been spent on the missile defense program in the last two decades.

The basic idea of NMD is appealing. Instead of ensuring peace by relying on the Cold War strategy of mutual assured destruction (MAD), where neither the

United States nor Russia can defend against nuclear attack but can destroy the other if attacked, NMD would protect the United States from missile attack with a defensive umbrella of antimissile missiles. This would give the United States an advantage over Russia or other nuclear powers not having any missile defense.

Russia is no longer seen as the main threat, even though Russia still has thousands of long-range missiles left over from the Cold War arms race. According to President Bush, the main threat to the United States comes from so-called rogue nations unfriendly to the United States, such as North Korea and Iraq. In view of the September 11 attacks, the al-Qaeda terrorist network of Osama bin Laden also should be considered a threat. Bin Laden has promised more terrorist attacks on the United States and has proclaimed a jihad against the United States. Even though these terrorists do not possess nuclear weapons or missiles at present (at least, as far as we know, they don't), it seems likely that they will acquire them in the future. Then they could hold America hostage by threatening a nuclear attack, or they might launch a surprise attack on an undefended American city such as New York City or Los Angeles.

Even though it seems like a good idea, NMD has problems. There is a good chance that it would not work in an actual attack. Two out of four major missile defense tests conducted so far have failed. Critics say that trying to hit a missile with another missile is like trying to shoot down a bullet with another bullet. It is difficult, to say the least. Countermeasures such as dummy missiles or balloons could fool the defense system. Low-tech missiles, the most likely to be used, do not follow a predictable path, so they would probably be missed by antimissile missiles.

Even if the defensive system worked perfectly, it would defend only against long-range missiles and not against nuclear weapons delivered by other means. For example, a short-range missile could be launched from a submarine just off the coast, or a weapon could be taken to its target by truck or a private shipper. The most likely scenario is that terrorists would assemble a nuclear weapon at the target and then explode it. Obviously, NMD is no defense against such terrorist attacks.

Finally, there are political problems. NMD violates the 1972 Antiballistic Missile Treaty with Russia. The treaty limits the testing and deployment of new defense systems. Russian President Vladimir Putin contends that violating the 1972 treaty will upset nuclear stability and result in a new arms race.

Given these problems and how much it will cost, is NMD a good idea? What is your position?

7. Mini-Nukes

(For more details, see Fred Kaplan, "Low-Yield Nukes," posted November 21, 2003, on http://www.slate.msn.com.)

In 1970, the United States signed the Non-Proliferation Treaty. This treaty involved a pact between nations having nuclear weapons and nations not having them. Nations not having them promised not to develop nuclear weapons, and nations already having them promised to pursue nuclear disarmament. In 1992, the United States unilaterally stopped nuclear testing, on orders of the first President Bush, and then formalized this in 1995 by signing the Comprehensive Test Ban Treaty. This latter treaty prohibits the testing and development of nuclear weapons indefinitely, and it was signed by 186 other nations.

In 2003, the second Bush administration insisted that Iran and North Korea halt their nuclear weapons programs, and argued that the invasion and occupation of Iraq were justified because Iraq had weapons of mass destruction (WMD), that is, chemical, biological, and nuclear weapons (or at least a nuclear weapons program). Yet, at the same time, the second Bush administration was actively developing a new generation of exotic nuclear weapons, including low-yield mini-nukes and earth-penetrating nukes, despite the fact that the country already had 7,650 nuclear warheads and bombs. Specifically, the fiscal year 2004 defense bill, passed by both houses of Congress in November 2003, did four things. First, it repealed the 1992 law banning the development of low-yield nuclear weapons. Second, the bill provided $15 million to develop an earth-penetrating nuclear weapon, a bunker buster. Third, it allocated $6 million to explore special-effects bombs, for example, the neutron bomb that enhances radiation. Finally, the bill provided $25 million for underground nuclear tests.

This renewed development of nuclear weapons and testing violated the 1970 and 1995 treaties, but the second Bush administration argued that it was necessary to do this for self-defense. The old warheads mounted on intercontinental missiles were designed to wipe out industrial complexes or destroy whole cities. Such weapons were never used, and it appeared that they no longer had any utility. Certainly they were not effective against suicide bombers or other terrorist attacks. What was needed, it was argued, was smaller warheads that could destroy underground bunkers or WMD storage sites.

Critics argued that the U.S. development of more nuclear weapons undermined the attempt to stop similar development in other nations. If the United States needed nuclear weapons for self-defense, then why didn't other nations need them too? The fact that the United States did not attack North Korea (which had

nuclear weapons) seemed to support the view that nations needed these weapons to deter attacks.

Furthermore, critics argued that mini-nukes or bunker busters were not necessary. Conventional weapons could do the job. The United States already had at least two non-nuclear smart bombs that could penetrate the earth before exploding. There was the GBU-24, a 2000-pound laser-guided bomb, and the BLU-109 JDAM, a 2000-pound satellite-guided bomb. Both of these bombs could be filled with incendiary explosive that would burn whatever biological or chemical agents might be stored in an underground site.

So why did the United States need to develop more nuclear weapons? Was this necessary or effective for self-defense? Explain your answer. Why did the United States continue to keep 7,650 nuclear warheads and bombs? Was it ever necessary to have so many weapons? Is it necessary now? What is your view?

8. The Gulf War

(For a book-length treatment of the Gulf War, including the view of it as jihad, see Kenneth L. Vaux, *Ethics and the Gulf War* [Boulder, CO: Westview Press, 1992].) In August 1990, the Iraqi army invaded and occupied Kuwait. Although the United States had received warnings, officials did not take them seriously. Saddam Hussein believed the United States would not intervene and apparently had received assurances to that effect. Hussein claimed that the invasion was justified because Kuwait had once been part of Iraq and because the Kuwaitis were exploiting the Rumalla oilfield, which extended into Iraq. The immediate response of the United States and its allies was to begin a ship embargo against Iraq. President George Bush, citing atrocities against the Kuwaitis, compared Hussein to Hitler. For his part, Hussein declared the war to be jihad and threatened the mother of all battles (as he put it) if the Americans dared to intervene. Iran's Ayatollah Khomeini, certainly no friend of the United States, seconded the claim of jihad, adding that anyone killed in battle would be a martyr and immediately go to paradise, the Islamic heaven.

In the months that followed, Iraq ignored repeated ultimatums to leave Kuwait. But Iraq did try to stall for time, following the Koranic teaching of "withholding

your hand a little while from war" (Vaux, 1992, p. 71). Thousands of foreign prisoners were released, and Iraq responded positively to French and Soviet peace initiatives. At the same time, Saddam Hussein continued to call it a holy war, saying that the United States was a satanic force attacking the religious values and practices of Islam.

On January 16, 1991, after a UN deadline had passed, the allied forces (American, British, French, Saudi, and Kuwaiti) launched a massive day-and-night air attack on military targets in Iraq, including the capital city of Baghdad. The forty days of air war that followed were very one-sided. The allied forces were able to bomb targets at will using advanced technical weapons such as radar-seeking missiles, laser-guided bombs, stealth fighters that avoided radar detection, and smart cruise missiles that could adjust their course. The Iraqi air force never got off the ground, but hid or flew to Iran. Iraqi Scud missiles killed twenty-two American soldiers sleeping in Saudi Arabia and civilians in Israel, but were mostly unreliable and ineffective. Finally, the ground war (Operation Desert Storm) lasted only 100 hours before the allied forces liberated Kuwait City. The Iraqis suffered more than 200,000 casualties (according to American estimates), whereas the allied forces sustained fewer than 200 casualties.

Can this war be justified using the just war theory? Carefully explain your answer. Keep in mind that some religious leaders at the time said that it was not a just war.

Was this really a jihad, as Saddam Hussein and the Ayatollah Khomeini said? Remember that Kuwait and Saudi Arabia are also Muslim countries.

Oil presented another consideration. Kuwait had about 20 percent of the world's known oil reserves at the time. Some said the war was really about the control and price of oil and argued that if Kuwait had not had valuable resources, the United States would not have intervened. (For example, the United States did nothing when China invaded and occupied a defenseless Tibet in 1949.)

☙ SUGGESTED READINGS

Several U.S. government websites post information and news about the ongoing wars and terrorism. See those of the Department of Defense (www.defense.gov), the CIA (www.cia.gov), the Department of Homeland Security (www.dhs.gov), the FBI (www.fbi.org), and the White House (www.whitehouse.gov). For antiwar and pacifist views, see www.antiwar.com and www.nonviolence.org. The Arab perspective is presented at www.iwpr.net.

Michael G. Knapp, "The Concept and Practice of Jihad in Islam," *Parameters*, Spring (2003): 82–84, surveys the concept of jihad in Islam. In the classical view, jihad was restricted to defensive war against non-Muslims. Modern militant Islam changed the concept to include wars of aggression. The movement reached an extreme with Osama bin Laden, who declared jihad, war, against the United States and its allies.

Louise Richardson, *What Terrorists Want: Understanding the Enemy, Containing the Threat* (New York: Random House, 2007), explains the causes of terrorism, proposes a definition, and discusses the proper response.

Claudia Card, "Questions Regarding a War on Terrorism," *Hypatia*, Vol. 18, No. 1 (Winger 2003): 164–169, critically examines the so-called *war on terrorism*.

William V. O'Brien, *The Conduct of Just and Limited War* (Westport, CT: Greenwood Publishing Group, 1981), gives an exhaustive and detailed explanation of traditional just war theory.

Michael W. Brough, John W. Lango, and Harry van der Linden, eds., *Rethinking the Just War Tradition* (Albany, NY: State University of New York Press, 2007), is a valuable collection of articles on just war theory, the distinction between combatants and noncombatants, and preventive war.

Timothy Shanahan, ed., *Philosophy 9/11* (Peru, IL: Open Court Publishing, 2005), is a collection of articles on terrorism, just war theory, terrorists, the war on terrorism, and counterterrorism.

Uwe Steinhoff, *On the Ethics of War and Terrorism* (Oxford: Oxford University Press, 2007), examines war and terrorism using just war theory. There are chapters on legitimate authority, just cause and right intention, innocents, double effect, and proportionality.

Seamus Miller, *Terrorism and Counter-Terrorism* (Oxford: Blackwell Publishing, 2009), critically examines various issues about terrorism. There are chapters on the varieties of terrorism, defining terrorism, terrorism and collective responsibility, terrorism-as-crime, and terrorism in war.

Pierre Allan and Alexis Keller, eds., *What Is a Just Peace?* (Oxford: Oxford University Press, 2008), is a collection of readings on the problem of determining a just peace. For example, what would be a just peace plan for ending the Israeli-Palestinian conflict?

Osama bin Laden, "To the Americans," in *Messages to the World*, ed. B. Lawrence (London: Verso, 2005), 162–172. This letter gives bin Laden's reasons for the 9/11 attacks. It was published in the *London Observer* on November 24, 2002. An al-Qaeda document that attempts to justify the 9/11 attacks is available in English translation at www.mepc.org.

Hans Blix, *Disarming Iraq* (New York: Pantheon Books, 2004), concludes that every claim made by the Bush administration about Iraq's weapons programs—the mobile biological labs, the yellowcake, the aluminum tubes—has proven to be false and that the Iraq war was unnecessary.

Richard A. Clarke, *Against All Enemies* (New York: Free Press, 2004). Clarke was the counterterrorism coordinator in both the Clinton and the second Bush administrations. He claims that President George W. Bush was obsessed with Iraq after the 9/11 attacks and eager to blame Iraq even though there was overwhelming evidence that al Qaeda was responsible and Saddam Hussein was not.

Christopher Hitchens, *A Long Short War* (London: Plume, 2003), is an enthusiastic supporter of the Iraq war. He claims that it liberated the Iraqis from oppression and prevented Iraq from attacking the United States with nuclear weapons.

Robert Kagan and William Kristol, "The Right War for the Right Reasons," in *The Right War*, ed. Gary Kosen (Cambridge: Cambridge University Press, 2005), 18–35, defend the Iraq war. They claim that Saddam Hussein had "undeniable ties" to terrorists, was a brutal dictator, and was pursuing weapons of mass destruction.

Jan Narveson, "Regime Change," in *A Matter of Principle*, ed. Thomas Cushman (Berkeley: University of California Press, 2005), 58–75, presents the case for regime change in Iraq. He argues that military intervention in Iraq was justified because it produced a decent regime "at modest cost to the Iraqis" and "at quite modest cost in lives to the Coalition" (p. 74).

C. A. J. Coady, "Terrorism and Innocence," *Journal of Ethics* 8 (2004): 37–58, discusses problems with defining terrorism and deciding who is innocent.

Burleigh Taylor Wilkins, *Terrorism and Collective Responsibility* (London: Routledge, 1992), argues that terrorism can be morally justified in certain circumstances. For example, terrorism aimed at defeating Hitler would have been justified.

Whitley R. P. Kaufman, "Terrorism, Self-Defense, and the Killing of the Innocent," *Social Philosophy Today* 20 (2004): 41–52, argues that terrorism violates the moral prohibition against harming the innocent, and as such is always morally impermissible.

Andrew Valls, "Can Terrorism Be Justified?" in *Ethics in International Affairs*, ed. Andrew Valls (Lanham, MD: Roman & Littlefield, 2000), 65–79, argues that if war can be justified using just war theory, then terrorism can be justified as well.

Virginia Held, "Legitimate Authority in Non-state Groups Using Violence," *Journal of Social Philosophy* 36, no. 2 (Summer 2005): 175–193, argues that in actual circumstances, such as the struggle to gain independence in South Africa, some uses of violence may be justified, and terrorism may be as justified as war.

Steve Coll, *Ghost Wars* (London: Penguin Press, 2004), explains the history of al Qaeda in Afghanistan, including how Saudi Arabia aided the rise of Osama bin Laden and Islamic extremism.

Ahmed Rashid, *Taliban: Militant Islam, Oil, and Fundamentalism in Central Asia* (New Haven, CT: Yale University Press, 2000), presents the history of the Taliban and explains their version of Islam. They believe they are God's invincible soldiers fighting an unending war against unbelievers.

Anthony H. Cordesman, *Terrorism, Asymmetric Warfare, and Weapons of Mass Destruction* (Westport, CT: Praeger, 2001), discusses previous commissions on terrorism, the details of homeland defense, and the risk of chemical and biological attacks.

Yossef Bodansky, *Bin Laden: The Man Who Declared War on America* (New York: Random House, 2001). This book is by a well-known expert on terrorism; it covers bin Laden's life and his pursuit of chemical, biological, and nuclear weapons.

Paul R. Pillar, *Terrorism and U.S. Foreign Policy* (Washington, DC: Brookings Institution, 2001), explains the causes of modern terrorism in countries such as Pakistan and Afghanistan and examines the new war against terrorism.

Peter Partner, *God of Battles: Holy Wars of Christianity and Islam* (Princeton, NJ: Princeton University Press, 1998), explains the doctrines of war in Christianity and Islam.

James Turner Johnson, *Mortality and Contemporary Warfare* (New Haven, CT: Yale University Press, 1999), presents the history and development of just war theory and its application in the real world.

Bryan Brophy-Baermann and John A. C. Conybeare, "Retaliating against Terrorism," *American Journal of Political Science* 38, no. 1 (February 1994): 196–210, argue that retaliation against terrorism produces a temporary deviation in attacks but no long-term effect.

Dilip Hiro, *Holy Wars: The Rise of Islamic Fundamentalism* (London: Routledge, 1989), explains the development of Islamic fundamentalism found today in Iran and Afghanistan, where Islam has emerged as a radical ideology of armed warfare.

Ayatollah Ruhollah Khomeini, "Islam Is Not a Religion of Pacifists," in *Holy Terror*, ed. Amir Taheri (Bethesda, MD: Adler & Adler, 1987), gives a clear statement of the Islamic doctrine of holy war. According to the Ayatollah Khomeini, Islam says, "Kill all the unbelievers just as they would kill you all!"

R. Peters, "Jihad," in *The Encyclopedia of Religion* (New York: Macmillan, 1989), gives a scholarly account of the Islamic concept of jihad and its application to war.

A. Mallory, *The Crusaders through Arab Eyes* (New York: Schocken Books, 1985), covers two centuries of hostility and war between Muslim Arabs and Christian Crusaders from the West (called Franks), starting with the fall of Jerusalem in 1099. It is a depressing history of invasion, counterinvasion, massacres, and plunder.

Michael Walzer, *Just and Unjust Wars: A Moral Argument with Historical Illustrations* (New York: Basic Books, 1977), develops and defends just war theory and applies the theory to numerous historical cases, such as the Six-Day War, the Vietnam War, the Korean War, and World War II. He argues that the Vietnam War can be justified as assistance to the legitimate government of South Vietnam.

Robert L. Phillips, *War and Justice* (Norman: University of Oklahoma Press, 1984), defends just war theory. He accepts two principles of the theory, the principle of proportionality and the principle of discrimination. The latter principle, however, in turn rests on the doctrine of double effect, which distinguishes between intending to kill and merely foreseeing that death will occur as an unintended consequence of an action.

James Johnson, *The Just War Tradition and the Restraint of War* (Princeton, NJ: Princeton University Press, 1981), explains the historical development of just war theory from the Middle Ages to the present.

Paul Ramsey, *The Just War: Force and Political Responsibility* (New York: Charles Scribner's Sons, 1968). This book is a collection of articles on just war theory, all written by Ramsey. He is a Christian who defends a version of the theory that has an absolute principle of discrimination against killing noncombatants. Yet having accepted this principle, he goes on to claim that the war in Vietnam was justified though it involved killing many noncombatants.

Paul Christopher, *The Ethics of War and Peace* (Englewood Cliffs, NJ: Prentice Hall, 1994). This textbook covers the just war tradition, the international laws on war, and moral issues such as war crimes; reprisals; and nuclear, biological, and chemical weapons.

Immanuel Kant, *Perpetual Peace* (New York: Liberal Arts Press, 1957). In a classic discussion, Kant maintains that war must not be conducted in a way that rules out future peace. Perpetual peace results when democratic countries let the people decide about going to war. Kant believes that the people will always vote for peace.

Albert Schweitzer, *The Teaching of Reverence for Life*, trans. Richard and Clara Masters (New York: Holt, Rinehart & Winston, 1965), argues that all taking of life is wrong because all life is sacred.

Leo Tolstoy, *The Law of Love and the Law of Violence*, trans. Mary Koutouzow Tolstoy (New York: Holt, Rinehart & Winston, 1971), explains his Christian pacifism.

Mohandas K. Gandhi, "The Practice of Satyagraha," in *Gandhi: Selected Writings*, ed. Ronald Duncan (New York: Harper & Row, 1971), presents his view of nonviolent resistance as an alternative to war.

T. R. Miles, "On the Limits to the Use of Force," *Religious Studies* 20 (1984): 113–120, defends a version of pacifism that is opposed to all war but not to all use of force. This kind of pacifism would require one to refuse to serve in the military but would not rule out serving as a police officer.

William Earle, "In Defense of War," *The Monist* 57, no. 4 (October 1973): 561–569 attacks pacifism (defined as the principled opposition to all war) and then gives a justification for the morality and rationality of war.

Jan Narveson, "In Defense of Peace," in *Moral Issues*, ed. Jan Narveson (Oxford: Oxford University Press, 1983), 59–71, replies to Earle. He does not defend pacifism; instead, he argues that whenever there is a war, at least one party is morally unjustified.

Jan Narveson, "Morality and Violence: War, Revolution, Terrorism," in *Matters of Life and Death: New Introductory Essays in Moral Philosophy*, ed. Tom Regan (New York: McGraw Hill, 1993), pp. 121–159. In this survey article, Narveson covers many different issues, including the nature and morality of violence, the right of self-defense, pacifism, just war theory, and terrorism.

Richard A. Wasserstrom, ed., *War and Morality* (Belmont, CA: Wadsworth, 1970), is a collection of articles on the morality of war and other issues. Elizabeth Anscombe discusses the doctrine of double effect as it applies to war. Wasserstrom argues that modern wars are very difficult to justify because innocents are inevitably killed.

Jean Bethke Elshtain, *Women and War* (New York: Basic Books, 1987). What is the feminist view of war? According to Elshtain, some feminists are pacifists working for world peace, whereas others want to reject the traditional noncombatant role of women and become warriors. As a result of the second position, the United States now has a higher percentage of women in the military than any other industrialized nation.

Sebastian Junger, *War* (New York: Hachette Book Group, 2010), gives a vivid account of the U.S. military operations in the Korengal Valley, the valley in Afghanistan where the Soviets were defeated. In 2010 the U.S. military abandoned its bases and withdrew from the valley.

Torture

INTRODUCTION

Factual Background

Humans have been torturing each other for a long time. Throughout the ages, the most common method has been beating. The Romans used the cat-of-nine-tails, a whip having nine tips embedded with lead, nails, and glass; it was used to flog people to extract information. The Chinese used bamboo sticks to beat people. During the Spanish Inquisition, torture was used to get confessions or religious conversions. One common method was called the *strappado*: The hands were bound behind the back, and the victim was suspended until the joints in the arms and shoulders dislocated. Other torture methods included the rack, the iron maiden, the thumbscrew, the boot, and red-hot pincers applied to the toes, ears, nose, or nipples. In modern times, electricity has become one of the most popular and painful tools of torturers. Prisoners are poked with electric cattle prods or have car battery leads attached to their bodies. Stun weapons are used to deliver shocks up to 75,000 volts. Psychological torture is common and includes prolonged solitary confinement, hooding, stress positions, withholding food and water, sleep deprivation, loud noise, bright light, hot and cold temperatures, nakedness, rape and sexual humiliation, mock executions, water boarding, and the use of dogs. Another method is to inject drugs such as sodium pentothal, which depresses the central nervous system and is supposed to make the subject easier to interrogate.

There are international agreements that prohibit torture. The United Nations Universal Declaration of Human Rights, Article 5, says, "No one shall be subjected to torture or cruel, inhuman, or degrading treatment or punishment." The Geneva Convention, Article 3, prohibits "cruel treatment and torture." It also bans "outrages upon personal dignity, in particular, humiliating and degrading treatment." (See the Problem Case.)

American soldiers at Abu Ghraib prison outside Baghdad, Iraq, violated these prohibitions. According to a 2003 report by Major General Antonio M. Taguba, there were numerous instances of "sadistic, blatant, and wanton criminal abuses," including pouring cold water or phosphoric liquid on naked detainees, threatening them with rape or death, sodomizing them with broomsticks, and using military dogs to bite them. There is the well-known picture of a hooded man forced to stand on a box with wires attached to his hands and neck. Reportedly, he was told that he would be electrocuted if he stepped or fell off the box. Former prisoners tell stories of U.S. soldiers beating prisoners, sometimes to death. Mohammed Unis Hassan says that he was cuffed to bars of his cell and then a female soldier poked his eye with her fingers so hard that he couldn't see afterward. Now his left eye is gray and glassy and his vision is blurred. He says he saw an old man forced to lie naked on his face until he died. Other naked prisoners were threatened and bitten by attack dogs.

Some of the mistreatment at Abu Ghraib involved sexual humiliation. There are photographs of naked Iraqi prisoners forced to simulate oral or anal sex. Private Lynndie England is shown giving a thumbs-up sign and pointing to the genitals of a naked and hooded Iraqi as he masturbates. In another picture, Private England is shown with Specialist Charles A. Graner, both grinning and giving the thumbs-up sign in front of a pile of naked Iraqis. Another picture shows Private England leading a naked man around on a dog leash.

Another place where prisoners have been tortured is the U.S. naval base at Guantánamo Bay, Cuba. FBI agents, Red Cross inspectors, and numerous released detainees have alleged that prisoners were chained in a fetal position on the floor or in a baseball catcher's position, subjected to extremes of temperature, made to walk on broken glass or barbed wire, subjected to loud music and flashing lights, given electrical shocks, chained and hanged from the ceiling, and beaten. One of the more bizarre acts was throwing the Koran in the toilet.

The revelation of torture at Abu Ghraib and Guantánamo Bay produced outrage among human rights activists. The response of the Bush administration was a Justice Department memo in 2002 asserting that inflicting moderate pain is not torture. According to the memo, mistreatment is torture only if it produces suffering "equivalent in intensity to the pain accompanying serious physical injury, such as organ failure, impairment of bodily function, or even death." On his talk show, Rush Limbaugh said that the sexual humiliation at Abu Ghraib was just harmless fun, similar to what goes on in college fraternities or secret societies.

In 2006, President Bush signed the McCain Detainee Amendment into law. It prohibits "cruel, inhuman or degrading" treatment of prisoners by U.S. officials or agents, but it is not clear what torture methods are prohibited. The amendment requires that military interrogations follow the U.S. Army's *Field Manual on Interrogation*, but this document is being rewritten and the section on interrogation techniques is classified. The McCain amendment authorizes any method on the highly classified list of techniques, no matter what they are.

The interrogation methods used by the United States are secret, and they have also been outsourced to other countries. The CIA has been operating covert prisons in eight countries, including Egypt, Thailand, Afghanistan, and several democracies in Eastern Europe. The existence and locations of these facilities, called "black sites," were classified, but President Bush revealed their existence in September 2006. He said in a speech that fourteen prisoners had been moved from the CIA's secret prisons in Europe to Guantánamo Bay. The prisoners included Khalid Sheik Mohammed, who confessed to planning the 9/11 attacks. (See the Problem Case.) President Bush said the fourteen prisoners were the last ones remaining in CIA custody, but Manfred Nowak, the UN special investigator on torture, said, "Of course there are many others." In his speech, President Bush said, "The United States does not torture," but he refused to say what specific methods had been used to get confessions from the prisoners.

The Readings

Alan Dershowitz defends the use of nonlethal torture to get lifesaving information from a terrorist. He gives two examples of instances in which torture can be morally justified. The examples are hypothetical, but they are based on actual situations. First, suppose the FBI tortured Zacarias Moussaoui before the 9/11 attacks and used the information gained from his torture to prevent the attacks. Dershowitz is confident that everyone will agree the torture was justified. Second, suppose a stolen Russian nuclear weapon is going to be detonated in New York City. The detonation of this "ticking bomb" can be prevented if we torture a terrorist and find out where it is located. Again, Dershowitz is sure that people will agree the torture was justified. In both cases, the justification is basically a simple appeal to costs and benefits; that is, to act utilitarianism. The pain of torture is bad, but the good produced, namely saving thousands of lives, makes the torture morally justified.

It can be objected that allowing torture in these cases turns it into a social practice or institution. This is undesirable because it leads to torture in other cases in which it is not justified. Dershowitz's reply to this slippery-slope objection is that principled lines have to be drawn between justified and unjustified torture. But whom can we trust to do this? Dershowitz proposes that judges issue "torture warrants" making torture legal in cases in which it is justified. Torture warrants are better than allowing secret torture because they protect the rights of the suspect and provide the open accountability and visibility that is important in a democracy.

David Luban does not agree that torture is morally justified in a ticking-bomb case like the one described by Dershowitz. He claims the ticking-bomb story is intellectual fraud that tricks us into thinking that torture can be justified and that the torturer is not a sadistic brute but a heroic public servant trying to save innocent lives. Luban claims that the story cheats by assuming too much—that officials know there is a bomb, that they have captured the one who planted it or knows where it is, that torture will make him talk, and so on. None of this is certain in the real world. Also, the story assumes that it is rational to choose between the certainty of torture versus the uncertainty of saving lives and that a decision can be made by calculating costs and benefits. All this is so remote from the real world that the wise course is to deny the possibility. It is a waste of time, insane, or frivolous to try to make a moral decision in this case. Besides, back in the real world, once it is granted that torture is permitted in the imaginary ticking-bomb case, we end up with a torture culture with torture practices, training, and institutions.

Uwe Steinhoff has a different position. Unlike Luban, he thinks torture is clearly justified in rare cases. There is the Dirty Harry case, where Harry saves an innocent girl's life by torturing the guilty kidnapper. As for the ticking-bomb case, Steinhoff argues that interrogative torture of a terrorist is morally justified even if we are not certain about the relevant facts—that we have the right person, that he knows where the bomb is located, and so on. Torturing a suspect who might be guilty of planting a bomb is like shooting a man who seems ready to kill the president. We have to act even if we are not certain. Steinhoff also attacks Dershowitz's proposal for torture warrants. Torture may be morally justified in rare cases, but that does not mean it should be legal. It can remain illegal and be excused in the rare cases in which it is justified. It is unnecessary to have torture warrants if torture is rarely used. Furthermore, torture warrants result in the institutionalization of torture, and this conflicts with the general prohibition of torture. Finally, torture warrants lead to a brutalization of the enforcers, which includes the state.

Heather MacDonald (see the Suggested Readings) defends the U.S. military's treatment of enemy combatants. She argues that the actual interrogational techniques used by the military are light-years away from real torture and are controlled by bureaucratic safeguards. The illegal acts at Abu Ghraib were not the result of any official decisions, but rather were caused by the anarchy of war. As for the alleged torture at Guantánamo, the interrogational techniques used there were not torture at all, in her view. They were merely stress techniques that included isolation, sleep deprivation, loud noise, prolonged standing, poking, grabbing, and so on. She admits, however, that the water boarding of Khalid Sheik Mohammed (see the Problem Case) arguably crossed the line into torture, and she notes that the CIA's behavior remains a "black box." She insists that to succeed in the war on terrorism, interrogators must be allowed to use these stress techniques on terrorists.

Philosophical Issues

What is torture? There is disagreement about how to define *torture* and what treatment is considered torture. MacDonald quotes a famous 2002 memo by Assistant Attorney General Jay S. Bybee, which interprets the 1984 Convention Against Torture as forbidding only physical pain equivalent to that "accompanying serious physical injury, such as organ failure, impairment of bodily function or even death," or mental pain resulting in "significant psychological harm of significant duration, e.g., lasting for months or even years." Following Luban, we can call this "torture heavy." Most people would classify water boarding, electrocution, and severe beating as torture heavy.

MacDonald and others argue that the interrogation techniques used at Guantánamo and other secret locations were not torture, or at least not torture heavy. What should we call being chained in a fetal position, or given electrical shocks, or being chained and hanged from the ceiling? Most people would say these treatments are a form of torture. Following Luban, we can call such treatment "torture lite."

Luban also discusses deceptive techniques designed to elicit emotions such as fear, hate, and love. He does not think they amount to torture, but they do create an environment of mind control. Then there is abuse, which seems to be a milder form of torture lite.

Dershowitz mentions inserting a needle under the fingernails to produce unbearable pain without any threat to life or health and drilling an unanesthetized tooth. These techniques seem to be torture heavy even though they are not lethal.

In contrast to the Bybee memo, the Human Rights Watch statement (also quoted by MacDonald) includes among the effects of torture "long-term depression, post-traumatic stress disorder, marked sleep disturbances and alterations in self-perceptions, not to mention feelings of powerlessness, of fear, guilt and shame." If those are the effects of torture, then all the techniques described by MacDonald, and certainly the techniques used by the CIA (see the Problem Case), count as torture.

What techniques should be allowed when interrogating terrorists? MacDonald's position is that torture lite should be permitted but not torture heavy. Dershowitz and Steinhoff seem to allow anything short of killing the terrorist. The Human Rights Watch position is that prisoners should not be tortured, and torture includes both torture lite and heavy. Luban argues that if we allow torture lite it will turn into torture heavy. In other words, there is a slippery slope where deception slides into abuse, abuse slides into torture lite, and torture lite slides into torture heavy. To avoid the slippery slope, we need to draw bright lines prohibiting abuse and torture.

Is torture morally wrong? Luban says that reverence for human rights and dignity makes torture morally unacceptable. Dershowitz and Steinhoff agree that it is usually morally wrong, but they both argue that it can be morally justified in some cases, for example, in the ticking-bomb case. Steinhoff says that cases of justified torture are very rare, while Dershowitz is willing to let a judge decide when torture is morally justified. It seems safe to say that all three would agree that sadistic torture—that is, torture done merely to cause suffering—is obviously wrong, even if the torturer enjoys it. (Kant famously gave sadistic torture as a counterexample to utilitarianism.) They would agree that torture done to punish a criminal is wrong as well. For one thing, it violates the Eighth Amendment prohibition of cruel and unusual punishment. They would condemn torturing a prisoner to produce a confession. Besides being cruel, torturing to produce a confession is worthless because people will confess to anything under torture. (See the book by William Sampson in the Suggested Readings.)

The debate about the morality of torture in the readings centers around interrogation torture and, specifically, whether torture is morally justified in a ticking-bomb case. This case was first discussed by Henry Shue (see the Suggested Reading). Shue argued that torture is permitted in this case, but like Steinhoff he had reservations. Even if it is permitted in this unusual case, this does not mean torture should be legalized. As we have seen, Dershowitz not only thinks torture is morally justified in cases in which lives can be saved, it also should be legal when authorized by a judge. Luban does not agree that torture is morally permitted in the ticking-bomb case, or in any other case for that matter. He characterizes the ticking-bomb case as a fraud, a picture that bewitches us. His position is that torture, whether heavy or lite, should be absolutely prohibited.

The Case for Torturing the Ticking Bomb Terrorist

ALAN DERSHOWITZ

Alan Dershowitz is the Felix Frankfurter Professor of Law at Harvard Law School. He is the author of 25 books and more than 100 articles. His most recent book is *The Case for Moral Clarity: Israel, Hamas and Gaza* (2009).

Dershowitz makes the case for torturing terrorists in cases in which many lives can be saved, for example, to prevent a nuclear bomb from being detonated in New York City. A simple cost-benefit analysis makes it obvious that torture is justified in such cases. It is better to torture a guilty terrorist than to allow millions of innocent victims to die. In reply to the slippery-slope objection that allowing torture in such cases will lead to unjustified torture, Dershowitz argues that clear lines must be drawn. To do this, he proposes that torture warrants (like search warrants) be issued by a judge. These warrants would help secure the safety of citizens, and at the same time recognize civil liberties and human rights. They would ensure the open account-ability required in a democracy, and be preferable to secret, off-the-books torture because they would actually reduce the mistreatment of suspects and protect their rights.

The arguments in favor of using torture as a last resort to prevent a ticking bomb from exploding and killing many people are both simple and simple-minded. Bentham constructed a compelling hypothetical case to support his utilitarian argument against an absolute prohibition on torture:

> Suppose an occasion were to arise, in which a suspicion is entertained, as strong as that which would be received as a sufficient ground for arrest and commitment as for felony—a suspicion that at this very time a considerable number of individuals are actually suffering, by illegal violence inflictions equal in intensity to those which if inflicted by the hand of justice, would universally be spoken of under the name of torture. For the purpose of rescuing from torture these hundred innocents, should any scruple be made of applying equal or superior torture, to extract the requisite information from the mouth of one criminal, who having it in his power to make known the place where at this time the enormity was practising or about to be practised, should refuse to do so? To say nothing of wisdom, could any pretence be made so much as to the praise of blind and vulgar humanity, by the man who to save one criminal, should determine to abandon 100 innocent persons to the same fate?[1]

If the torture of one guilty person would be justified to prevent the torture of a hundred innocent persons, it would seem to follow—certainly to Bentham—that it would also be justified to prevent the murder of thousands of innocent civilians in the ticking bomb case. Consider two hypothetical situations that are not, unfortunately, beyond the realm of possibility. In fact, they are both extrapolations on actual situations we have faced.

Several weeks before September 11, 2001, the Immigration and Naturalization Service detained Zacarias Moussaoui after flight instructors reported suspicious statements he had made while taking flying lessons and paying for them with large amounts of cash.[2] The government decided not to seek a warrant to search his computer. Now imagine that they had, and that they discovered he was part of a plan to destroy large occupied buildings, but without any further details. They interrogated him, gave him immunity from prosecution, and offered him large cash

Source: From Why Terrorism Works: Understanding the Threat, Responding to the Challenge by Alan Dershowitz. Copyright © 2003. New Haven, CT: Yale University Press.

rewards and a new identity. He refused to talk. They then threatened him, tried to trick him, and employed every lawful technique available. He still refused. They even injected him with sodium pentothal and other truth serums, but to no avail. The attack now appeared to be imminent, but the FBI still had no idea what the target was or what means would be used to attack it. We could not simply evacuate all buildings indefinitely. An FBI agent proposes the use of nonlethal torture—say, a sterilized needle inserted under the fingernails to produce unbearable pain without any threat to health or life, or the method used in the film *Marathon Man*, a dental drill through an unanesthetized tooth.

The simple cost-benefit analysis for employing such nonlethal torture seems overwhelming: it is surely better to inflict nonlethal pain on one guilty terrorist who is illegally withholding information needed to prevent an act of terrorism than to permit a large number of innocent victims to die.[3] Pain is a lesser and more remediable harm than death; and the lives of a thousand innocent people should be valued more than the bodily integrity of one guilty person. If the variation on the Moussaoui case is not sufficiently compelling to make this point, we can always raise the stakes. Several weeks after September 11, our government received reports that a ten-kiloton nuclear weapon may have been stolen from Russia and was on its way to New York City, where it would be detonated and kill hundreds of thousands of people. The reliability of the source, code named Dragonfire, was uncertain, but assume for purposes of this hypothetical extension of the actual case that the source was a captured terrorist—like the one tortured by the Philippine authorities—who knew precisely how and where the weapon was being brought into New York and was to be detonated. Again, everything short of torture is tried, but to no avail. It is not absolutely certain torture will work, but it is our last, best hope for preventing a cataclysmic nuclear devastation in a city too large to evacuate in time. Should nonlethal torture be tried? Bentham would certainly have said yes.

The strongest argument against any resort to torture, even in the ticking bomb case, also derives from Bentham's utilitarian calculus. Experience has shown that if torture, which has been deemed illegitimate by the civilized world for more than a century, were now to be legitimated—even for limited use in one extraordinary type of situation—such legitimation would constitute an important symbolic setback in the worldwide campaign against human rights abuses. Inevitably, the legitimation of torture by the world's leading democracy would provide a welcome justification for its more widespread use in other parts of the world. Two Bentham scholars, W. L. Twining and P. E. Twining, have argued that torture is unacceptable even if it is restricted to an extremely limited category of cases:

> There is at least one good practical reason for drawing a distinction between justifying an isolated act of torture in an extreme emergency of the kind postulated above and justifying the *institutionalisation* of torture as a regular practice. The circumstances are so extreme in which most of us would be prepared to justify resort to torture, if at all, the conditions we would impose would be so stringent, the practical problems of devising and enforcing adequate safeguards so difficult and the risks of abuse so great that it would be unwise and dangerous to entrust any government, however enlightened, with such a power. Even an out-and-out utilitarian can support an absolute prohibition against institutionalised torture on the ground that no government in the world can be trusted not to abuse the power and to satisfy in practice the conditions he would impose.[4]

Bentham's own justification was based on *case* or *act* utilitarianism—a demonstration that in a *particular case*, the benefits that would flow from the limited use of torture would outweigh its costs. The argument against any use of torture would derive from *rule* utilitarianism—which considers the implications of establishing a precedent that would inevitably be extended beyond its limited case utilitarian justification to other possible evils of lesser magnitude. Even terrorism itself could be justified by a case utilitarian approach. Surely one could come up with a singular situation in which the targeting of a small number of civilians could be thought necessary to save thousands of other civilians—blowing up a German kindergarten by the relatives of inmates in a Nazi death camp, for example, and threatening to repeat the targeting of German children unless the death camps were shut down.

The reason this kind of single-case utilitarian justification is simple-minded is that it has no inherent limiting principle. If nonlethal torture of one person is justified to prevent the killing of many important people, then what if it were necessary to use lethal torture—or at least torture that posed a substantial risk of death? What if it were necessary to torture the suspect's mother or children to get him to divulge the information? What if it took threatening to kill his family, his friends, his entire village?[5] Under a simple-minded quantitative case utilitarianism, anything goes as long as the number of people tortured or killed does not exceed the number that would be saved. This is morality by numbers, unless there are other constraints on what we can properly do. These other constraints can come from rule utilitarianisms or other principles of morality, such as the prohibition against deliberately punishing the innocent. Unless we are prepared to impose some limits on the use of torture or other barbaric tactics that might be of some use in preventing terrorism, we risk hurtling down a slippery slope into the abyss of amorality and ultimately tyranny. Dostoevsky captured the complexity of this dilemma in *The Brothers Karamazov* when he had Ivan pose the following question to Alyosha: "Imagine that you are creating a fabric of human destiny with the object of making men happy in the end, giving them peace at least, but that it was essential and inevitable to torture to death only one tiny creature—that baby beating its breast with its fist, for instance—and to found that edifice on its unavenged tears, would you consent to be the architect [under] those conditions? Tell me the truth."

A willingness to kill an innocent child suggests a willingness to do anything to achieve a necessary result. Hence the slippery slope.

It does not necessarily follow from this understandable fear of the slippery slope that we can never consider the use of nonlethal infliction of pain, if its use were to be limited by acceptable principles of morality. After all, imprisoning a witness who refuses to testify after being given immunity is designed to be punitive—that is painful. Such imprisonment can, on occasion, produce more pain and greater risk of death than nonlethal torture. Yet we continue to threaten and use the pain of imprisonment to loosen the tongues of reluctant witnesses.[6]

It is commonplace for police and prosecutors to threaten recalcitrant suspects with prison rape. As one prosecutor put it: "You're going to be the boyfriend of a very bad man." The slippery slope is an argument of caution, not a debate stopper, since virtually every compromise with an absolutist approach to rights carries the risk of slipping further. An appropriate response to the slippery slope is to build in a principled break. For example, if nonlethal torture were legally limited to convicted terrorists who had knowledge of future massive terrorist acts, were given immunity, and still refused to provide the information, there might still be objections to the use of torture, but they would have to go beyond the slippery slope argument.[7]

The case utilitarian argument for torturing a ticking bomb terrorist is bolstered by an argument from analogy—an *a fortiori* argument. What moral principle could justify the death penalty for past individual murders and at the same time condemn nonlethal torture to prevent future mass murders? Bentham posed this rhetorical question as support for his argument. The death penalty is, of course, reserved for convicted murderers. But again, what if torture was limited to convicted terrorists who refused to divulge information about future terrorism? Consider as well the analogy to the use of deadly force against suspects fleeing from arrest for dangerous felonies of which they have not yet been convicted. Or military retaliations that produce the predictable and inevitable collateral killing of some innocent civilians. The case against torture, if made by a Quaker who opposes the death penalty, war, self-defense, and the use of lethal force against fleeing felons, is understandable. But for anyone who justifies killing on the basis of a cost-benefit analysis, the case against the use of nonlethal torture to save multiple lives is more difficult to make. In the end, absolute opposition to torture—even nonlethal torture in the ticking bomb case—may rest more on historical and aesthetic considerations than on moral or logical ones.

In debating the issue of torture, the first question I am often asked is, "Do you want to take us back to the Middle Ages?" The association between any form of torture and gruesome death is powerful in the minds of most people knowledgeable of the history of its abuses. This understandable association makes it difficult for many people to think about nonlethal torture as a technique for *saving* lives.

The second question I am asked is, "What kind of torture do you have in mind?" When I respond by describing the sterilized needle being shoved under the fingernails, the reaction is visceral and often visible—a shudder coupled with a facial gesture of disgust. Discussions of the death penalty on the other hand can be conducted without these kinds of reactions, especially now that we literally put the condemned prisoner "to sleep" by laying him out on a gurney and injecting a lethal substance into his body. There is no breaking of the neck, burning of the brain, bursting of internal organs, or gasping for breath that used to accompany hanging, electrocution, shooting, and gassing. The executioner has been replaced by a paramedical technician, as the aesthetics of death have become more acceptable. All this tends to cover up the reality that death is forever while nonlethal pain is temporary. In our modern age death is underrated, while pain is overrated.

I observed a similar phenomenon several years ago during the debate over corporal punishment that was generated by the decision of a court in Singapore to sentence a young American to medically supervised lashing with a cane. Americans who support the death penalty and who express little concern about inner-city prison conditions were outraged by the specter of a few welts on the buttocks of an American. It was an utterly irrational display of hypocrisy and double standards. Given a choice between a medically administered whipping and one month in a typical state lockup or prison, any rational and knowledgeable person would choose the lash. No one dies of welts or pain, but many inmates are raped, beaten, knifed, and otherwise mutilated and tortured in American prisons. The difference is that we don't see—and we don't want to see—what goes on behind their high walls. Nor do we want to think about it. Raising the issue of torture makes Americans think about a brutalizing and unaesthetic phenomenon that has been out of our consciousness for many years.[8]

THE THREE—OR FOUR—WAYS

The debate over the use of torture goes back many years, with Bentham supporting it in a limited category of cases, Kant opposing it as part of his categorical imperative against improperly using people as means for achieving noble ends, and Voltaire's views on the matter being "hopelessly confused."[9] The modern resort to terrorism has renewed the debate over how a rights-based society should respond to the prospect of using nonlethal torture in the ticking bomb situation. In the late 1980s the Israeli government appointed a commission headed by a retired Supreme Court justice to look into precisely that situation. The commission concluded that there are "three ways for solving this grave dilemma between the vital need to preserve the very existence of the state and its citizens, and maintain its character as a law-abiding state." The first is to allow the security services to continue to fight terrorism in "a twilight zone which is outside the realm of law." The second is "the way of the hypocrites: they declare that they abide by the rule of law, but turn a blind eye to what goes on beneath the surface." And the third, "the truthful road of the rule of law," is that the "law itself must insure a proper framework for the activity" of the security services in seeking to prevent terrorist acts.[10]

There is of course a fourth road: namely to forgo any use of torture and simply allow the preventable terrorist act to occur.[11] After the Supreme Court of Israel outlawed the use of physical pressure, the Israeli security services claimed that, as a result of the Supreme Court's decision, at least one preventable act of terrorism had been allowed to take place, one that killed several people when a bus was bombed.[12] Whether this claim is true, false, or somewhere in between is difficult to assess.[13] But it is clear that if the preventable act of terrorism was of the magnitude of the attacks of September 11, there would be a great outcry in any democracy that had deliberately refused to take available preventive action, even if it required the use of torture. During numerous public appearances since September 11, 2001, I have asked audiences for a show of hands as to how many would support the use of nonlethal torture in a ticking bomb case. Virtually every hand is raised. The few that remain down go up when I ask how many believe that torture would actually be used in such a case.

Law enforcement personnel give similar responses. This can be seen in reports of physical abuse directed against some suspects that have been detained following September 11, reports that have been taken quite seriously by at least one federal judge.[14] It is confirmed by the willingness of U.S. law enforcement officials to facilitate the torture of terrorist suspects by repressive regimes allied with our intelligence agencies. As one former CIA operative with thirty years of experience reported: "A lot of people are saying we need someone at the agency who can pull fingernails out. Others are saying, 'Let others use interrogation methods that we don't use.' The only question then is, do you want to have CIA people in the room?" The real issue, therefore, is not whether some torture would or would not be used in the ticking bomb case—it would. The question is whether it would be done openly, pursuant to a previously established legal procedure, or whether it would be done secretly, in violation of existing law.[15]

Several important values are pitted against each other in this conflict. The first is the safety and security of a nation's citizens. Under the ticking bomb scenario this value may require the use of torture, if that is the only way to prevent the bomb from exploding and killing large numbers of civilians. The second value is the preservation of civil liberties and human rights. This value requires that we not accept torture as a legitimate part of our legal system. In my debates with two

prominent civil libertarians, Floyd Abrams and Harvey Silverglate, both have acknowledged that they would want nonlethal torture to be used if it could prevent thousands of deaths, but they did not want torture to be officially recognized by our legal system. As Abrams put it: "In a democracy sometimes it is necessary to do things off the books and below the radar screen." Former presidential candidate Alan Keyes took the position that although torture might be *necessary* in a given situation it could never be *right*. He suggested that a president *should* authorize the torturing of a ticking bomb terrorist, but that this act should not be legitimated by the courts or incorporated into our legal system. He argued that wrongful and indeed unlawful acts might sometimes be necessary to preserve the nation, but that no aura of legitimacy should be placed on these actions by judicial imprimatur.

This understandable approach is in conflict with the third important value: namely, open accountability and visibility in a democracy. "Off-the-book actions below the radar screen" are antithetical to the theory and practice of democracy. Citizens cannot approve or disapprove of governmental actions of which they are unaware. We have learned the lesson of history that off-the-book actions can produce terrible consequences. Richard Nixon's creation of a group of "plumbers" led to Watergate, and Ronald Reagan's authorization of an off-the-books foreign policy in Central America led to the Iran-Contra scandal. And these are only the ones we know about!

Perhaps the most extreme example of such a hypocritical approach to torture comes—not surprisingly—from the French experience in Algeria. The French army used torture extensively in seeking to prevent terrorism during a brutal colonial war from 1955 to 1957. An officer who supervised this torture, General Paul Aussaresses, wrote a book recounting what he had done and seen, including the torture of dozens of Algerians. "The best way to make a terrorist talk when he refused to say what he knew was to torture him," he boasted. Although the book was published decades after the war was over, the general was prosecuted—but not for what he had done to the Algerians. Instead, he was prosecuted for *revealing* what he had done, and seeking to justify it.[16]

In a democracy governed by the rule of law, we should never want our soldiers or our president to take any action that we deem wrong or illegal. A good test of whether an action should or should not be done is whether we are prepared to have it disclosed—perhaps not immediately, but certainly after some time has passed. No legal system operating under the rule of law should ever tolerate an "off-the-books" approach to necessity. Even the defense of necessity must be justified lawfully. The road to tyranny has always been paved with claims of necessity made by those responsible for the security of a nation. Our system of checks and balances requires that all presidential actions, like all legislative or military actions, be consistent with governing law. If it is necessary to torture in the ticking bomb case, then our governing laws must accommodate this practice. If we refuse to change our law to accommodate any particular action, then our government should not take that action.[17]

Only in a democracy committed to civil liberties would a triangular conflict of this kind exist. Totalitarian and authoritarian regimes experience no such conflict, because they subscribe to neither the civil libertarian nor the democratic values that come in conflict with the value of security. The hard question is: which value is to be preferred when an inevitable clash occurs? One or more of these values must inevitably be compromised in making the tragic choice presented by the ticking bomb case. If we do not torture, we compromise the security and safety of our citizens. If we tolerate torture, but keep it off the books and below the radar screen, we compromise principles of democratic accountability. If we create a legal structure for limiting and controlling torture, we compromise our principled opposition to torture in all circumstances and create a potentially dangerous and expandable situation.

In 1678, the French writer Francois de La Rochefoucauld said that "hypocrisy is the homage that vice renders to virtue." In this case we have two vices: terrorism and torture. We also have two virtues: civil liberties and democratic accountability. Most civil libertarians I know prefer hypocrisy, precisely because it appears to avoid the conflict between security and civil liberties, but by choosing the way of the hypocrite these civil libertarians compromise the value of democratic accountability. Such is the nature of tragic choices in a complex world. As Bentham put it more than two centuries ago: "Government throughout is but a choice of evils." In a democracy, such choices must be made, whenever possible, with openness and democratic accountability, and subject to the rule of law.[18]

Consider another terrible choice of evils that could easily have been presented on September 11, 2001—and may well be presented in the future: a hijacked passenger jet is on a collision course with a densely occupied office building; the only way to prevent the destruction of the building and the killing of its occupants is to shoot down the jet, thereby killing its innocent passengers. This choice now seems easy, because the passengers are certain to die anyway and their somewhat earlier deaths will save numerous lives. The passenger jet must be shot down. But what if it were only *probable*, not certain, that the jet would crash into the building? Say, for example, we know from cell phone transmissions that passengers are struggling to regain control of the hijacked jet, but it is unlikely they will succeed in time. Or say we have no communication with the jet and all we know is that it is off course and heading toward Washington, D.C., or some other densely populated city. Under these more questionable circumstances, the question becomes *who* should make this life and death choice between evils—a decision that may turn out tragically wrong?

No reasonable person would allocate this decision to a fighter jet pilot who happened to be in the area or to a local airbase commander—unless of course there was no time for the matter to be passed up the chain of command to the president or the secretary of defense. A decision of this kind should be made at the highest level possible, with visibility and accountability.

Why is this not also true of the decision to torture a ticking bomb terrorist? Why should that choice of evils be relegated to a local policeman,

FBI agent, or CIA operative, rather than to a judge, the attorney general, or the president?

There are, of course, important differences between the decision to shoot down the plane and the decision to torture the ticking bomb terrorist. Having to shoot down an airplane, though tragic, is not likely to be a recurring issue. There is no slope down which to slip.[19] Moreover, the jet to be shot down is filled with our fellow citizens—people with whom we can identify. The suspected terrorist we may choose to torture is a "they"—an enemy with whom we do not identify but with whose potential victims we do identify. The risk of making the wrong decision, or of overdoing the torture, is far greater, since we do not care as much what happens to "them" as to "us."[20] Finally, there is something different about torture—even nonlethal torture—that sets it apart from a quick death. In addition to the horrible history associated with torture, there is also the aesthetic of torture. The very idea of deliberately subjecting a captive human being to excruciating pain violates our sense of what is acceptable. On a purely rational basis, it is far worse to shoot a fleeing felon in the back and kill him, yet every civilized society authorizes shooting such a suspect who poses dangers of committing violent crimes against the police or others. In the United States we execute convicted murderers, despite compelling evidence of the unfairness and ineffectiveness of capital punishment. Yet many of us recoil at the prospect of shoving a sterilized needle under the finger of a suspect who is refusing to divulge information that might prevent multiple deaths. Despite the irrationality of these distinctions, they are understandable, especially in light of the sordid history of torture.

We associate torture with the Inquisition, the Gestapo, the Stalinist purges, and the Argentine colonels responsible for the "dirty war." We recall it as a prelude to death, an integral part of a regime of gratuitous pain leading to a painful demise. We find it difficult to imagine a benign use of nonlethal torture to save lives.

Yet there was a time in the history of Anglo-Saxon law when torture was used to save life, rather than to take it, and when the limited administration of nonlethal torture was supervised by judges, including some who are well remembered in history.[21] This fascinating story has been recounted by Professor John Langbein of Yale Law School, and it is worth summarizing here because it helps inform the debate over whether, if torture would in fact be used in a ticking bomb case, it would be worse to make it part of the legal system, or worse to have it done off the books and below the radar screen.

In his book on legalized torture during the sixteenth and seventeenth centuries, *Torture and the Law of Proof*, Langbein demonstrates the trade-off between torture and other important values. Torture was employed for several purposes. First, it was used to secure the evidence necessary to obtain a guilty verdict under the rigorous criteria for conviction required at the time—either the testimony of two eyewitnesses or the confession of the accused himself. Circumstantial evidence, no matter how compelling, would not do. As Langbein concludes, "no society will long tolerate a legal system in which there is no prospect in convicting unrepentant persons who commit clandestine crimes. Something had to be done to extend the system to those cases. The two-eyewitness rule was hard to compromise or evade, but the confession invited 'subterfuge.'" The subterfuge that was adopted permitted the use of torture to obtain confessions from suspects against whom there was compelling circumstantial evidence of guilt. The circumstantial evidence, alone, could not be used to convict, but it was used to obtain a torture warrant. That torture warrant was in turn used to obtain a confession, which then had to be independently corroborated—at least in most cases (witchcraft and other such cases were exempted from the requirement of corroboration).[22]

Torture was also used against persons already convicted of capital crimes, such as high treason, who were thought to have information necessary to prevent attacks on the state.

Langbein studied eighty-one torture warrants, issued between 1540 and 1640, and found that in many of them, especially in "the higher cases of treasons, torture is used for discovery, and not for evidence." Torture was "used to protect the state" and "mostly that meant preventive torture to identify and forestall plots and plotters." It was only when the legal system loosened its requirement of proof (or introduced the "black box" of the jury system) and when perceived threats against the state diminished that torture was no longer deemed necessary to convict guilty defendants against whom there had previously been insufficient evidence, or to secure preventive information.[23]

The ancient Jewish system of jurisprudence came up with yet another solution to the conundrum of convicting the guilty and preventing harms to the community in the face of difficult evidentiary barriers. Jewish law required two witnesses and a specific advance warning before a guilty person could be convicted. Because confessions were disfavored, torture was not an available option. Instead, the defendant who had been seen killing by one reliable witness, or whose guilt was obvious from the circumstantial evidence, was formally acquitted, but he was then taken to a secure location and fed a concoction of barley and water until his stomach burst and he died. Moreover, Jewish law permitted more flexible forms of self-help against those who were believed to endanger the community.[24]

Every society has insisted on the incapacitation of dangerous criminals regardless of strictures in the formal legal rules. Some use torture, others use informal sanctions, while yet others create the black box of a jury, which need not explain its commonsense verdicts. Similarly, every society insists that, if there are steps that can be taken to prevent effective acts of terrorism, these steps should be taken, even if they require some compromise with other important principles.

In deciding whether the ticking bomb terrorist should be tortured, one important question is whether there would be less torture if it were done as part of the legal system, as it was in sixteenth- and seventeenth-century England, or off the books, as it is in many countries today. The Langbein study does not definitively answer this question, but it does provide some suggestive insights. The English system of torture was more visible and thus more subject to public accountability, and it is likely that torture was employed less frequently in England than in France.

"During these years when it appears that torture might have become routinized in English criminal procedure, the Privy Council kept the torture power under careful control and never allowed it to fall into the hands of the regular law enforcement officers," as it had in France. In England "no law enforcement officer . . . acquired the power to use torture without special warrant." Moreover, when torture warrants were abolished, "the English experiment with torture left no traces." Because it was under centralized control, it was easier to abolish than it was in France, where it persisted for many years.[25]

It is always difficult to extrapolate from history, but it seems logical that a formal, visible, accountable, and centralized system is somewhat easier to control than an ad hoc, off-the-books, and under-the-radar-screen nonsystem. I believe, though I certainly cannot prove, that a formal requirement of a judicial warrant as a prerequisite to nonlethal torture would decrease the amount of physical violence directed against suspects. At the most obvious level, a double check is always more protective than a single check. In every instance in which a warrant is requested, a field officer has already decided that torture is justified and, in the absence of a warrant requirement, would simply proceed with the torture. Requiring that decision to be approved by a judicial officer will result in fewer instances of torture even if the judge rarely turns down a request. Moreover, I believe that most judges would require compelling evidence before they would authorize so extraordinary a departure from our constitutional norms, and law enforcement officials would be reluctant to seek a warrant unless they had compelling evidence that the suspect had information needed to prevent an imminent terrorist attack. A record would be kept of every warrant granted, and although it is certainly possible that some individual agents might torture without a warrant, they would have no excuse, since a warrant procedure would be available. They could not claim "necessity," because the decision as to whether the torture is indeed necessary has been taken out of their hands and placed in the hands of a judge. In addition, even if torture were deemed totally illegal without any exception, it would still occur, though the public would be less aware of its existence.

I also believe that the rights of the suspect would be better protected with a warrant requirement. He would be granted immunity, told that he was now compelled to testify, threatened with imprisonment if he refused to do so, and given the option of providing the requested information. Only if he refused to do what he was legally compelled to do—provide necessary information, which could not incriminate him because of the immunity—would he be threatened with torture. Knowing that such a threat was authorized by the law, he might well provide the information.[26] If he still refused to, he would be subjected to judicially monitored physical measures designed to cause excruciating pain without leaving any lasting damage.

NOTES

1. Quoted in W.L. Twining and P.E. Twining, "Bentham on Torture," *Northern Ireland Legal Quarterly*, Autumn 1973, p. 347. Bentham's hypothetical question does not distinguish between torture inflicted by private persons and by governments.
2. David Johnston and Philip Shenon, "F.B.I. Curbed Scrutiny of Man Now a Suspect in the Attacks," *New York Times*, 10/6/2001.
3. It is illegal to withhold relevant information from a grand jury after receiving immunity. See *Kastigar v. U.S.* 406 U.S. 441 (1972).
4. Twining and Twining, "Bentham on Torture," pp. 348–49. The argument for the limited use of torture in the ticking bomb case falls into a category of argument known as "argument from the extreme case," which is a useful heuristic to counter arguments for absolute principles.
5. To demonstrate that this is not just in the realm of the hypothetical: "The former CIA officer said he also suggested the agency begin targeting close relatives of known terrorists and use them to obtain intelligence. 'You get their mothers and their brothers and their sisters under your complete control, and then you make that known to the target,' he said. 'You imply or you directly threaten [that] his family is going to pay the price if he makes the wrong decision,'" Bob Drogin and Greg Miller, "Spy Agencies Facing Questions of Tactics," *Los Angeles Times*, 10/28/2001.
6. One of my clients, who refused to testify against the mafia, was threatened by the government that if he persisted in his refusal the government would "leak" false information that he was cooperating, thus exposing him to mob retaliation.
7. *USA v. Cobb.*
8. On conditions in American prisons, see Alan M. Dershowitz, "Supreme Court Acknowledges Country's Other Rape Epidemic," *Boston Herald*, 6/12/1994.

The United States may already be guilty of violating at least the spirit of the prohibition against torture. In a recent case the Canadian Supreme Court refused to extradite an accused person to the United States because of threats made by a judge and a prosecutor regarding the treatment of those who did not voluntarily surrender themselves to the jurisdiction of the U.S. court. First, as he was sentencing a co-conspirator in the scheme, the American judge assigned to their trial commented that those fugitives who did not cooperate would get the "absolute maximum jail sentence." Then, the prosecuting attorney hinted during a television interview that uncooperative fugitives would be subject to homosexual rape in prison:

> Zubrod [prosecutor]: I have told some of these individuals, "Look, you can come down and you can put this behind you by serving your time in prison and making restitution to the victims, or you can wind up serving a great deal longer sentence under much more stringent conditions," and describe those conditions to them.
>
> MacIntyre [reporter]: How would you describe those conditions?
>
> Zubrod: *You're going to be the boyfriend of a very bad man if you wait out your extradition.*
>
> MacIntyre: And does that have much of an impact on these people?
>
> Zubrod: Well, out of the 89 people we've indicted so far, approximately 55 of them have said, "We give up."

After reading the transcripts, the Supreme Court of Canada held: "The pressures were not only inappropriate but also, in the case of the statements made by the prosecutor on the eve of the opening of the judicial hearing in Canada, unequivocally amounted to an abuse of the process of the court. We do not condone the threat of sexual violence as a means for one party before the court to persuade any opponent to abandon his or her right to a hearing. Nor should we expect litigants to overcome well-founded fears of violent reprisals in order to be participants in a judicial process. Aside from such intimidation itself, it is plain that a committal order requiring a fugitive to return to face such an ominous climate—which was created by those who would play a large, if not decisive role in determining the fugitive's ultimate fate—would not be consistent with the principles of fundamental justice." *USA v. Cobb,* 1 S.C.R. 587 (2001). (Thanks to Craig Jones, a student, for bringing this matter to my attention.)

 9. John Langbein, *Torture and the Law of Proof* (Chicago: University of Chicago Press, 1977), p. 68. Voltaire generally opposed torture but favored it in some cases.

10. A special edition of the *Israel Law Review* in 1989 presented a written symposium on the report on the Landau Commission, which investigated interrogation practices of Israel's General Security Services from 1987 to 1989.

11. A fifth approach would be simply to never discuss the issue of torture—or to postpone any such discussion until after we actually experience a ticking bomb case—but I have always believed that it is preferable to consider and discuss tragic choices before we confront them, so that the issue can be debated without recriminatory emotions and after-the-fact finger-pointing.

12. "The Supreme Court of Israel left the security services a tiny window of opportunity in extreme cases. Citing the traditional common-law defense of necessity, the Supreme Court left open the possibility that a member of the security service who honestly believed that rough interrogation was the only means available to save lives in imminent danger could raise this defense. This leaves each individual member of the security services in the position of having to guess how a court would ultimately resolve his case. That is extremely unfair to such investigators. It would have been far better had the court required any investigator who believed that torture was necessary in order to save lives to apply to a judge. The judge would then be in a position either to authorize or refuse to authorize a 'torture warrant.' Such a procedure would require judges to dirty their hands by authorizing torture warrants or bear the responsibility for failing to do so. Individual interrogators should not have to place their liberty at risk by guessing how a court might ultimately decide a close case. They should be able to get an advance ruling based on the evidence available at the time.

"Perhaps the legislature will create a procedure for advance judicial scrutiny. This would be akin to the warrant requirement in the Fourth Amendment to the United States Constitution. It is a traditional role for judges to play, since it is the job of the judiciary to balance the needs for security against the imperatives of liberty. Interrogators from the security service are not trained to strike such a delicate balance. Their mission is single-minded: to prevent terrorism. Similarly, the mission of civil liberties lawyers who oppose torture is single-minded: to vindicate the individual rights of suspected terrorists. It is the role of the court to strike the appropriate balance. The Supreme Court of Israel took a giant step in the direction of striking that balance. But it—or the legislature—should take the further step of requiring the judiciary to assume responsibility in individual cases. The essence of a democracy is placing responsibility for difficult choices in a visible and neutral institution like the judiciary." Dershowitz, *Shouting Fire,* pp. 476–77.

13. Charles M. Sennott, "Israeli High Court Bans Torture in Questioning; 10,000 Palestinians Subjected to Tactics," *Boston Globe,* 9/7/1999.

14. Osama Awadallah, a green-card holder living in San Diego, has made various charges of torture, abuse, and denial of access to a lawyer. Shira Scheindlin, a federal district court judge in New York, has confirmed the seriousness and credibility of the charges, saying Awadallah may have been "unlawfully arrested, unlawfully searched, abused by law enforcement officials, denied access to his lawyer and family." Lewis, "Taking Our Liberties."

15. Drogin and Miller, "Spy Agencies Facing Questions of Tactics." Philip Heymann is the only person I have debated thus far who is willing to take the position that no form of torture should ever be permitted—or used—even if thousands of lives could be saved by its use. Philip B. Heymann, "Torture Should Not Be Authorized," *Boston Globe,* 2/16/2002. Whether he would act on that principled view if he were the responsible government official who was authorized to make this life and death choice—as distinguished from an academic with the luxury of expressing views without being accountable for their consequences—is a more difficult question. He has told me that he probably would authorize torture in an actual ticking bomb case, but that it would be wrong and he would expect to be punished for it.

16. Suzanne Daley, "France Is Seeking a Fine in Trial of Algerian War General," *New York Times*, 11/29/2001.

17. The necessity defense is designed to allow interstitial action to be taken in the absence of any governing law and in the absence of time to change the law. It is for the nonrecurring situation that was never anticipated by the law. The use of torture in the ticking bomb case has been debated for decades. It can surely be anticipated. See Dershowitz, *Shouting Fire*, pp. 474–76.

   Indeed, there is already one case in our jurisprudence in which this has occurred and the courts have considered it. In the 1984 case of *Leon v. Wainwright*, Jean Leon and an accomplice kidnapped a taxicab driver and held him for ransom. Leon was arrested while trying to collect the ransom but refused to disclose where he was holding the victim. At this point, several police officers threatened him and then twisted his arm behind his back and choked him until he told them the victim's whereabouts. Although the federal appellate court disclaimed any wish to "sanction the use of force and coercion by police officers," the judges went out of their way to state that this was not the act of "brutal law enforcement agents trying to obtain a confession." "This was instead a group of concerned officers acting in a reasonable manner to obtain information they needed in order to protect another individual from bodily harm or death." Although the court did not find it necessary to invoke the "necessity defense," since no charges were brought against the policemen who tortured the kidnapper, it described the torture as having been "motivated by the immediate *necessity* to find the victim and save his life."

   Leon v. *Wainwright*, 734 F.2d 770, 772–73 (11th Circuit 1984) (emphasis added). If an appellate court would so regard the use of police brutality—torture—in a case involving one kidnap victim, it is not difficult to extrapolate to a situation in which hundreds or thousands of lives might hang in the balance.

18. Quoted in Twining and Twining, "Bentham on Torture," p. 345.

19. For an elaboration of this view, see Dershowitz, *Shouting Fire*, pp. 97–99.

20. The pilot who would have been responsible for shooting down the hijacked plane heading from Pennsylvania to Washington, D.C., on September 11, 2001, has praised the passengers who apparently struggled with the hijackers, causing the plane to crash. These brave passengers spared him the dreadful task of shooting down a plane full of fellow Americans. The stakes are different when it comes to torturing enemy terrorists.

21. Sir Edward Coke was "designated in commissions to examine particular suspects under torture." Langbein, *Torture and the Law of Proof*, p. 73.

22. Ibid., p. 7.

23. Ibid., p. 90, quoting Bacon.

24. Din Rodef, or Law of the Pursuer, refers to the halachic principle that one may kill a person who is threatening someone else's life. This rule was set forth in the twelfth century by Moses Maimonides, a great Talmudic scholar.

25. Langbein, *Torture and the Law of Proof*, pp. 136–37, 139.

26. When it is known that torture is a possible option, terrorists sometimes provide the information and then claim they have been tortured, in order to be able to justify their complicity to their colleagues.

⚜ REVIEW QUESTIONS

1. Dershowitz discusses three cases in which torture can be justified. What are they?

2. According to Dershowitz, what is the strongest argument against any resort to torture? How does he reply?

3. Explain Dershowitz's argument from analogy for torturing a ticking-bomb terrorist.

4. In what four ways can a state respond to terrorism, according to Dershowitz? Why does he reject forgoing any use of torture?

5. What are the important values involved in the debate about allowing torture, according to Dershowitz? Why does he not object to secret torturing by the state?

6. Explain Dershowitz's proposal for torture warrants. Why does he think they will decrease the amount of violence directed at suspects and protect their rights?

1. Does rule utilitarianism provide a good argument for the absolute prohibition of torture? Why or why not?
2. Would you torture a baby to death if this would make all men happy? Explain your answer.
3. Would torture be justified to prevent the 9/11 attacks? What does Dershowitz say? What do you think?
4. Are torture warrants a good idea? Why or why not?

Liberalism, Torture and the Ticking Bomb

DAVID LUBAN

For biographical information on David Luban, see his reading in Chapter 1.

Luban attacks what he calls the liberal ideology of torture, which on its surface seems to respect human rights and prohibit torture, but at a deeper level accepts torture in hypothetical ticking-bomb cases and ends up creating a torture culture. In Luban's view, the ticking-bomb story rests on so many assumptions that it amounts to an intellectual fraud. The story unrealistically assumes that the authorities know there is a bomb, that they have captured the man who planted it, that the man will talk when tortured, that lives will be saved, and so on. But this is all uncertain in the real world. We are asked to decide between the certainty of cruel torture and the mere possibility of saving lives, by totting up costs and benefits.

Trying to make a decision in the ticking-bomb case is just a mistake. The wise course is to deny that it is possible or at least so unlikely that trying to make a decision is insane and frivolous. Furthermore, once we grant the permissibility of torture in a hypothetical case, we end up in the real world with a torture culture that includes trained torturers and prisons like Abu Ghraib.

INTRODUCTION

Torture used to be incompatible with American values. Our Bill of Rights forbids cruel and unusual punishment, and that has come to include all forms of corporal punishment except prison and death by methods purported to be painless. Americans and our government have historically condemned states that torture; we have granted asylum or refuge to those who fear it. The Senate ratified the Convention Against Torture, Congress enacted anti-torture legislation, and judicial

opinions spoke of "the dastardly and totally inhuman act of torture."

Then came September 11. Less than one week later, a feature story reported that a quiz in a university ethics class "gave four choices for the proper U.S. response to the terrorist attacks: A.) execute the perpetrators on sight; B.) bring them back for trial in the United States; C.) subject the perpetrators to an international tribunal; or D.) torture and interrogate those involved." Most students chose A and D—execute them on sight and torture them. Six weeks after September 11, the press reported that frustrated FBI interrogators were considering harsh interrogation tactics; a few weeks after that, the *New York Times* reported that torture had become a topic of conversation "in bars, on commuter trains, and at dinner tables." By mid-November 2001, the *Christian Science Monitor* found that thirty-two percent of surveyed Americans favored torturing terror suspects. Alan Dershowitz reported in 2002 that "[d]uring numerous public appearances since September 11, 2001, I have asked audiences for a show of hands as to how many would support the use of nonlethal torture in a ticking-bomb case. Virtually every hand is raised." American abhorrence to torture now appears to have extraordinarily shallow roots.

To an important extent, one's stance on torture runs independent of progressive or conservative ideology. Alan Dershowitz suggests that torture should be regulated by a judicial warrant requirement. Liberal Senator Charles Schumer has publicly rejected the idea "that torture should never, ever be used." He argues that most U.S. senators would back torture to find out where a ticking time bomb is planted. By contrast, William Safire, a self-described "conservative . . . and card-carrying hard-liner," expresses revulsion at "phony-tough" pro-torture arguments, and forthrightly labels torture "barbarism." Examples like these illustrate how vital it is to avoid a simple left-right reductionism. For the most part, American conservatives belong no less than progressives to liberal culture, broadly understood. Henceforth, when I speak of "liberalism," I mean it in the broad sense used by political philosophers from John Stuart Mill on, a sense that includes conservatives as well as progressives, so long as they believe in limited government and the importance of human dignity and individual rights. . . .

On its surface, liberal reverence for individual rights makes torture morally unacceptable; at a deeper level, the same liberal ideas seemingly can justify interrogational torture in the face of danger. These ideas allow us to construct a liberal ideology of torture, by which liberals reassure themselves that essential interrogational torture is detached from its illiberal roots. The liberal ideology of torture is expressed perfectly in so-called "ticking-bomb hypotheticals" designed to show that even perfectly compassionate liberals (like Senator Schumer) might justify torture to find the ticking bomb.

I will criticize the liberal ideology of torture and suggest that ticking-bomb stories are built on a set of assumptions that amount to intellectual fraud. Ticking-bomb stories depict torture as

an emergency exception, but use intuitions based on the exceptional case to justify institutionalized practices and procedures of torture. In short, the ticking bomb begins by denying that torture belongs to liberal culture, and ends by constructing a torture culture. . . .

THE TICKING BOMB

Suppose the bomb is planted somewhere in the crowded heart of an American city, and you have custody of the man who planted it. He won't talk. Surely, the hypothetical suggests, we shouldn't be too squeamish to torture the information out of him and save hundreds of lives. Consequences count, and abstract moral prohibitions must yield to the calculus of consequences.

Everyone argues the pros and cons of torture through the ticking time bomb. Senator Schumer and Professor Dershowitz, the Israeli Supreme Court and indeed every journalist devoting a think-piece to the unpleasant question of torture, begins with the ticking time bomb and ends there as well. The Schlesinger Report on Abu Ghraib notes that "[f]or the U.S., most cases for permitting harsh treatment of detainees on moral grounds begin with variants of the 'ticking time-bomb' scenario." At this point in my argument, I mean to disarm the ticking time bomb and argue that it is the wrong thing to think about. If so, then the liberal ideology of torture begins to unravel.

But before beginning these arguments, I want to pause and ask why this jejune example has become the alpha and omega of our thinking about torture. I believe the answer is this: The ticking time bomb is proffered against liberals who believe in an absolute prohibition against torture. The idea is to force the liberal prohibitionist to admit that yes, even he or even she would agree to torture in at least this one situation. Once the prohibitionist admits that, then she has conceded that her opposition to torture is not based on principle. Now that the prohibitionist has admitted that her moral principles can be breached, all that is left is haggling about the price. No longer can the prohibitionist claim the moral high ground; no longer can she put the burden of proof on her opponent. She is down in the mud with them, and the only question left is how much further down she will go. Dialectically, getting the prohibitionist to address the ticking time bomb is like getting the vegetarian to eat just one little oyster because it has no nervous system. Once she does that—*gotcha!*

The ticking time-bomb scenario serves a second rhetorical goal, one that is equally important to the proponent of torture. It makes us see the torturer in a different light—one of the essential points in the liberal ideology of torture because it is the way that liberals can reconcile themselves to torture even while continuing to "put cruelty first." Now, he is not a cruel man or a sadistic man or a coarse, insensitive brutish man. The torturer is instead a conscientious public servant, heroic the way that New York firefighters were heroic, willing to do desperate things only because the plight is so desperate and so many innocent lives are weighing on the public servant's conscience. The time bomb clinches the great divorce between torture and cruelty; it placates liberals, who put cruelty first.

Wittgenstein once wrote that confusion arises when we become bewitched by a picture. He meant that it's easy to get seduced by simplistic examples that look compelling but actually misrepresent the world in which we live. If the subject is the morality of torture, philosophical confusions can have life-or-death consequences. I believe the ticking time bomb is the picture that bewitches us.

I don't mean that the time-bomb scenario is completely unreal. To take a real-life counterpart: in 1995, an al Qaeda plot to bomb eleven U.S. airliners and assassinate the Pope was thwarted by information tortured out of a Pakistani bomb-maker by the Philippine police. According to journalists Marites Dañguilan Vitug and Glenda M. Gloria, the police had received word of possible threats against the Pope. They went to work. "For weeks, agents hit him with a chair and a long piece of wood, forced water into his mouth, and crushed lighted cigarettes into his private parts. . . . His ribs were almost totally broken that his captors were surprised that

he survived. . . . Grisly, to be sure—but if they hadn't done it, thousands of innocent travelers might have died horrible deaths.

But look at the example one more time. The Philippine agents were surprised he survived—in other words, they came close to torturing him to death *before* he talked. And they tortured him *for weeks*, during which time they didn't know about any specific al Qaeda plot. What if he too didn't know? Or what if there had been no al Qaeda plot? Then they would have tortured him for weeks, possibly tortured him to death, for nothing. For all they knew at the time, that is exactly what they were doing. You cannot use the argument that preventing the al Qaeda attack justified the decision to torture, because *at the moment the decision was made* no one knew about the al Qaeda attack.

The ticking-bomb scenario cheats its way around these difficulties by stipulating that the bomb is there, ticking away, and that officials know it and know they have the man who planted it. Those conditions will seldom be met. Let us try some more realistic hypotheticals and the questions they raise:

1. The authorities know there may be a bomb plot in the offing, and they have captured a man who may know something about it, but may not. Torture him? How much? For weeks? For months? The chances are considerable that you are torturing a man with nothing to tell you. If he doesn't talk, does that mean it's time to stop, or time to ramp up the level of torture? How likely does it have to be that he knows something important? Fifty-fifty? Thirty-seventy? Will one out of a hundred suffice to land him on the waterboard?

2. Do you really want to make the torture decision by running the numbers? A one-percent chance of saving a thousand lives yields ten statistical lives. Does that mean that you can torture up to nine people on a one-percent chance of finding crucial information?

3. The authorities think that one out of a group of fifty captives in Guantanamo might know where Osama bin Laden is hiding, but they do not know which captive. Torture them all? That is: Do you torture forty-nine captives with

nothing to tell you on the uncertain chance of capturing bin Laden?

4. For that matter, would capturing Osama bin Laden demonstrably save a single human life? The Bush administration has downplayed the importance of capturing bin Laden because American strategy has succeeded in marginalizing him. Maybe capturing him would save lives, but how certain do you have to be? Or does it not matter whether torture is intended to save human lives from a specific threat, as long as it furthers some goal in the War on Terror? This last question is especially important once we realize that the interrogation of al Qaeda suspects will almost never be employed to find out where the ticking bomb is hidden. Instead, interrogation is a more general fishing expedition for any intelligence that might be used to help "unwind" the terrorist organization. Now one might reply that al Qaeda is itself the ticking time bomb, so that unwinding the organization meets the formal conditions of the ticking-bomb hypothetical. This is equivalent to asserting that any intelligence that promotes victory in the War on Terror justifies torture, precisely because we understand that the enemy in the War on Terror aims to kill American civilians. Presumably, on this argument, Japan would have been justified in torturing American captives in World War II on the chance of finding intelligence that would help them shoot down the Enola Gay; I assume that a ticking-bomb hardliner will not flinch from this conclusion. But at this point, we verge on declaring all military threats and adversaries that menace American civilians to be ticking bombs whose defeat justifies torture. The limitation of torture to emergency exceptions, implicit in the ticking-bomb story, now threatens to unravel, making torture a legitimate instrument of military policy. And then the question becomes inevitable: Why not torture in pursuit of any worthwhile goal?

5. Indeed, if you are willing to torture forty-nine innocent people to get information from the one who has it, why stop there? If suspects will not break under torture, why not torture their loved ones in front of them? They are no more innocent than the forty-nine you have already shown you are prepared to torture. In fact, if only the numbers matter, torturing loved ones is almost a no-brainer if you think it will work. Of course, you won't know until you try whether torturing his child will break the suspect. But that just changes the odds; it does not alter the argument.

The point of the examples is that in a world of uncertainty and imperfect knowledge, the ticking-bomb scenario should not form the point of reference. The ticking bomb is the picture that bewitches us. The real debate is not between one guilty man's pain and hundreds of innocent lives. It is the debate between the certainty of anguish and the mere possibility of learning something vital and saving lives. And, above all, it is the question about whether a responsible citizen must unblinkingly think the unthinkable and accept that the morality of torture should be decided purely by totaling up costs and benefits. Once you accept that only the numbers count, then anything, no matter how gruesome, becomes possible. "Consequentialist rationality," as Bernard Williams notes sardonically, "will have something to say even on the difference between massacring seven million, and massacring seven million and one."

I am inclined to think that the path of wisdom instead lies in Holocaust survivor David Rousset's famous caution that normal human beings do *not* know that everything is possible. As Williams says, "there are certain situations so monstrous that the idea that the processes of moral rationality could yield an answer in them is insane" and "to spend time thinking what one would decide if one were in such a situation is also insane, if not merely frivolous."

TORTURE AS A PRACTICE

There is a second, insidious, error built into the ticking-bomb hypothetical. It assumes a single, ad hoc decision about whether to torture, by officials who ordinarily would do no such thing except in a desperate emergency. But in the real world of interrogations, decisions are not made on-off. The real world is a world of policies, guidelines, and directives. It is a world of *practices*, not of ad hoc emergency measures. Therefore, any responsible discussion of torture must address the practice of torture, not the ticking-bomb hypothetical. I am not saying anything original here; other writers have made exactly this point. But somehow, we always manage to forget this and circle back to the ticking time bomb. Its rhetorical power has made it indispensable to the sensitive liberal soul, and we would much rather talk about the ticking bomb than about torture as an organized social practice.

Treating torture as a practice rather than as a desperate improvisation in an emergency means changing the subject from the ticking bomb to other issues like these: Should we create a professional cadre of trained torturers? That means a group of interrogators who know the techniques, who learn to overcome their instinctive revulsion against causing physical pain, and who acquire the legendary surgeon's arrogance about their own infallibility. It has happened before. Medieval executioners were schooled in the arts of agony as part of the trade: how to break men on the wheel, how to rack them, and even how to surreptitiously strangle them as an act of mercy without the bloodthirsty crowd catching on. In Louis XVI's Paris, torture was a hereditary family trade whose tricks were passed on from father to son. Who will teach torture techniques now? Should universities create an undergraduate course in torture? Or should the subject be offered only in police and military academies? Do we want federal grants for research to devise new and better techniques? Patents issued on high-tech torture devices? Companies competing to manufacture them? Trade conventions in Las Vegas? Should there be a medical sub-specialty of torture doctors, who ensure that captives do not die before they talk? The questions amount to this: Do we really want to create a torture culture and the kind of people who inhabit it? The ticking time bomb distracts us from the real issue, which is not about emergencies, but about the normalization of torture.

Perhaps the solution is to keep the practice of torture secret in order to avoid the moral corruption that comes from creating a public culture of torture. But this so-called "solution" does not reject the normalization of torture. It accepts it, but layers on top of it the normalization of state

secrecy. The result would be a shadow culture of torturers and those who train and support them, operating outside the public eye and accountable only to other insiders of the torture culture.

Just as importantly: Who guarantees that casehardened torturers, inured to levels of violence and pain that would make ordinary people vomit at the sight, will know where to draw the line on when torture should be used? They rarely have in the past. They didn't in Algeria. They didn't in Israel, where in 1999, the Israeli Supreme Court backpedaled from an earlier consent to torture lite because the interrogators were running amok and torturing two-thirds of their Palestinian captives. In the Argentinian Dirty War, the tortures began because terrorist cells had a policy of fleeing when one of their members had disappeared for forty-eight hours, leaving authorities two days to wring the information out of the captive. Mark Osiel, who has studied the Argentinean military in the Dirty War, reports that many of the torturers initially had qualms about what they were doing, until their priests reassured them that they were fighting God's fight. By the end of the Dirty War, the qualms were gone, and, as John Simpson and Jana Bennett report, hardened young officers were placing bets on who could kidnap the prettiest girl to rape and torture. Escalation is the rule, not the aberration.

There are two fundamental reasons for this: one rooted in the nature of bureaucracy and the other in social psychology. The liberal ideology of torture presupposes a torturer impelled by the desire to stop a looming catastrophe, not by cruelty. Implicitly, this image presumes that the interrogator and the decisionmaker are the same person. But the defining fact about real organizations is the division of labor. The person who decides whether this prisoner presents a genuine ticking-bomb case is not the interrogator. The decision about what counts as a ticking-bomb case—one where torture is the lesser evil—depends on complex value judgments, and these are made further up the chain of command. The interrogator simply executes decisions made elsewhere.

Interrogators do not inhabit a world of loving kindness, or of equal concern and respect for all human beings. Interrogating resistant prisoners non-violently and non-abusively still requires a relationship that in any other context would be morally abhorrent. It requires tricking information out of the subject, and the interrogator does this by setting up elaborate scenarios to disorient the subject and propel him into an alternative reality. The subject must be deceived into thinking that his high-value intelligence has already been revealed by someone else, so that it is no longer of any value. He must be fooled into thinking that his friends have betrayed him or that the interrogator is his friend. The interrogator disrupts his sense of time and place, disorients him with sessions that never take place at predictable times or intervals, and manipulates his emotions. The very names of interrogation techniques show this: "Emotional Love," "Emotional Hate," "Fear Up Harsh," "Fear Up Mild," "Reduced Fear," "Pride and Ego Up," "Pride and Ego Down," "Futility." The interrogator may set up a scenario to make the subject think he is in the clutches of a much-feared secret police organization from a different country ("False Flag"). Every bit of the subject's environment is fair game for manipulation and deception, as the interrogator aims to create the total lie that gets the subject talking.

Let me be clear that I am not objecting to these deceptions. None of these practices rises to the level of abuse or torture lite, let alone torture heavy, and surely tricking the subject into talking is legitimate if the goals of the interrogation are legitimate. But what I have described is a relationship of totalitarian mind-control more profound than the world of Orwell's *1984*. The interrogator is like Descartes' Evil Deceiver, and the subject lives in a false reality reminiscent of *The Matrix*. The liberal fiction that interrogation can be done by people who are neither cruel nor tyrannical runs aground on the fact that regardless of the interrogator's character off the job, on the job, every fiber of his concentration is devoted to dominating the mind of the subject.

Only one thing prevents this from turning into abuse and torture, and that is a clear set of bright-line rules, drummed into the interrogator

with the intensity of a religious indoctrination, complete with warnings of fire and brimstone. American interrogator Chris Mackey reports that warnings about the dire consequences of violating the Geneva Conventions "were repeated so often that by the end of our time at [training school] the three syllables 'Leaven-worth' were ringing in our ears."

But what happens when the line is breached? When, as in Afghanistan, the interrogator gets mixed messages about whether Geneva applies, or hears rumors of ghost detainees, of high-value captives held for years of interrogation in the top-secret facility known as "Hotel California," located in some nation somewhere? Or when the interrogator observes around him the move from deception to abuse, from abuse to torture lite, from torture lite to beatings and waterboarding? Without clear lines, the tyranny innate in the interrogator's job has nothing to hold it in check. Perhaps someone, somewhere in the chain of command, is wringing hands over whether this interrogation qualifies as a ticking-bomb case; but the interrogator knows only that the rules of the road have changed and the posted speed limits no longer apply. The liberal fiction of the conscientious interrogator overlooks a division of moral labor in which the person with the fastidious conscience and the person doing the interrogation are not the same.

The fiction must presume, therefore, that the interrogator operates only under the strictest supervision, in a chain of command where his every move gets vetted and controlled by the superiors who are actually doing the deliberating. The trouble is that this assumption flies in the face of everything that we know about how organizations work. The basic rule in every bureaucratic organization is that operational details and the guilty knowledge that goes with them get pushed down the chain of command as far as possible. As sociologist Robert Jackall explains,

> [i]t is characteristic . . . that details are pushed down and credit is pulled up. Superiors do not like to give detailed instructions to subordinates. . . . [O]ne of the privileges of authority is the divestment of humdrum intricacies.

. . . Perhaps more important, pushing details down protects the privilege of authority to declare that a mistake has been made. . . . Moreover, pushing down details relieves superiors of the burden of too much knowledge, particularly guilty knowledge.

We saw this phenomenon at Abu Ghraib, where military intelligence officers gave military police vague orders like: "'Loosen this guy up for us.' 'Make sure he has a bad night.' 'Make sure he gets the treatment.'" Suppose that the eighteen-year-old guard interprets "[m]ake sure he has a bad night" to mean, simply, "keep him awake all night." How do you do that without physical abuse? Furthermore, personnel at Abu Ghraib witnessed far harsher treatment of prisoners by "other governmental agencies" (OGA), a euphemism for the Central Intelligence Agency. They saw OGA spirit away the dead body of an interrogation subject, and allegedly witnessed a contract employee rape a youthful prisoner. When that is what you see, abuses like those in the Abu Ghraib photos will not look outrageous. Outrageous compared with what?

This brings me to the point of social psychology. Simply stated, it is this: we judge right and wrong against the baseline of whatever we have come to consider "normal" behavior, and if the norm shifts in the direction of violence, we will come to tolerate and accept violence as a normal response. The psychological mechanisms for this re-normalization have been studied for more than half a century, and by now they are reasonably well understood. Rather than detour into psychological theory, however, I will illustrate the point with the most salient example—one that seems so obviously applicable to Abu Ghraib that the Schlesinger Commission discussed it at length in an appendix to its report. This is the famous Stanford Prison Experiment. Male volunteers were divided randomly into two groups who would simulate the guards and inmates in a mock prison. Within a matter of days, the inmates began acting like actual prison inmates—depressed, enraged, and anxious. And the guards began to abuse the inmates to such an alarming degree that the researchers had to halt the two-week experiment after just seven days. In the words of the experimenters:

> The use of power was self-aggrandising and self-perpetuating. The guard power, derived initially from an arbitrary label, was intensified whenever there was any perceived threat by the prisoners and this new level subsequently became the baseline from which further hostility and harassment would begin. . . . [T]he absolute level of aggression as well as the more subtle and "creative" forms of aggression manifested, increased in a spiralling function.

It took only five days before a guard, who prior to the experiment described himself as a pacifist, was forcing greasy sausages down the throat of a prisoner who refused to eat; and in less than a week, the guards were placing bags over prisoners' heads, making them strip, and sexually humiliating them in ways reminiscent of Abu Ghraib.

My conclusion is very simple. Abu Ghraib is the fully predictable image of what a torture culture looks like. Abu Ghraib is not a few bad apples—it is the apple tree. And you cannot reasonably expect that interrogators in a torture culture will be the fastidious and well-meaning torturers that the liberal ideology fantasizes.

This is why Alan Dershowitz has argued that judges, not torturers, should oversee the permission to torture, which in his view must be regulated by warrants. The irony is that Jay S. Bybee, who signed the Justice Department's highly permissive torture memo, is now a federal judge. Politicians pick judges, and if the politicians accept torture, the judges will as well. Once we create a torture culture, only the naive would suppose that judges will provide a safeguard. Judges do not fight their culture—they reflect it.

For all these reasons, the ticking-bomb scenario is an intellectual fraud. In its place, we must address the real questions about torture—questions about uncertainty, questions about the morality of consequences, and questions about what it does to a culture and the torturers themselves to introduce the practice. Once we do so, I suspect that few Americans will be willing to accept that everything is possible.

⚜ REVIEW QUESTIONS

1. What happened to the American view of torture after 9/11, according to Luban?
2. How does Luban define "liberalism"? Who is a liberal on his definition?
3. Explain Luban's view of the "liberal ideology of torture."
4. What is the basic ticking-bomb story? According to Luban, what assumptions does the story make? What questions are left unanswered?
5. Besides being unrealistic, what second error is built into the ticking-bomb story?
6. What is Luban's point about the Stanford Prison Experiment?

⚜ DISCUSSION QUESTIONS

1. Does the ticking-bomb story amount to intellectual fraud, as Luban says? Or does it describe a situation that could actually happen? What is your view?
2. Should we train professional torturers so that we will be able to effectively torture terrorists to get information about possible or actual attacks?

Torture—The Case for Dirty Harry and against Alan Dershowitz

UWE STEINHOFF

Uwe Steinhoff is Senior Associate in the Oxford University Leverhulme Programme on the Changing Character of War. He is the author of *On the Ethics of War and Terrorism* (2007).

Steinhoff begins with an attack on the absolute moral prohibition of torture. He argues that there are two cases in which interrogative torture is morally justified. First, there is the Dirty Harry case: Harry saves an innocent girl's life by torturing the guilty kidnapper. Second, there is the ticking-bomb case. Steinhoff's view is in sharp contrast to Luban's position. Steinhoff argues that interrogative torture of a terrorist is morally justified even if we are not certain about the reliability of the information or sure that we have the right person. It is morally justified even if the terrorist has not planted the bomb and does not know where it is. In Steinhoff's view, there is no relevant moral difference between shooting a man who seems ready to shoot the president and torturing a terrorist who might have planted a bomb. However, just because torture is morally justified in these rare cases does not mean that it should be legal. It can be excused in the rare cases even if it is illegal. Steinhoff goes on to critically examine Alan Dershowitz's proposal to make torture legal by introducing legal torture warrants. Steinhoff thinks this is a bad idea. We do not need torture warrants because the cases in which torture is morally justified are rare. Also, the institutionalizing of torture with torture warrants undermines the general prohibition of torture and leads to a brutalization of the enforcer.

Consider the Dirty Harry case. In the Don Siegel movie *Dirty Harry* someone kidnaps a female child and puts her in a place where she will suffocate if not rescued in time. There is not much time left, according to the very claims of the kidnapper. The police officer Harry

Source: Torture — The Case for Dirty Harry and against Alan Dershowitz by Uwe Steinhoff from JOURNAL OF APPLIED PHILOSOPHY, Vol. 23, No 3, pp 342–352. Copyright © 2006. Reprinted by permission of John Wiley & Sons.

(Clint Eastwood) is to deliver the ransom to the kidnapper. When they finally meet at night in a park, the kidnapper knocks Harry down with his gun and tells him that he will let the girl die anyway. He also tells Harry that he wants him to know that before he kills him too. In the moment he is about to shoot Harry, who lies defenceless and badly beaten to his feet, Harry's partner interferes (and is shot). The kidnapper can escape, wounded. Harry pursues him. Finally he corners him, and the kidnapper raises his arms to surrender. Harry shoots him in the leg. The kidnapper is frightened to death, tells Harry not to kill him and that he has rights. Harry asks him where the girl is. The kidnapper talks only about his rights. Harry sees the kidnapper's leg wound and puts his foot on it, torturing the kidnapper. The camera retreats. In the next scene, the girl is saved.

The Dirty Harry case, it seems to me, is a case of morally justified torture. But isn't the kidnapper right? Does not even he have rights? Yes, he has, but in these circumstances he does not have the right not to be tortured. Again, the situation is analogous to self-defence. The aggressor does not lose all of his rights, but his right to life weighs less than the innocent defender's right to life. The aggressor culpably brings about a situation where one of the two—he or the defender—will die. It is only just and fair that the harm that will befall in this situation upon one of the two is diverted to the person who is responsible for the harm—the aggressor. In the Dirty Harry case, the kidnapper brings about a situation where a person is tortured or will continue to be tortured until death (being slowly suffocated in a small hole *is* torture). It is only just and fair that this harm befalls the person responsible for the situation—the kidnapper. Moreover, the choice is made even easier by the fact that being tortured for a small period of time is better than being tortured until death. Harry made the right decision.

Two replies might be made at this point. The first one—repeated like a litany by certain opponents of torture—is that interrogative torture simply does not work. That, however, is simply wrong. Sometimes interrogative torture does work, and the torturer gets the information he was looking for.[1]

Well, one might say, but at least interrogative torture is not very reliable. Apart from the fact that even that is not so clear, it would not even help. Consider the following case: An innocent person is being attacked by an aggressor, who fires a deadly weapon at him (and misses him at first but keeps firing). The attacked person's only possibility to save his life is by using the One-Million-Pains-To-One-Kill-Gun that he happens to have with him. On average, you have to pull the trigger of this gun one million times in order to have one immediately incapacitating projectile come out of it (it incapacitates through the infliction of unbearable pain). All the other times it fires projectiles that only ten seconds after hitting a human target cause the target unbearable pain. Thus, firing this gun at the aggressor will certainly cause the aggressor unbearable pain, but the probability that it will save the life of the defender is only 1:1,000,000. I must admit that I cannot even begin to make sense of the suggestion that, given these odds, the defender should not use the gun against the aggressor. Yes, the pain inflicted by the weapon on the aggressor is extremely unlikely to secure the survival of the defender, but there still *is* a chance that it will, so why should the *defender* forgo this chance for the benefit of the *aggressor*? Obviously, there is no reason (at least none that I could see). Again, the application to the torture of ticking bomb terrorists and Dirty Harry kidnappers is obvious.

What is the second reply? Richard H. Weisberg takes issue with the example of the ticking bomb case:

> . . . the hypothetical itself lacks the virtues of intelligence, appropriateness, and especially sophistication. Here, as in *The Brothers Karamazov—pace* Sandy Levinson—it is the complex rationalizers who wind up being more naive than those who speak strictly, directly, and simply against injustice. 'You can't know whether a person knows where the bomb is', explains Cole in a recent piece in the *Nation*, 'or even if they're telling the truth. Because of this, you wind up sanctioning torture in general'.[2]

To begin with, by allowing torture in the ticking bomb case one does *not* necessarily wind up sanctioning it in general. Killing (of certain people) is sanctioned in war but not in general. The actual second reply I was referring to, however, is *that you do not know whether you have the right person.* (That you do not know whether the person speaks the truth is simply the first reply. We have already dealt with it.) But what does it mean: 'You don't know'? Does it mean you do not know for certain? If not knowing for certain whether you have the right person would be sufficient reason not to harm that person, we would not only have to abstain from self-defence but also from punishment. You *never* know for certain!

Take the example of a man who draws a gun in front of a head of states and aims at him. The bodyguards simply cannot know (for certain) whether this person wants to shoot, they cannot even know whether it is a real gun. Maybe the 'attacker' is only a retard with a water pistol. So the bodyguards of the head of state (whom we want to assume innocent) should not shoot at such a person who, for all they *can* know, seems to be attacking the person they are to protect? Actually, if shooting (and probably killing) him is the only way to make sure that he is not able to pull the trigger, they *should* shoot him.

One might say that this person, even if he does not really want to shoot and has no real gun, at least *feigns* an attack, and this makes him liable to counter-attack. Whoever credibly feigns an attack on another person cannot later, after having suffered from severe countermeasures, complain that he 'only' feigned it. He shouldn't have feigned it at all. We can, however, have a comparable situation with a terrorist. If a person says to other persons that he is going to build a powerful bomb to blow up a kindergarten and has the necessary skills and buys the necessary chemicals, he had better not, when the security service storms his hideout where he is surrounded by his bomb-making equipment, sneeringly say: 'You are too late. I have already planted the bomb. It will go off in 12 hours and kill hundreds of children'. If he then is tortured by the security service, which wants to find out where the bomb is, he is not, it seems, in a particularly good position to complain about that *even if he has not planted a bomb.*[3] Moreover, even if a real or supposed terrorist has

not made that particularly threatening statement, hanging around with the wrong people in the wrong situations can also make you liable to attack. Suppose an innocent woman is hunted by a mob. Maybe they do not like her skin colour, her ethnic group, her religion or whatever. The mob has already killed other people for the same reason. She hides with the hand grenade she fortunately has, behind a bush. Suddenly one of the group sees her, points his finger at her, shouts 'There she is', and the armed members of the group raise their guns to shoot at her. Not all members of the group have guns. Some are unarmed and shout: 'Kill her, kill her!' Others do not even shout but sneer, foaming at the mouth (I am not talking about completely innocent people, who just 'happen' to be there for no fault of their own). The only way she can save herself is to throw the grenade at the mob, which will kill all of them, including the unarmed ones. Is she justified in doing so? I would think so. Being a member of certain groups that collectively undertake aggressive acts or intentionally pose a threat to innocent people makes one liable to severe countermeasures. Consequently, a member of a terrorist group might be liable to torture in the ticking bomb case, even if he does not know were the bomb is.

It helps, by the way, very little to aver at this point that torture is simply not compatible with liberalism. David Luban, for example, claims that torture aims 'to strip away from its victim all the qualities of human dignity that liberalism prizes' and that 'torture is a microcosm, raised to the highest level of intensity, of the tyrannical political relationships that liberalism hates the most'.[4] However, prisons are also 'microcosms' of tyranny; yet, most liberals do not find them incompatible with liberalism. Where is the difference? Maybe it lies in the fact that in torture tyranny is 'raised to the highest level'. But, first, it is far from clear that one hour of torture is more tyrannical than 15 years of prison. Second, even if torture were more tyrannical than prison, and liberalism abhorred tyranny, there remained still the fact that liberalism can accommodate quite intense forms of tyranny, such as incarceration for life (or for a decade and more). Why should it not also be able to accommodate the most extreme form of tyranny? 'Because it is the most extreme form' is in itself no answer to this question.

More importantly, liberalism is not so much about 'dignity'—which is a quite elusive concept, anyway (in particular, I deny that the dignity of the culpable aggressor is violated by Dirty Harry's action any more than it would be violated by Dirty Harry's killing him in self-defence)—but about liberty. It is called liberalism, not 'dignism'. It is also not about just anybody's liberty. It is about the liberty of the innocent. This is why there is no particular problem in liberalism to kill aggressors or to deprive them of their liberty if this is the only way to protect innocent people from these aggressors. The core value of the liberal state is the protection of the liberty and the rights of *innocent* individuals against *aggressors*. The state can be such an aggressor, but the state can and must also protect against other aggressors. To keep Dirty Harry in the situation described from torturing the kidnapper, therefore, would run against the liberal state's own *raison d'être*. The state would help the aggressor, not the victim; it would help the aggressor's tyranny over the innocent and therefore actually abet the relationship it hates the most.

Since my description of the core value of liberalism, as I submit, is at least as plausible as Luban's (and I think it is historically much more plausible), the appeal to liberalism cannot help absolute opponents of torture. To claim that liberalism 'correctly understood' absolutely prohibits torture simply engages in an attempt of persuasive definition and begs the question. Besides, why could liberalism, 'correctly understood', not be wrong?

But—speaking about the innocent—what about the risk of torturing a completely *innocent* person, a person that made itself *not* liable? Yes, that risk exists, as it does in the case of punishment. In the latter case, the risk of punishing innocent persons has to be weighed against the risk of not at all punishing the non-innocent and of not at all deterring potential criminals. In the case of interrogative torture in the context of a ticking bomb situation, the risk of torturing an innocent person has to be weighed against

the risk of letting other innocent persons die in an explosion. If the weighing process in the former case can justify punishment, it is unclear why the weighing process in the latter case could not sometimes justify torture. If the odds are high enough, it does. In fact, the justification in the latter case might even be easier—easier at least than justifying capital punishment, for death, as already noted, is worse than torture (at least for most people who are confronted with a decision between their death and being tortured for a limited time). It might even be easier than justifying incarceration for one or two decades, for it is not clear that many persons would not prefer some hours or even days of torture to that alternative.

To sum up the discussion so far: A compelling argument for an absolute *moral* prohibition of torture cannot be made. Under certain circumstances torture can be justified. *Justified*, not only excused. I emphasise this because some philosophers claim that situations of so-called necessity or emergency can only *excuse* torture (and some other extreme measures). But there is nothing in the meaning of the terms 'necessity' or 'emergency' themselves that could warrant that view. For example, the German penal code distinguishes between 'justifying emergency' and 'excusing emergency'. § 34 reads:

> Whosoever, in order to avert a not otherwise avoidable present danger to life, body, freedom, honour, property, or another legally protected interest, acts so as to avert the danger to himself or others, does not act illegally if, upon consideration of the conflicting interests, namely of the threatened legally protected interests and of the degree of the threatened danger, the protected interest substantially outweighs the infringed interest. This, however, is true only if the act is an adequate [in the sense of means-end rationality ('angemessen')] means to avert the danger.[5]

He does not act illegally, and that means his act is legally justified. If the protected interests do not substantially outweigh the infringed interest, however, he can at best be excused. The moral case is not different. There can be situations where torture is an instrumentally adequate and the only means to avert a certain danger from certain morally protected interests and

where the protected interests substantially outweigh the infringed ones. Therefore, if the odds
are high enough, torture can be not only excused
but morally justified.

No doubt, an absolutist opponent of torture will not be particularly impressed by the
argument offered so far. In fact, absolutists normally (although perhaps not always) do not even
try to refute the arguments adduced against
their absolutist positions; they tend to just per-
sistently and dramatically reaffirm their positions. The writer and poet Ariel Dorfman is a
good example:

> I can only pray that humanity will have the
> courage to say no, no to torture, no to torture
> under any circumstance whatsoever, no to tor-
> ture, no matter who the enemy, what the accusa-
> tion, what sort of fear we harbor; no to torture no
> matter what kind of threat is posed to our safety;
> no to torture anytime, anywhere; no to torture
> anyone; no to torture.[6]

Moral absolutism is a dangerous and mistaken view. If, for example, humanity would face
the choice (maybe posed by some maniac with
the ultimate weapon or by an alien race, or what
have you) between being exterminated or torturing one particularly bad man (let us say Idi Amin)
for an hour or a day, it is far from clear why any
person in his right mind—both intellectually *and*
morally—should pray that humanity said 'no to
torture'.[7] And what, by the way, if the choice is
between all human beings (that includes children) being *tortured* by the alien race or only one
particularly bad man being tortured by some humans? Consequences count; they cannot simply
be ignored for the benefit of some allegedly absolute rule, especially if they might be catastrophic.
Fiat justitia, pereat mundus is an irrational and
immoral maxim.

To say it again: A compelling argument for
an absolute *moral* prohibition of torture cannot
be made. But what about the legal prohibition of
torture? If torture can be morally justified under
certain circumstances, should it also be legalised?

It could seem that torture is already legal under the German penal code. For if, as I
claimed, the interests which are protected by
torturing a terrorist can substantially outweigh

the infringed interests (most notably of the
terrorist), then torture must be legal. However,
the fact that this outweighing can occur from a
moral perspective does not yet mean that it can
also occur from the legal perspective of a certain penal code. Each system of laws is in principle free to stipulate an *absolute* prohibition of
torture. The German law does this in so far as
it accepts certain international absolute prohibitions of torture as binding. That is, according to
German law *nothing* can (legally) outweigh the
interest of not being tortured (or at least of not
being tortured by state officials or agents acting
on behalf of a state). That torture is illegal under all circumstances in a given system of law,
however, does not exclude the possibility that
the practice might under some circumstances be
excused by the law. It seems to me that it would
be reasonable to excuse it under some circumstances.[8] I shall, however, say nothing further on
this topic here. . . .

Instead, I shall say something about the proposal to *justify torture before the act* (rather than
excusing it *ex post*). The lawyer Alan Dershowitz
made the infamous suggestion to introduce legal
'torture warrants', issued by judges.

. . . it is important to ask the following
question: if torture is being or will be prac-
ticed, is it worse to close our eyes to it and
tolerate its use by low-level law enforcement
officials without accountability, or instead to
bring it to the surface by requiring that a warrant of some kind be required as a precondition
to the infliction of any type of torture under
any circumstances?[9]

And he states:

> My own belief is that a warrant requirement, if
> properly enforced, would probably reduce the fre-
> quency, severity, and duration of torture. I can-
> not see how it could possibly increase it, since a
> warrant requirement simply imposes an additional
> level of prior review . . . here are two examples
> to demonstrate why I think there would be less
> torture with a warrant requirement than without
> one. Recall the case of the alleged national secu-
> rity wiretap being placed on the phones of Martin
> Luther King by the Kennedy administration
> in the early 1960s. This was in the days when
> the attorney general could authorize a national

security wiretap without a warrant. Today no judge would issue a warrant in a case as flimsy as that one. When Zacarias Moussaoui was detained after trying to learn how to fly an airplane, without wanting to know much about landing it, the government did not even seek a national security wiretap because its lawyers believed that a judge would not have granted one.[10]

A few things must be said concerning this argument. First, closing one's eyes to the practice of torture is not the only alternative to the introduction of torture warrants. Unfortunately, Dershowitz seems to have difficulties grasping the difference between closing one's eyes on the one hand and exposing and condemning on the other. To wit, he criticises William Schulz, the executive director of Amnesty International USA, who asks whether Dershowitz would also favour brutality warrants and prisoner rape warrants. (Dershowitz answers with a 'heuristic yes', whatever that is supposed to be.)[11] And he quotes himself saying: 'My question back to Schulz is do you prefer the current situation in which brutality, testilying and prisoner rape are rampant, but we close our eyes to these evils?'[12] Who is 'we'? Certainly not Schulz or Amnesty International.[13]

Second, Dershowitz admits that he 'certainly cannot prove . . . that a formal requirement of a judicial warrant as prerequisite to nonlethal torture would decrease the amount of physical violence directed against suspects'.[14] It seems, however, that Dershowitz should offer something more than his personal 'belief' and two examples to back the quite grave proposal to legalise torture. That he does not displays a lightness about the matter which is out of place. To be sure, he also adduces John H. Langbein's historical study of torture,[15] and although he concedes that it 'does not definitely answer' 'whether there would be less torture if it were done as part of the legal system', he thinks that it 'does provide some suggestive insights'.[16] Yet, before drawing 'suggestive insights' from Langbein's study and from history, one should get both straight. Dershowitz does not.[17] In fact, Langbein leaves no doubt that torture was *not* part of the judicial system in England. Not only 'law enforcement officers' but

also the courts (and judges) could not warrant torture. Langbein even states:

> The legal basis, such as it was, for the use of torture in the eighty-one known cases appears to have been the notion of sovereign immunity, a defensive doctrine that spared the authorities from having to supply justification for what they were doing.[18]

The facts, then, are that torture was never part of the English judicial system (if it was ever legal in England at all) whereas it *was* part of the Continental legal system. Extensive (not to say epidemic) use was made of torture on the Continent but not in England. Obviously, these facts suggest insights quite different from the ones Dershowitz comes up with.

Moreover, it is also funny that Dershowitz thinks that his two examples *support* his case. What his examples show (if they show anything) is that an attorney general who is *authorised* to put a wiretap without judicial warrant is more likely to put a wiretap than an attorney general who does need a warrant. However, the question to be answered is whether torture would be less likely under a requirement of a judicial warrant than *under a total ban*. To suggest a positive answer to this question by way of an analogy, Dershowitz would have to compare a legal arrangement in which the attorney general is *prohibited* from putting a wiretap with a legal arrangement where he is authorised to do so if he has a warrant. Dershowitz does not do that. It is he who engages in 'tortured reasoning', to use his term,[19] not his critics.

Finally, why shouldn't state agents who do not get a warrant torture anyway? They do not get a warrant today, and some of them torture anyway. Dershowitz answers that:

> . . . the current excuse being offered—we had to do what we did to get information—would no longer be available, since there would be an authorized method of securing information in extraordinary cases by the use of extraordinary means.[20]

First, people who escape detection are not in need of excuses to wriggle out of punishment in the first place. Besides, the excuse *would* be available. It would be: 'Since the judge didn't give us the warrant—he did not realise the seriousness of the situation (or there wasn't enough time)—we just had to torture under these circumstances without a warrant in order to get the information and to avoid a great evil'.

In short, Dershowitz has not offered the slightest bit of evidence—not even anecdotal—for his bold claim that the introduction of torture warrants would reduce torture or as much as increase accountability. Yet there is very good evidence to the contrary. Since Dershowitz invited us to draw suggestive insights from history, especially on the basis of Langbein's study, it might be worthwhile to note what Langbein himself has to say:

> 'Another insight from history is the danger that, once legitimated, torture could develop a constituency with a vested interest in perpetuating it.'[21]

And that, to draw the conclusion Dershowitz isn't able to draw, would hardly help to reduce torture or to increase accountability.

But why *should* we try to reduce torture? After all, in the first part of this paper I have argued that no compelling argument for an absolute moral prohibition of torture can be made; yes, not even for a prohibition in the Dirty Harry cases. I have also argued that torture is not worse than death and probably not worse than a decade of incarceration. So since we have legal incarceration, why shouldn't we have legal torture too?

One very straightforward answer is: because we don't need it. The ticking bomb case or the Dirty Harry case is a very rare case. In fact, it is safe to assume that all the torture that happened or happens in Abu Ghraib, Afghanistan and Guantanamo simply has nothing to do with ticking bombs or hostages who are about to die. The same holds for the overwhelming majority of all other cases of torture. Ticking bomb and Dirty Harry cases are *exceptions*. An emergency or necessity paragraph along the lines of § 35 of the German penal code can deal with such exceptions, and perhaps not even that is needed. If the stakes are high enough and no other option is available, police officers or other state agents will probably use torture even if they face prosecution if caught (that is, incidentally, what Dershowitz himself

claims). Besides, if punished, they might still be allowed the benefit of mitigating circumstances.

Second, that being tortured (or torturing someone) is not necessarily worse than being killed or incarcerated for a long time (or than killing someone or incarcerating him for a long time) does not imply that introducing a *wider practice* of torture is not worse than introducing or maintaining a wider practice of incarceration or killing. Dershowitz, for example, acknowledges:

> Experience has shown that if torture, which has been deemed illegitimate by the civilized world for more than a century, were now to be legitimated—even for limited use in one extraordinary type of situation—such legitimation would constitute an important symbolic setback in the worldwide campaign against human rights abuses.[22]

However, he thinks:

> It does not necessarily follow from this understandable fear of the slippery slope that we can never consider the use of nonlethal infliction of pain, if its use were to be limited by acceptable principles of morality. After all, imprisoning a witness who refuses to testify after being given immunity is designed to be punitive—that is painful. Such imprisonment can, on occasion, produce more pain and greater risk of death than nonlethal torture.[23]

It does indeed not follow that we can never consider the use of non-lethal infliction of pain, but it does follow that *institutionalising* torture—for example with torture warrants—is a bad idea. In particular, the analogy with the practice of coercing witnesses through imprisonment into testifying is misleading. The practice is designed to be punitive, yes, but that is not the same as being designed to be *painful*. Not every aversive treatment causes pain. It is important not to blur the distinctions. Further, the very fact that imprisonment produces only *on occasion* more pain and greater risk of death than non-lethal torture (although I suppose that non-lethal imprisonment would carry no risk of death) shows that it is not designed to produce pain and death. After all, being released can, on occasion, also produce more pain and greater risk of death than non-lethal torture. But how is that supposed to support the case for torture or for torture warrants? Thus, by using imprisonment as a method of punishment we are *not* already on the slippery slope.

Even if legalising torture puts us on a slippery slope, couldn't we stop the slide downwards? Dershowitz proposes a 'principled break':

> For example, if nonlethal torture were legally limited to convicted terrorists who had knowledge of future massive terrorist acts, were given immunity, and still refused to provide the information, there might still be objections to the use of torture, but they would have to go beyond the slippery slope argument.[24]

Actually, one argument that could be made here is that a *convicted* terrorist will hardly be a ticking bomb terrorist, unless, of course, he has set the time fuse on a few months or even years in the future *or* his conviction was made without due process. Giving up due process, however, does not look very much like a 'principled break', at least if the principle is supposed to be compatible with the rule of law. That notwithstanding, it has to be admitted that 'massive terrorist acts' will have to be planned long enough in advance so that a convicted terrorist might have knowledge of them. Consequently, torturing him might be a means to thwart the attacks.

However, Dershowitz's talk about a 'principled break' does, in fact, not address the problem of an 'important symbolic setback in the world-wide campaign against human rights abuses' at all. The symbolic setback consists precisely in undermining the *absolute* prohibition on torture and cannot be compensated, probably not even mitigated, by recourse to alleged 'principled breaks'. Moreover, the whole idea of a 'principled break' in connection with 'security laws' that cut down on civil liberties and individual rights is rather naïve. (I put 'security laws' in quotation marks because cutting down on civil liberties and individual rights hardly increases an individual's security from the state—the political entity, it should be remembered, that has slaughtered more people than any other political entity in history and is certainly more dangerous than any subnational terrorist organisation.) Experience shows that

measures introduced against putative terrorists in alleged conditions of emergency tend to be doubly extended, namely, beyond the emergency and to crimes or offences of lesser seriousness. In the UK, for example, emergency anti-terrorist measures, such as limitations on the right to silence, admissibility of confession evidence and extended periods of pre-judicial detention, have infiltrated ordinary criminal law and procedure.[25] Once advertised as being targeted only against terrorists, they can now befall any citizen who gets involved in criminal procedure.

It is to be expected, then, that the legalisation of torture for certain specific circumstances will, just like other so-called security laws, come with an inherent 'metastatic tendency'[26] that in time extends it beyond those circumstances. Apart from this dangerous tendency of 'security laws' in general there is, in addition, something very *special* about torture. Jeremy Waldron has argued that the prohibition of torture is archetypical of the idea:

> . . . that even where law has to operate forcefully, there will not be the connection that has existed in other times or places between law and brutality. People may fear and be deterred by legal sanctions . . . they may even on occasion be forced . . . to do things or go places against their will. But even when this happens, they will not be herded like cattle or broken like horses; they will not be beaten like dumb animals or treated as bodies to be manipulated. Instead, there will be an enduring connection between the spirit of law and respect for human dignity—respect for human dignity even in extremis, where law is at its most forceful and its subjects at their most vulnerable.[27]

That the prohibition of torture is a legal *archetype* means that it has 'a significance stemming from the fact that it sums up or makes vivid to us the point, purpose, principle, or policy of a whole area of law'.[28] For example, Waldron shows that decisive court rulings against lesser forms of police brutality—lesser, that is, than torture—were made with reference to torture. The similarities with torture were invoked to reject those other brutalities. This, of course, would not be possible if torture itself became regularised and justified by law, for the similarity with a regular legal practice could hardly count against some other practice. As Waldron puts it:

> The idea is that our confidence that what lies at the bottom of the slope (torture) is wrong informs and supports our confidence that the lesser evils that lie above torture are wrong too.[29]

Thus, by undermining the archetype of the prohibition of torture one also undermines the prohibition of lesser forms of brutality. The whole set of injunctions against brutality would unravel and the character of the legal system would be corrupted.[30]

What is so frightening about such a brutalisation of the legal system is that it is also the brutalisation of its *enforcer*—which, in modern societies, is ultimately the *state*. It is one thing to grant to an individual in a certain situation the moral justification to torture another individual; it is a completely different thing to allow the state to legally institutionalise torture in certain circumstances. Dirty Harry has to justify himself not only morally but also legally. He might face legal charges, and that might make him think twice before he tortures someone. This, in fact, ensures that the slope of the moral permission of torture in certain cases does not become too slippery to be acceptable. Dirty Harry takes his decision as an individual, not as an agent of the state. The state is not behind him. But if law enforcers can resort to torture knowing in advance that the state is behind them, the worst has to be expected—on a large and inevitably growing scale. Here it is worth noting that the argument that the prohibition of torture is an archetype and the argument that the legal introduction of torture would have a metastatic tendency reinforce each other. The further the practice of torture extends, the more it will undermine the archetypical character of the prohibition; the more that happens, the further the practice will extend. It is not only a slippery slope but also a slope that on its way down gets exponentially steeper. One of the functions of the rule of law is to keep the power of the state under control. But this doesn't work with *any* law. It doesn't work with a brutal or brutalised one. Torture warrants are indeed a 'stunningly bad idea'.[31]

NOTES

1. See S. Levinson, 'Contemplating torture: an introduction' in Levinson (2004) op. cit. (see n. 1), pp. 23–43, at pp. 33ff., and the further references there.
2. R. H. Weisberg, 'Loose professionalism' in Levinson (2004) op. cit, pp. 299–305, at p. 304.
3. Jeff McMahan agrees that this person cannot complain under the circumstances but thinks that this still does not make him liable to be tortured, the reason being that 'torturing him serves no purpose under the circumstances'. (Personal communication) However, if he cannot complain, he cannot be being wronged (for then he obviously could complain); and I think that the only possible reason why someone is not wronged by an attack (for example in the form of torture) is that he is liable to the attack. In fact, this seems to be pretty much the meaning of 'liable to attack'. Besides, if someone unjustly shoots at me and I shoot back, hitting him in the shoulder, and he continues shooting and kills me, then my counterattack has served no purpose under the circumstances (if it had, I would not be dead). That makes my counterattack hardly unjust or the attacker not liable to be shot at (otherwise every unsuccessful defender would also be an unjust defender, which is absurd).
4. D. Luban, (2005) 'Liberalism and the unpleasant question of torture', http://ethics.stanford.edu/newsletter/_old/december, accessed on 2 October 2005, electronic resource. A comparable argument is put forward by K. Seth, 'Too close to the rack and the screw: constitutional constraints on torture in the war on terror', *University of Pennsylvania Journal of Constitutional Law* 6 (2003–2004): 278–325.
5. The translation is mine.
6. A. Dorfman, 'The tyranny of terror: is torture inevitable in our century and beyond?' in Levinson (2004) op. cit., pp. 3–18, at p. 17.
7. Torturing this person would, of course, be a case of self-preservation and not of self- or other-defence (or something close to it) as in the Dirty Harry case.
8. That seems to be the position of Shue op. cit., pp. 58f., and R. A. Posner, 'Torture, terrorism, and interrogation' in Levinson (2004) op. cit., pp. 291–298, at pp. 297f.; and it is the position of O. Gross, 'The prohibition on torture and the limits of the law' in Levinson (2004) op. cit., pp. 229–253, esp. at pp. 231 and 239–250.

9. A. Dershowitz, 'Tortured reasoning' in Levinson (2004) op. cit., pp. 257–280, at p. 257. He emphasises that *that* was his question and not the 'old, abstract' one 'over whether torture can ever be justified', and he complains about 'misleading' descriptions of his proposals. *Ibid.,* p. 266. Maybe the next time he addresses the former question instead of the latter he could help to avoid 'misleading' descriptions of his intentions by not using titles like 'Should the Ticking Bomb Terrorist Be Tortured?' See A. Dershowitz, *Why Terrorism Works: Understanding the Threats, Responding to the Challenge* (New Haven, CT: Yale University Press, 2002) p. 131.

10. Dershowitz (2004) op. cit., pp. 270f.

11. *Ibid.,* pp. 266f.

12. *Ibid.,* p. 267, '"Testilying" is a term coined by New York City police to describe systematic perjury regarding the circumstances that led to a search, seizure, or interrogation'. *Ibid.,* p.278, n. 13.

13. Compare E. Scarry, 'Five errors in the reasoning of Alan Dershowitz' in Levinson (2004) op. cit., pp. 281–290, at p. 288.

14. Dershowitz (2002) op. cit., p. 158.

15. J. H. Langbein, *Torture and the Law of Proof: Europe and England in the Ancien Régime* (Chicago, IL: University of Chicago Press, 1977).

16. Dershowitz (2002) op. cit., p. 158.

17. On Dershowitz's misreading of Langbein see also J. Waldron, 'Torture and positive law: jurisprudence for the White House', *Columbia Law Review* 105 (2005): 1739, n. 250.

18. J. H. Langbein, 'The legal history of torture' in Levinson (2004) op. cit., pp. 93–103, at p. 100.

19. Dershowitz (2004) op. cit., p. 257.

20. *Ibid.,* p. 276.

21. Langbein (2004) op. cit., p. 101.

22. Dershowitz (2002) op. cit., p. 145.

23. *Ibid.,* p. 147.

24. *Ibid.*

25. P. Hillyard, 'The normalization of special powers from Northern Ireland to Britain' in N. Lacey (ed.) *A Reader on Criminal Justice* (Oxford: Oxford University Press, 1994); O. Gross, 'Cutting down trees: law-making under the shadow of great calamities' in R. J. Daniels, P. Macklem and K. Roach (eds.), *The Security of Freedom: Essays on Canada's Anti-Terrorism Bill* (Toronto: Toronto University Press, 2001), pp. 39–61, esp. at 47ff. I owe the references to these articles to L. Zedner, 'Securing liberty in the face of terror: reflections from criminal justice', pp. 7 and 15, and to C. Warbrick, 'Terrorism, counter-terrorism, international law', p. 9, unpublished papers held at the colloquium *Moral and Legal Aspects of Terrorism,* Corpus Christi College, Oxford, 5 March 2005.

26. Shue op. cit., p. 58.

27. Waldron op. cit., pp. 1726f.

28. *Ibid.,* p. 1723.

29. *Ibid.,* p. 1735.

30. *Ibid.,* p. 1728-1739.

31. J. B. Elshtain, 'Reflections on the problem of "dirty hands"' in Levinson (2004) op. cit., pp. 77–89, at p. 83. I owe thanks to patrick Lenta, Jeff McMahan and David Rodin for helpful comments on an earlier draft of this paper.

⚜ REVIEW QUESTIONS

1. Why does Steinhoff think that interrogative torture is morally justified in the Dirty Harry case?

2. How does Steinhoff reply to the objection that torture does not work?

3. What is Steinhoff's reply to the objection that interrogative torture is not reliable? How does this reply apply to the ticking-bomb case?

4. What is Weisberg's criticism of the ticking-bomb case? How does Steinhoff reply?

5. What is Luban's objection to torture? How does Steinhoff respond?

6. Why does Steinhoff think that interrogative torture is justified in the ticking-bomb case?

7. Why does Steinhoff hold that moral absolutism is dangerous and mistaken?

8. Explain Alan Dershowitz's proposal. Why does Steinhoff reject it as a bad idea?

⚜ DISCUSSION QUESTIONS

1. Are you convinced that Harry is morally justified in torturing the kidnapper? Should this behavior be legal? Explain your answers.
2. Unlike Luban, Steinhoff thinks torturing terrorists is morally justified even given various uncertainties. Do you agree? Why or why not?
3. Is moral absolutism always dangerous and mistaken? What is your view?
4. Is Dershowitz's proposal really a bad idea? What do you think?

PROBLEM CASES

1. A Nuclear Bomb

Al Qaeda terrorists have planted a small nuclear device in an apartment building in London, and it is set to go off in two hours. If it goes off, it will kill thousands of people and injure thousands more. It will destroy a large part of the city. The terrorist group that planted the bomb has been under surveillance by the police. The police suspect that a devastating terrorist act has been planned; they have been monitoring telephone conversations and e-mails for months. They decide to bring in one of the terrorists for questioning. They know he has planned terrorist attacks in the past, and they have good evidence that a nuclear attack is going to happen in London and that he knows about it. The terrorist has been questioned before, and he knows the routine. If he refuses to talk, then the bomb will go off as he planned; his terrorist mission will be accomplished. Time is running out. There is not enough time to evacuate the city. The police are reasonably confident that the suspect knows where the bomb is and when it is set to go off. One of the policemen happens to have experience in torturing, although torture is illegal and not normally used. The policeman believes the terrorist will talk if tortured.

Should the terrorist be tortured or not? If he does not talk, the bomb will go off as planned and thousands will die or be injured. But if he does reveal the location of the bomb, experts will rush to the location and they will be able to prevent it from detonating. Is torture justified in this situation? Why or why not?

2. The Extraordinary Rendition Program

(See Jane Mayer, "Outsourcing Torture," *The New Yorker*, February 14, 2005.) The extraordinary rendition program began as far back as 1995. Originally, it was directed at suspects having outstanding foreign arrest warrants, but after 9/11, the program was expanded to target suspected terrorists. Suspicious "enemy combatants" were captured and confined and interrogated in secret CIA prisons called "black sites" outside the United States. President Bush admitted the existence of such prisons in a September 2006 speech. The most common destinations for suspects are Egypt, Jordan, Syria, and Morocco; all are known to practice torture and have been cited for human rights violations by the State Department. An estimated 150 people have been rendered since 2001.

The legal status of the rendering program is controversial. In 1998, Congress passed legislation saying that the policy of the United States is not to expel, extradite, or otherwise affect the involuntary return of any person to a country where the person would be in danger of being subjected to torture. The American Civil Liberties Union claims that the United States is violating federal and international law by engaging in secret abductions and torture. But Alberto Gonzales, the U.S. attorney general, argues that U.S. and international laws and prohibitions against torture do not apply to "enemy combatants" and do not apply to American interrogations of confined suspects overseas. In this view, suspected terrorists are basically outside the scope of the law. They can be detained indefinitely, without counsel, without charges of wrongdoing, and interrogated using CIA methods.

CIA sources have described six "Enhanced Interrogation Techniques" that are used to interrogate al-Qaeda suspects confined in the secret prisons. The CIA interrogators are supposed to be trained and authorized to use these techniques:

1. Attention Grab: The interrogator forcefully grabs the shirt front of the prisoner and shakes him. Violent shaking can cause whiplash injuries.
2. Attention Slap: The prisoner is slapped in the face with the aim of causing pain and fear.
3. Belly Slap: The naked prisoner is slapped hard in the stomach to cause pain. A punch to the stomach can produce permanent internal damage.
4. Long Time Standing: This technique is very effective. Prisoners are forced to stand handcuffed with their feet shackled to an eyebolt in the floor for more than forty hours. They become exhausted and sleep deprived.
5. The Cold Cell: The naked prisoner is made to stand in a cell kept below fifty degrees and is regularly doused with cold water. The prisoner can die of hypothermia.
6. Water Boarding: The prisoner is bound to an inclined board with the feet raised and the head slightly below the feet. Cellophane is wrapped over the face. Water is poured on the face from a hose or a bucket. The gag reflex quickly kicks in with a terrifying fear of drowning. After a short time, the victim pleads for the treatment to stop.

Are these CIA methods torture or not? Suppose that these methods produce valuable information about al-Qaeda terrorists and their future plans for attacks. If so, are these methods justified? What is your view? Should the United States continue the rendering program? Why or why not?

3. Khalid Sheik Mohammed

(See the Wikipedia article with links to news reports.) According to a transcript released by the military on March 15, 2007, Mr. Mohammed confessed to directing the 9/11 attacks and thirty-one other terrorist attacks and plans. He testified at the Guantánamo Bay detention facility that he was "responsible for the 9/11 attacks from A to Z." He described himself as al Qaeda's military operational commander for foreign operations. He claimed that he personally decapitated Daniel Pearl, the American journalist who was kidnapped and murdered in 2002 in Pakistan. He said he was responsible for several other operations, including the 2001 Richard Reid shoe-bomber attempt to blow up an airliner, the 2002 Bali nightclub bombing in Indonesia, and the 1993 World Trade Center attack. He said he was involved in more than two dozen uncompleted terrorist plots, including ones that targeted offices in New York City, Los Angeles, and Chicago. He plotted to blow up nuclear power plants. He planned assassination attempts of several U.S. presidents. He planned to explode London's Big Ben tower and destroy the Panama Canal.

Mr. Mohammed was arrested in Pakistan in 2003 and "disappeared" to a semisecret prison in Jordan where he was interrogated by the CIA. His confession came after four years of captivity, including six months at Guantánamo Bay. CIA officials told ABC news that Mr. Mohammed's interrogation included water boarding. The technique involves strapping a prisoner on an inclined board with the head below the feet. The face is wrapped in cellophane and water poured over it. This produces an intense gag reflex and fear of drowning, but it is not supposed to result in permanent physical damage. The CIA officers who subjected themselves to the procedure lasted an average of fourteen seconds before giving up. Mr. Mohammed impressed the interrogators when he was able to last between two and two-and-a-half minutes before begging to confess.

The Human Rights Watch says that Mr. Mohammed was tortured. Do you agree? Should water boarding be acknowledged as torture? Why or why not?

The CIA officials admit that confessions resulting from torture or mistreatment may not be reliable. For example, Ibn al Shaykh al Libbi was water boarded and then made to stand naked in a cold cell overnight where he was regularly doused with cold water. After two weeks of "enhanced interrogation," his confessions became the basis for the Bush administration claim that Iraq trained al-Qaeda members to use biochemical weapons. Later, it was established that he had no knowledge of such training or weapons and had fabricated the statements to avoid further harsh treatment.

Some commentators are skeptical about Mr. Mohammed's rambling and wide-ranging confessions. For example, Michigan Representative Mike Rogers, a Republican on the terrorism panel of the House Intelligence Committee, found the confessions to be exaggerated or self-promotional. He doubted that Mr. Mohammed had a role in so many terrorist acts and plans. One CIA official admitted that some of Mr. Mohammed's claims during interrogation were "white noise" designed to send the interrogators on "wild goose chases" or to "get him through the day's interrogation sessions."

If Mr. Mohammed's confessions were not useful or reliable, then was the CIA interrogation justified?

Suppose that the confessions in question produced useful information that prevented terrorist attacks. Would that fact justify the treatment Mr. Mohammed received at the hands of the CIA interrogators?

Now that he has confessed to crimes including murder, what should be done with Mr. Mohammed? The Bush administration position was that he is an "enemy combatant" without any legal rights. This means that he could be executed without a trial. Is this the right thing to do?

The Obama administration has announced that it expects Mohammed to be given a trial, found guilty, and executed. But there was confusion about how to do this. In 2010, all charges against Mohammed by military commissions were withdrawn without prejudice, which allows officials to try Mohammed and the other suspects in a civilian court. But where should he be tried? The plan to have the trial in New York City was abandoned after a wave of protests. Another problem is that confessions or evidence based on torture are not admissible in U.S. civilian courts. In the meantime, he is being held at Guantánamo Bay.

Should Mohammed be given a trial or not? If so, should he be found guilty and executed? Another option is to hold him indefinitely without a trial at Guantánamo Bay. What should be done with him?

4. The Geneva Convention and the UN Convention

The United States ratified the Geneva Convention relative to the Treatment of Prisoners of War in 1955. It prohibits "cruel treatment and torture." It also prohibits "outrages upon personal dignity, in particular, humiliating and degrading treatment."

The United Nations Convention Against Torture and Other Cruel, Inhuman or Degrading Treatment or Punishment was adopted by the UN General Assembly in 1984. To date, 142 nations have ratified it, including the United States.

Article 1 defines torture (in part) as "any act by which severe pain or suffering, whether physical or mental, is intentionally inflicted on a person for such purposes as obtaining from him or a third person information or a confession."

Article 2 requires each state to take "effective legislative, administrative, judicial or other measures to prevent acts of torture." It also says that no circumstances whatever, whether a state of war or a threat of war or any other public emergency, may be used to justify torture.

Article 3 prohibits a state from extraditing a person to another state to be tortured.

Article 16 states that each state that is a party to the agreement "shall undertake to prevent in any territory under its jurisdiction other acts of cruel, inhuman or degrading treatment or punishment which do not amount to torture as defined in Article 1."

Should the United States follow these conventions or not? Are violations of these conventions war crimes? What is your position?

☙ SUGGESTED READINGS

The *Stanford Encyclopedia of Philosophy* (http://plato .stanford.edu) has an excellent article on torture written by Seamus Miller. The CIA website (www.cia.gov) has detailed information on torture, including personal anecdotes, methods used, and information gained. The World Organization Against Torture (www.omct.org) is a global network fighting against torture and other human rights violations. The Human Rights Watch (www.hrw.org) has reports on the use of torture around the world.

Heather MacDonald, "How to Interrogate Terrorists," *City Journal*, Winter 2005: 1–8, argues that to succeed in the war on terror, the U.S. military must be allowed to use stress techniques on unlawful combatants, including sleep deprivation, loud noise, prolonged kneeling or standing, and so on. These techniques are not torture in her view, but she admits that water boarding may cross the line into torture.

Henry Shue, "Torture," *Philosophy and Public Affairs* 7, no. 2 (Winter 1978): 124–143, argues that torture is morally worse than killing in a just war because it violates the prohibition against assaulting the defenseless, but he suggests that there is at least one imaginable case in which interrogational torture might be justified: the now-famous ticking-bomb case. As Shue describes the case, there is a fanatic who has hidden a nuclear bomb set to explode in Paris, and the only way to prevent the destruction of Paris is to torture the fanatic to find out where the bomb is hidden so that it can be found and deactivated.

Bob Brecher, *Torture and the Ticking Bomb* (London: Wiley-Blackwell, 2007), gives a detailed critique of the ticking-bomb story used by Dershowitz and others to justify torture.

Kenneth Roth and Minky Worden, eds., *Torture* (New York: New Press, 2005). This is a collection of twelve articles on torture, including Michael Ignatieff on justifying torture, Jean Mendez on the victim's perspective, Jamie Feiner on torture in U.S. prisons, and David Rieff on the inadequacies of the human rights view.

Sanford Levison, ed., *Torture* (Oxford: Oxford University Press, 2006). This is a useful collection of seventeen essays covering the morality, legality, and practice of torture.

Fritz Allhoff, "Terrorism and Torture," *International Journal of Applied Philosophy* 17, no. 1 (2003): 105–118, supports the use of torture to get information about imminent and significant threats but not to force confession or to deter crime.

Fritz Allhoff, "A Defense of Torture," *International Journal of Applied Philosophy* 19, no. 2 (Fall 2005): 243–264, argues for the permissibility of torture in ticking-bomb cases.

Michael Davis, "The Moral Justification of Torture and Other Cruel, Inhuman, or Degrading Treatment," *International Journal of Applied Philosophy* 19, no. 2 (2005): 161–178, argues that the ticking-bomb case proves nothing because it relies on intuition, which is unreliable and fails to provide any justification.

Christopher W. Tindale, "Tragic Choices," *International Journal of Applied Philosophy* 19, no. 2 (Fall 2005): 209–222, defends an absolute prohibition of interrogational torture; he argues that the ticking-bomb scenarios are ill considered.

Larry May, "Torturing Detainees During Interrogation," *International Journal of Applied Philosophy* 19, no. 2 (Fall 2005): 193–208, argues that our humanity demands that suspected terrorists not be subject to torture when they are captured and imprisoned.

David Sussman, "What's Wrong with Torture?" *Philosophy and Public Affairs* 33 (December 2005): 1–33, defends the intuition that torture is a special type of wrong, and this explains why we find it more morally offensive than other ways of inflicting harm.

Seamus Miller, "Is Torture Ever Morally Justified?" *International Journal of Applied Philosophy* 19, no. 2 (2005): 179–192, argues that torture is morally justified in extreme emergencies, but it ought not to be legalized.

Jeremy Waldron, "Torture and Positive Law," *Columbia Law Review* 105, no. 6 (2005): 1681–1750, defends the legal prohibition of torture. This prohibition is not just one rule among others; it is a legal archetype that is emblematic of a basic commitment to nonbrutality in the legal system.

Alan M. Dershowitz, *Why Terrorism Works* (New Haven, CT: Yale University Press, 2002), devotes a chapter to defending the use of torture on terrorists to get information about imminent attacks.

Howard J. Curzer, "Admirable Immorality, Dirty Hands, Ticking Bombs, and Torturing

Innocents," *Southern Journal of Philosophy* 44, no. 1 (Spring 2006): 31–56, argues that torturing is morally required and should be done when it is the only way to avert disasters. He admits that it is odd to hold that a vicious act like torture is morally required.

Jessica Wolfendale, "Training Torturers," *Social Theory and Practice* 322, no. 2 (April 2006): 269–287, argues that ticking-bomb arguments ignore the fact that permitting torture requires training torturers. This fact casts doubt on the arguments.

Karen J. Greenberg and Joshua L. Drafel, eds., *The Torture Papers* (Cambridge: Cambridge University Press, 2006), documents the abuse of prisoners at Abu Ghraib and Guantánamo.

Mark Danner, *Torture and Truth* (New York: New York Review of Books, 2004), argues that torture is part of a planned policy of the Bush administration.

Karen J. Greenberg, ed., *The Torture Debate in America* (Cambridge: Cambridge University Press, 2006), presents different perspectives on torture, from absolute prohibition to a useful weapon in the war on terrorism.

Colin Dayan, *The Story of Cruel and Unusual* (Boston: MIT Press, 2007), argues that recent Supreme Court decisions have dismantled the Eighth Amendment protection against "cruel and unusual" punishment. The result is the abuse and torture of prisoners at Abu Ghraib and Guantánamo.

William Sampson, *Confession of an Innocent Man* (Toronto: McClellan & Stewart, 2005). This is the horrifying story of an innocent Canadian man arrested, imprisoned, and tortured into confessing to car bombings he did not commit. Later, he was officially exonerated of the crimes.

Alfred McCoy, *A Question of Torture* (New York: Owl Books, 2006), describes the development of the torture methods used by the CIA.

Susan Sontag, "Regarding the Torture of Others," *The New York Times Magazine*, May 24, 2004, discusses the implications and meaning of the famous photographs of prisoners at Abu Ghraib.

CHAPTER THREE

Assassination

- **Introduction**
  - ○ Factual Background
  - ○ The Readings
  - ○ Philosophical Issues

WHITLEY R. P. KAUFMAN   **Rethinking the Ban on Assassination**

DANIEL STATMAN   **Targeted Killing**

PROBLEM CASES

SUGGESTED READINGS

INTRODUCTION

Factual Background

Assassination (or *targeted killing*) is the killing of a political or military leader or other public figure. There have been numerous assassinations throughout recorded history. On the Ides of March (March 15) 44 BCE, the Roman dictator Julius Caesar was stabbed to death by members of the Senate. The event is famously presented in Shakespeare's play *Julius Caesar*. In the Middle Ages, the French kings Henry III and Henry IV were assassinated. In Russia, four emperors were killed within 200 years. In modern times, the assassination of Franz Ferdinand is blamed for starting World War I. In 1948, an assassin shot and killed India's Mohandas K. Gandhi. In the United States, four presidents have been assassinated: Abraham Lincoln, James Garfield, William McKinley, and John F. Kennedy. An assassin also killed Robert Kennedy. Martin Luther King, Jr., the civil rights leader, was shot and killed by James Earl Ray in 1968.

Assassination is prohibited in international law. Article 23b of the Hague Regulations prohibits "assassination, proscriptions, or outlawry of an enemy, or putting a price upon an enemy's head, as well as offering a reward of an enemy 'dead or alive.'" U.S. law also makes assassination illegal. In 1976, President Ford issued an executive order that states: "No employee of the United States Government shall engage in, or conspire to engage in, political assassination." President Carter reaffirmed the prohibition. In 1981, President Reagan reiterated the prohibition in almost the same language: "No person employed by or acting on behalf of the United States Government shall engage in, or conspire to engage in, assassination."

Despite the legal prohibition of assassination, both Israel and the United States have assassinated political leaders and others, or tried to do so. In 1986, the Reagan administration dropped bombs on Libyan leader Muammar Qaddafi's home in retaliation for the bombing of a Berlin discotheque that killed a U.S. soldier. The attack killed Qaddafi's adopted infant daughter and fifteen others but not Qaddafi. According to Mark Bowden (see the Suggested Readings), a U.S. Delta Force sniper shot and killed Colombian drug lord Pablo Escobar in l993. The CIA tried for nearly half a century to assassinate Fidel Castro, using bizarre methods such as an exploding cigar (see the Problem Case). In 2003, the U.S. military hit a Baghdad restaurant with Tomahawk missiles in an attempt to kill Saddam Hussein and his sons. The explosions killed fourteen civilians but not Hussein and his sons. The Israeli military has targeted and killed several Hamas leaders, including Salah Shehada (2002; see the Problem Case), Ahmed Yassin (2004; see the Problem Case), Abdel Aziz al-Rantissi (2004), and Adman al-Ghoul (2004). In 2009, Israel used a one-ton bomb to flatten the home of Hamas leader Nizar Rayan, killing him and four of his children and two of his wives. During the war in Iraq, CIA or Blackwater hit teams armed with sawed-off M-4 automatic weapons with silencers made nightly raids to kill or capture suspected insurgents.

After the 9/11 attacks, President George W. Bush authorized "lethal covert actions" without formally rescinding the executive orders of Presidents Ford, Carter, and Reagan making assassination illegal. He said that bin Laden was wanted "dead or alive." Later, "wanted" posters were put up in Afghanistan promising $25 million for information leading to the capture of bin Laden. In June 2009, CIA director Leon Panetta revealed a secret CIA assassination program. Teams of assassins were to be deployed around the world to track down and kill suspected terrorist leaders. Members of Congress were angry because they had not been informed of the program. The furor grew when it was learned that the CIA had outsourced the program to Blackwater (now called Xe Services), the controversial private contractor. Panetta claimed that he had cancelled the program, but left open the possibility of reviving it.

In addition to assassins, bombs, and cruise missiles, the U.S. government uses Predator and Reaper drones for assassination. (The U.S. military prefers to call it "targeted killing" to avoid the negative connotations of "assassination.") The Predator is an unmanned aerial vehicle or plane that can fire two Hellfire missiles. The Reaper is four times heavier than the Predator and carries four Hellfire missiles and two 500-pound bombs. These unmanned drones have been frequently used in Pakistan and Afghanistan to target al-Qaeda and Taliban leaders. According to Pakistani authorities, there were more than sixty Predator or Reaper strikes in Pakistan between January 14, 2006, and April 8, 2009. Only ten were able to hit their actual targets, killing fourteen al-Qaeda leaders. The other 50 attacks went wrong because of faulty intelligence information, and thus killed 687 innocent civilians, including women and children. To give one example, in 2006 a Predator aircraft attacked the northern Pakistani village of Damadola and two other villages. The target was Ayman al-Zawahiri, al Qaeda's second in command after bin Laden. It is believed that he was killed but this has not been officially confirmed. Pakistani intelligence claimed that Abu Khabab al-Masri, al Qaeda's chief bomb maker and chemical weapons expert, was killed in the attacks. Pakistani officials also said the attacks killed eighteen civilians, including five children. According to a United Nations report issued in February 2009, targeted air strikes have killed more than 800 civilians in Afghanistan.

About 160 innocent civilians have been killed in Afghanistan since President Obama took office in January 2009.

In 2010, the number of drone strikes in the North Waziristan area of Pakistan increased dramatically. The drones, operated by the CIA, were flying twenty-four hours a day looking for targets, as compared to one flight a week in 2009. The fleet of Reaper aircraft was doubled. This increase in strikes and aircraft was in response to the suicide bombing of seven Americans in Afghanistan on December 30, 2009. According to Pakistani news reports, about ninety suspected terrorists were killed in January 2010.

Thus far we have discussed the use of Predators or Reapers by the U.S. military, which is publicly acknowledged. According to Jane Mayer (see the Suggested Readings), there is also a secret private program, run by Xe Services, aimed at terrorists around the world. The program is classified as covert, meaning that the CIA does not reveal where it operates, how it selects a target, who is in charge, or how many people have been killed. (Still, it is not exactly secret; see Scott Shane in the Suggested Readings.) Nevertheless, the CIA reported the assassination of Taliban leader Baitullah Mehsud by a missile strike in August 2009. He was hit while he was on a drip infusion for his kidney disease. The attack also killed Mehsud's wife and his parents-in-law. According to a study completed by the New American Foundation, a policy group in Washington, the Obama administration has sanctioned at least 41 CIA missile strikes in Pakistan that killed about 500 people, many of them innocent bystanders and including children. (In response to this report, CIA spokesman Paul Gimigliano said that there have been only twenty civilian deaths from Predator strikes.)

The Readings

Whitley R. P. Kaufman uses the term *assassination* to mean targeted killing without reference to treachery. He is primarily concerned about the morality of the premeditated, extrajudicial killing of individuals in positions of political or military leadership. He addresses the issue using just war doctrine. In that doctrine, the use of violence is justified only if it meets the requirements of necessity, proportionality, noncombatant immunity, and right motive. Revenge, punishment, or maximization of good consequences cannot provide a legitimate basis for violence. He argues that assassination is justified in just war theory only if the targeted individual is an aggressor and poses an imminent threat. Thus, just war doctrine generally prohibits assassination. It is legitimate only in very limited circumstances.

Daniel Statman uses the term *targeted killing* rather than *assassination*. He finds it puzzling that people are willing to accept the morality and legality of killing in a conventional war, such as the Falkland Islands War, and yet reject it when it comes to the targeted killing of terrorist leaders. After all, the threat to the United States posed by al Qaeda is greater than the threat the Argentinean invasion of the Falkland Islands posed to the British. In his view, the war on terror is analogous to conventional war. Both are responses to threats, and in both it is legitimate to target aggressors in self-defense. If one accepts the moral legitimacy of large-scale killing of combatants in conventional wars, then one should accept the moral legitimacy of targeted killing of terrorist leaders in wars against terror. Unlike Kaufman, Statman also accepts retribution as a moral justification for the targeted killing of Palestinian terrorists. In fact, he believes that the killing of activist terrorists is more justified than the killing of enemy combatants in conventional wars.

Philosophical Issues

What is assassination? There is disagreement about what counts as an assassination or how to define the term *assassination*. As Whitley R. P. Kaufman uses the term, the targeted killing of a political or military leader is an assassination. An assassination does not essentially involve the use of treachery; rather, it is the premeditated, extra-judicial killing of leaders.

Daniel Statman chooses to use the term *targeted killing* rather than *assassination* to avoid the negative moral connotation of the latter term, that is, the presumption that assassination is morally wrong. If assassination is murder, then by definition it is morally wrong. *Targeted killing* is a more neutral term that leaves open the question of whether it is morally wrong. As we have seen, Statman argues that targeted killing is not always morally wrong.

Amnesty International (see the Suggested Readings) refers to the targeted killing of political or military leaders by governments such as Israel or the United States as *state* assassination, as distinguished from assassinations done by private individuals. Jane Mayer (see the Suggested Readings) speaks of *targeted* assassinations of terror-ists. Others call the targeted killing of suspected terrorists extrajudicial executions.

The main issue raised in the readings is whether assassination or targeted kill-ing can be morally justified. Kaufman argues that it is generally unjustified if one adheres to the principles of just war doctrine. As he understands those principles, the targeted assassination or killing of a military or political leader could be justified only if it were done to prevent an imminent unjust attack with the motive of protect-ing oneself or others from death or serious harm. The force must be necessary, such that there is no less violent means of preventing attack (such as capturing the tar-get). It must be proportionate, in the sense that the harm produced is proportion-ate to the harm prevented. With those restrictions in mind, it seems that targeted killing that results in the deaths of innocent bystanders is not morally justified. This means that almost all of the targeted killing done by the United States and Israel is not morally justified.

Statman defends targeted killing. It is not only morally justified, it is even more defensible than the killing that goes on in all-out conventional wars. If one accepts the large-scale killing of combatants and noncombatants in conventional wars, then it is hard to see why the targeted killing of guilty terrorists is not mor-ally justified, too. Furthermore, killing terrorists satisfies the desire for revenge or retribution. This consideration provides further support for the moral justification of targeted killing.

Steven de Wijze (see the Suggested Reading) offers a third alternative to the moral complexity of targeted killing. Unlike Statman, he does not think that tar-geted killing is entirely morally justified, but he does not believe it should be un-equivocally condemned, either. Instead, he suggests that the government and agents who engage in such actions end up having "dirty hands." They have done some-thing wrong in order to do right. They have chosen the lesser of two evils, and par-adoxically this is morally justified and at the same time morally reprehensible. The moral emotion produced is "tragic remorse," the anguish produced by necessary wrongdoing.

Rethinking the Ban on Assassination

WHITLEY R. P. KAUFMAN

Whitley R. P. Kaufman is chair and associate professor of philosophy at the University of Massachusetts, Lowell. He is the author of *Justified Killing: The Paradox of Self-Defense* (2009) and about twenty articles, many of them on the topic of self-defense, punishment, and just war doctrine.

Kaufman argues that assassination or targeted killing is generally impermissible under just war doctrine, but may be legitimate in certain limited circumstances. He distinguishes between a punishment rationale, a self-defense rationale, and a consequentialist rationale for assassination. In just war theory, only the self-defense rationale can morally justify assassination: Assassination is morally justified if the target is an aggressor and poses an imminent threat. Even if the target is a combatant, there remain serious concerns about the morality of assassination: the fact that it is premeditated, the duty to use minimum harm, the danger of misuse, and the problem of a slippery slope of killing.

The September 11, 2001, terrorist attacks appear to have undermined, at least in the United States, what had previously been a firm moral and legal consensus against the use of political assassination. Though it is banned under international law[1] and has been prohibited as a matter of U.S. policy since 1976 when President Ford signed an executive order banning assassination, U.S. policy appears to have reversed course in response to the increase in terrorist attacks. President Clinton revealed at a news conference in 2001 following the Trade Center attacks that his administration in 1998, following the bombing of U.S. embassies, had authorized the "arrest and, if necessary, the killing of Osama bin Laden," though a lack of intelligence prevented the successful completion of the mission. In October 2001 George Bush authorized the CIA to carry out missions to assassinate Osama bin Laden and his supporters (and indeed publicly declared that bin Laden "was wanted, dead or alive"). In addition, Israel has increasingly resorted to the use of assassination of terrorist leaders among the Palestinians to prevent suicide bombing attacks. Vigorous debates have also arisen over the question of the potential assassination of political leaders such as Saddam Hussein or Muammar Qaddafi. More fundamentally, these actions have taken place in a shifting moral environment, in which the earlier assumption that assassination is morally impermissible no longer seems convincing in an age of terrorism.

In this essay I will analyze the ethics of political assassination from within the context of the just war tradition. Just war doctrine involves a strong presumption against the use of violence or killing (in peacetime or in war) outside of certain limited contexts, specifically the punishment of the guilty, defense against an unjust attacker, and the enforcement of natural justice or law. Even in those contexts, the use of violence is subject to the just war requirements including last resort (aka necessity), proportionality, noncombatant immunity, and right motive. Crucially, just war doctrine rejects the Realist/consequentialist position that an action can be justified merely because it leads to good overall results (though of course consequences are morally relevant in just war doctrine). Given that the most commonly stated rationale for assassination

Source: Rethinking the Ban on Assassination: Just War Principles in the Age of Terror by Whitley R.P. Kaufman from Rethinking the Just War Tradition by Michael W. Brough, John W. Lango and Harry Van Der Linden. Copyright © 2007. NY: State University of New York Press.

is consequentialist in nature—that is, that assassination would be the most efficient means of achieving one's goals—the practice of assassination would then seem to be ruled out in just war doctrine. But is this in fact the case, and even if it is, does the rise of terrorism and weapons of mass destruction require a modification of the tradition? On one extreme is the view that assassination is never morally permissible, no matter the circumstances; at the other extreme is the position that the conditions of the present day are so dangerous that traditional moral constraints must be sacrificed where necessary. I will argue here that neither position is correct; assassination is not automatically prohibited by just war doctrine, though it will be morally permissible only under very limited circumstances.

A first issue is, of course, the problem of defining *assassination*, a concept which is very difficult to pin down. Traditionally, the term *assassination* was held to refer to killing by means of treachery, betrayal, or perfidy. Some commentators have argued that this prohibition reflected a concern for honor or chivalry, and that it was not meant to prohibit targeting military or political leaders per se. Thus Caspar Weinberger has argued that when assassination is forbidden in the law of armed conflict, what is meant is "murder by treacherous means,"[2] and that therefore there is nothing wrong with assassination per se, so long as it does not involve "treachery." This argument however is a red herring. Whatever the concerns about the use of treachery in war, the central moral issue at stake is not the betrayal of trust, but rather the morality of premeditated, extrajudicial killing of specific individuals (i.e., those in leadership positions). Such an action would seem far removed from the paradigmatic case of justified killing: the soldier on the battlefield with a weapon in hand. Alberico Gentili, for example, allowed for seeking out the leader on the battlefield, but disapproved of the killing of the leader if he were "remote from arms and happened to be swimming in the Tiber," for this is killing an "unarmed man remote from war."[3] Such actions would ordinarily be considered simply murder, and the question is whether there is sufficient moral basis for permitting such a prima

facie wrongful act. Some commentators have adopted the term *targeted killing* so as to avoid any connotations of treachery associated with the term *assassination*.[4] However, in this essay I will use the terms *assassination* and *targeted killing* interchangeably, whether or not "treachery" is involved. The moral question is then whether assassinations—the premeditated, extrajudicial killings of a named individual—are permissible or not under just war doctrine.

A second issue we will have to examine is whether there is an essential difference between military and political leaders as regards the legitimacy of assassination. It is often assumed that military leaders, as they are obviously combatants under just war principles, are legitimate targets in wartime, and therefore it is permissible to assassinate them. Political leaders such as Saddam Hussein or Fidel Castro, some have argued, are different: they are not obviously combatants, even where they have ultimate control over the military. Similar difficult questions concern countries where the commander of the military is a civilian, as in the United States. The question is of course further complicated by the problem of assigning combatant status at all when there is not a state of war, especially as regards the problem of terrorism, which takes place in what William Banks calls the "twilight zone between war and peace."[5] But even within terrorist groups one can distinguish between political and military leaders. Israel's policy to date has been to accept just such a distinction within terrorist organizations such as Hamas, so that it does not try to kill political leaders who do not direct suicide bombers. This Israeli policy may however be breaking down currently, and many advocates of assassination reject the political/military distinction as artificial.

The question to be faced then is the following: is there a moral basis for a policy of premeditated, extrajudicial killing, and does it depend on whether the target is a military or merely political leader? Discussion of this question is often muddled by a failure to clearly distinguish the punishment rationale from the self-defense rationale for assassination. Indeed, the idea of justifying a policy of assassination under the rubric of punishment would seem to run into intractable moral problems, for a policy of summary execution without trial or any significant procedural constraints would not ordinarily be considered a legitimate form of punishment. Consider for example Caspar Weinberger's discussion: he begins with a just war defensive rationale for targeting leaders (on the grounds that they are combatants), then switches to a punishment argument ("there is every reason to punish the leaders for the acts that brought on the war"), and ends with a consequentialist rationale for assassination ("killing leaders may end a war with a big saving of soldiers' lives").[6] He concludes that if killing the leaders would not violate the laws of armed conflict, "then clearly the taking of any enemy commander (without any treachery) and holding him for trial conducted under normal national rules would not violate any moral or legal prohibition."[7] But the confusions in this argument are legion. The just war tradition, as I have said, does not obviously dictate that heads of state are combatants, and in any case Weinberger's invocation of consequentialist justifications are clearly ruled out under just war doctrine. More importantly, the syllogism with which Weinberger concludes his essay—that if killing the leader is permissible, then trying him is permissible—is not to the point. What is clear is that capturing an enemy commander and placing him on trial is morally and legally permissible. What is not clear is whether intentionally killing him—without benefit of trial—is permissible.

Given that the punishment rationale for extrajudicial assassination seems so obviously inapt, and given that most commentators do not want to resort to the Realist/consequentialist reasoning that Weinberger invokes, it is no surprise that most defenders of the assassination policy invoke a self-defense rationale. Thus, for example, Secretary of Defense Donald Rumsfeld reportedly told CNN that "the US would be acting in self-defense" in carrying out missions to assassinate bin Laden and other terrorists.[8] Yet even this line of argument is repeatedly conflated with nondefensive justifications. Brenda Godfrey, for example, defends Rumsfeld's position, and correctly distinguishes self-defense from backward-looking motives of reprisal or retaliation.[9] Yet she too

fails to clearly distinguish defense from forward-looking consequentialist or punishment motives. When there is an imminent threat of a terrorist attack, she argues, force is justified "in order to prevent the attack or to deter further attacks."[10] But the deterrence rationale is not obviously part of the doctrine of self-defense. Rather, deterrence belongs to the sphere of punishment and of consequentialist reasoning. Godfrey also appears to conflate the preventive use of force with the consequentialist justification that whatever leads to the best results is thereby morally permissible, as evidenced by her claim that "use of force should include the covert killing of the terrorist because it is the most efficient means of averting future harm."[11] Thomas Wingfield similarly invokes deterrence, consequentialist, and punishment rationales for assassination: "The proportionality doctrine of international law supports a conclusion that it is wrong to allow the slaughter of 10,000 relatively innocent soldiers and civilians if the underlying aggression can be brought to an end by the elimination of one guilty individual."[12] So, too, does Louis Beres confuse self-defense with consequentialism, arguing that the right of self-defense in Article 51 of the United Nations Charter authorizes assassination, given that a "utilitarian or balance-of-harms criterion could surely favor assassination" over large-scale uses of defensive force.[13]

Beres further asserts that in certain circumstances, the resort to assassination would be "decidedly rational and humane."[14] It is important to acknowledge just how tempting the idea of assassination is even from a moral standpoint. It offers a trade of a single death to avoid the death of millions, and as former White House press secretary Ari Fleischer put it, "The cost of one bullet, if the Iraqi people take it on themselves, is substantially less" than going to war.[15] The televangelist Pat Robertson recently on his television program called for the assassination of Venezuelan President Hugo Chavez, on the grounds that assassination is "a whole lot cheaper than starting a war."[16] Perhaps more pertinently, it appears to vindicate our moral sense, in that assassination goes directly after the responsible, indeed morally guilty, parties rather than after the "innocent" soldiers who in most cases are merely following orders, often under duress (as for instance in the Iraqi army). Jeff McMahan, for example, far too quickly assumes that morality favors targeting the guilty in war rather than those presenting a direct threat: "morality concedes that certain morally noninnocent noncombatants, like the political leader who initiates an unjust war, may be attacked."[17]

However, as tempting as these arguments sound, they do not in fact provide a moral basis for killing in war. Under just war doctrine, the primary justification for killing in war is defensive; it follows that neither of the aforementioned factors is morally relevant. The rationale of self-defense, as we have said, is distinct from the consequentialist or Realist rationale that aims to minimize overall costs and permits adopting any means so long as the ultimate end is permissible. Equally important, moral guilt, while it is the basis for the justification of punishment, is not the rationale for the use of defensive force. Defensive force in general is justified by the fact of aggression, not by the guilt of the aggressor. Hence soldiers may be killed even if they are not morally guilty of any wrong. "Innocence" in just war doctrine (and in self-defense doctrine generally) is a term of art, meaning one who is not presently threatening harm (from the Latin *nocere* = to harm). Thus it is crucial to understand the nature of the justification for killing and avoid conflating incompatible moral theories.

Thus we may conclude that the just war rationale for killing enemies in conflict is that the enemy poses a direct, unjust threat that can be countered by no other means than violence. While this rationale is often described as *defensive*, this term must be understood in a broad sense. That is, it is not necessarily limited to imminent or immediate threats, but can include preventive force against potential future threats. Thus the just war tradition has long recognized the legitimacy of *preventive* force against a potential future threat (assuming one has also satisfied the conditions of last resort, proportionality, and other requirements for going to war).[18] One is legitimately entitled to act so as to protect oneself against an unjust threat, even if that threat is in the future and not

yet imminent. However, it is crucial to note the distinction between the preventive rationale and the consequentialist justification. For the consequentialist, any use of force is justified so long as it leads to a net balance of good results. The just war preventive rationale, in contrast, insists that one is also constrained by a moral duty only to use harm against unjust threats. It is this distinction that accounts for why terrorism (intentionally targeting civilians for political or military purposes) is prohibited under just war doctrine, whereas terrorism in principle would be morally permissible for consequentialism. For just war doctrine, the preventive or defensive use of force must be targeted only against an unjust attacker.

Hence the question facing us, in order to determine whether assassination is permissible, is whether political or military leaders are legitimate military targets, that is, whether they are unjust attackers. It is often taken as uncontroversial and unproblematic that military leaders are legitimate military targets, given their presence in the chain of command—and sometimes this is extended to political leaders, too, so long as they direct the military. Thomas Wingfield, for instance, approvingly cites Schmitt: "lawful targeting in wartime has never required that the individual actually be engaged in combat. Rather, it depends on combatant status. The general directing operations miles from battle is as valid a target as the commander leading his troops in combat. The same applies to Saddam Hussein. Once he became a combatant, the law of war clearly permitted targeting him."[19] But, even apart from the logical leap between military commanders and heads of state, the chief error in this passage is what we might call the *formalist fallacy*. Just war doctrine indeed is often accused of formalism (sometimes called *essentialism*), of making combatancy simply determined by one's formal role, as if one can simply read off one's combatant status by identifying the essence of one's role. But this is I think a mischaracterization of just war doctrine.

Stephen Kershnar, for example, accuses the just war doctrine of holding that certain roles have "essences" that in turn determine one's status as combatant or noncombatant.[20] A doctor's essential role is to heal, a farmer's essential role is to grow food; hence they are not combatants. But a soldier's—and a military leader's—essential role is to fight, thus making him a combatant. The question of whether a political leader is a legitimate target then comes down to the question of whether his role is essentially one connected to aggression. Kershnar rightfully criticizes this view as clumsy and unconvincing. Indeed, it is not even clear in this view whether the political leader is a combatant or not. Is the nature of his role political leadership or military leadership? The formalist doctrine is also unhelpful in its application to terrorism, where there is no war and thus no combatancy in the technical sense. But it is also wrong, I would argue, because it mischaracterizes just war doctrine.

In the just war doctrine, combatancy is not determined by one's formal status, but rather by one's current and ongoing actions: that is, whether they constitute aggression or not. A soldier who lays down his weapons, or is no longer a threat, is no longer a combatant for purposes of exercising one's right to use deadly force. He may be captured, but he may not be shot. Correspondingly, a civilian who takes up arms and attempts aggressive action is a legitimate target, despite not being a combatant in the formal or essential sense. In other words, there is no avoiding a substantive analysis of the notion of combatancy. One is a combatant to the extent one is engaging in unjustified aggression; one is a noncombatant to the extent one is not a present or imminent threat. The paradigm of the combatant, then, is the soldier with the weapon pointed at you. On this view, it is not automatically true that a military leader is a combatant in the strict sense, and it is even more difficult to say whether a political leader—who is typically unarmed and not a fighter, nor himself an imminent threat—constitutes a combatant. Thus law professor Abram Chayes, appearing on *Nightline*, argued that "if Saddam was out leading his troops and he got killed in the midst of an engagement, well, that's one thing. But if he is deliberately and selectively targeted, I think that's another."[21] Chayes goes too far, for surely actual presence on the battlefield is not the only way one can constitute a direct threat. The problem, of course, is to say

just under what circumstances a leader is himself a direct threat sufficient to justify making him a legitimate military target.

But how can we answer such a question? What I would suggest is that we must resort to the substantive criteria for aggression. Jeffrie Murphy's definition of aggression provides a good starting point: "What I mean by this [i.e., aggression] is that the links of the chain (like the links between motives and actions) are held together logically and not merely causally, i.e., all held together, in this case, under the notion of who it is that is engaged in an attempt to destroy you."[22] The idea here is that the criteria are more than merely causal (or else doctors and farmers would be aggressors), but have to do with the nature of one's agency. Is one a direct agent in the unjustified aggression? Thomas Wingfield concedes that merely being a "regime elite" does not render one a legitimate target; this only applies to those members "participating in or taking an active role in directing military operations."[23] But even this is too weak. The further away we get from this paradigm case of the soldier wielding a weapon, the more suspect must be the use of force against someone. With those in a supervisory role, the presumption must be against killing them, unless their role is immediate and direct in the act of aggression. It is more plausible to consider them aggressors where it is they who are actually initiating the acts, that is, issuing orders to subordinates to carry out specific acts of violence. (It should be noted that *aggression* can refer either to external and internal violence: attacks on other countries, or unjustified attacks on one's own people, as say Hitler's policy of genocide or Hussein's use of chemical weapons on the Kurds.)

Clearly, military leaders will be far more likely to qualify as part of the direct chain of aggression than will political leaders. On this analysis, there can be no simple answer as to whether a given political leader is an aggressor, and hence a legitimate target in war. The answer will depend on the extent of involvement with the waging and oversight of the aggression, including, importantly, the extent to which he provides the initiative for the war itself, or for particular acts of aggression within it. The political structure of the society will obviously be relevant; in a dictatorship, there is far more centralized control of state functions, and thus a much stronger presumption of direct responsibility on the part of the ruler. In a democracy, in contrast, the leader may be acting as the agent of the legislature or the people in general. Even having the ultimate responsibility for giving the green light to war does not necessarily constitute the leader as an aggressor—this will depend on such factors as whether he is the initiator of the aggression or merely a figurehead. But it seems that in general political leaders are sufficiently different from military leaders such that the ordinary presumption of combatancy does not apply to the former category. Arguably Saddam Hussein was a legitimate target in that he appeared to maintain "operational control over military action"[24] and was himself directly responsible for the immediate or future potential harm. This would be even more justifiable where a leader is on the verge of ordering a nuclear strike, or authorizing an act of terrorism—assuming that he is genuinely the initiator and motivating force of the action, not merely a bureaucrat providing formal approval. It is true that in the age of modern warfare, the traditional paradigm of the target as one who is on the battlefield or even wielding a weapon is less useful, given the capacity of a political leader to order the launching of weapons of mass destruction from behind the lines (though this is not so much due to terrorism, but to the development of high technology, especially WMD). But of course the standard must be set very high here; the further removed a person is from direct control over the attack, the stronger the presumption must be against treating him as a direct threat and therefore a legitimate target.

Nonetheless, there remain serious concerns about the idea of assassination even if we decide that the leader is a legitimate target; these concerns apply to the assassination of military leaders as well as political leaders. The fact of premeditation is troublesome; in any case of homicide, premeditation often indicates a motive to kill whether or not such killing is strictly necessary. A primary moral duty with respect to any use of force is to use the minimum necessary

harm. An assassination order, or a bounty offered for the target "dead or alive," is in itself not morally permissible, because it violates this duty. Any planned assassination must be one in which killing is only a last resort; the order must be to capture alive if at all possible. (Some questions were raised, for example, about the killing of Hussein's sons: was every reasonable effort made to capture them alive?) This is to say, a premeditated killing is always suspect; the aim must be to capture if at all possible, and to kill only to prevent the target from escaping and carrying out further harm.[25]

A second concern is the danger of the slippery slope: if assassinations are permitted, will this undermine the just war limits on killing? The worry here is about breaking down the barrier between legitimate killing in self-defense or prevention of future harm (or, more controversially, punishment in the context of war crimes tribunals) versus the sort of illegitimate killing of which terrorism is a prime example, and which can simply be called *murder*. Assassination, given its premeditated character, is uncomfortably close to the side of illegitimacy. This is not necessarily a reason to reject the legitimacy of all assassinations, but it is a reason to reiterate the strict limitations on the policy. To the extent a person is in a role distant from the actual aggression itself (i.e., a supervisory role), there must be a direct connection between him and the acts of violence. A mere figurehead leader, as Wingfield suggests, is not a legitimate target, nor ordinarily is a civilian commander in a democratic state. The ordinary assumption must be that one may use defensive force only against those who are the agents threatening unjust violence. In just war doctrine, targeting of political leaders should be especially avoided. The Israeli policy of assassination of Hamas terrorist leaders has been defended on the grounds that it is designed to prevent imminent unjust attacks on civilians, that these leaders are directly responsible for planning and authorizing attacks, and that all reasonable alternatives have been exhausted (including issuing arrest warrants to Palestinian authorities, requesting extradition, etc.). To the extent these claims are true, they would seem to constitute a legitimate case of justifiable assassination.

In conclusion, it appears that the policy of assassination or targeted killing, though it raises serious moral concerns, can in some circumstances be a legitimate tool of war. However, the justification for such acts cannot be consequentialist in nature, aiming at a more "efficient" victory or at waging war "on the cheap." Much of the recent shift in opinion in favor of the use of assassination can be revealed for what it is: a newly emboldened effort of the Realists and the consequentialists to make inroads into the just war doctrine.[26] Nonetheless, the targeting of military or political leaders can in certain circumstances be a morally legitimate tool of war, justified as a preventive use of force against the initiator or controlling force of unjust aggression (even where there is not an imminent threat). Indeed, a murderous tyrant such as Hussein would seem to provide just such a case: where the political leader exerts near-total control over military and political decisions, where he is clearly the initiator of the unjust aggression, and where his capture or prevention is not possible other than by killing him. While we must reject the Realist idea that assassination is simply another tool of war to be used wherever effective, we must also reject the view that assassination is wholly prohibited under just war doctrine. It is only under very limited circumstances that the assassination of a political leader will be morally permissible.

NOTES

1. Article 23b, Annex to the Hague Convention IV (1907), prohibits "assassination, proscription, or outlawry of an enemy, or putting a price upon an enemy's head, as well as offering a reward for an enemy 'dead or alive.'"
2. Weinberger, "When Can We Target the Leaders?" *Strategic Review* (Spring 2001): 21–24, p. 23. See also Thomas Wingfield, "Taking Aim at Regime Elites," *Maryland Journal of International Law and Trade* 22 (1999): 287–317, p. 287.
3. *De Jure Belli Libri Tres* (1612), Book II Chapter VIII, in *The Classics of International Law*, trans. J. Rolfe (Oxford: Oxford University Press, 1950), 171.
4. See, e.g., Williams Banks, "Targeted Killing and Assassination: The U.S. Legal Framework," *University of Richmond Law Review* 37 (March 2003): 667–749, p. 671.
5. Ibid.
6. Weinberger, "When Can We Target the Leaders?," 22.
7. Ibid., 24.
8. Quoted in Brenda Godfrey, "Authorization to Kill Terrorist Leaders," *San Diego International Law Journal* 4 (2003): 491–512, p. 491.
9. Ibid., 501.
10. Ibid., 504.
11. Ibid.
12. Wingfield, "Taking Aim at Regime Elites," 312. Note the two distinct errors in this claim: (1) a conflation of self-defense with the punishment-based notions of guilt and innocence, and (2) a misunderstanding of the proportionality constraint as a consequentialist provision.
13. Beres, "On International Law and Nuclear Terrorism," *Georgia Journal of International and Comparative Law* 24 (1994): 1–36, p. 33.
14. Ibid.
15. See http://www.whitehouse.gov/news/releases/2002/10/20021001-4.html.
16. See, e.g., "A Call for Assassination Brings a Cry of Outrage," *Los Angeles Times*, 24 August 2005, 1.
17. McMahan, "Realism, Morality, and War," in *The Ethics of War and Peace*, ed. Terry Nardin (Princeton: Princeton University Press, 1996). 90.
18. See my "What's Wrong with Defensive War?" *Ethics and International Affairs* 19:3 (2005), for a discussion on the legitimacy of the use of preventive force in war.
19. Wingfield, "Taking Aim at Regime Elites," 314.
20. "The Moral Argument for a Policy of Assassination," paper delivered at APA Central Division Meeting, 2003. This paper has since been published in *Reason Papers* 27 (Fall 2004): 45–67.
21. Program on 4 February 1991. Wingfield dismisses Chayes's example too quickly (see Wingfield, "Taking Aim at Regime Elites," 314).
22. Murphy, "The Killing of the Innocent," in *War, Morality, and the Military Profession*, ed. Malham Wakin (Boulder: Westview Press, 1986), 346.
23. Wingfield, "Taking Aim at Regime Elites," 311.
24. Sebastien Jodoin, "The Legality of Saddam Hussein's Assassination," Part II, 3 (available at http://www.law.mcgill.ca/quid/archive/2003/03040805.html).
25. One might argue that the "dead or alive" idea means that the ultimate goal is to get the target, however necessary. Still, it implies indifference as between the two, even a veiled preference for "dead." Clearly, the moral rule requires the aim of capturing alive if at all possible.

26. See, for example, John Yoo's assertion that "a nation at war may use force against members of the enemy at any time, regardless of their proximity to hostilities or their activity at the time of attack." Yoo is believed to have authorized a Justice Department opinion justifying the use of assassinations in wartime. See Paul Barrett, "Opinion Maker: A Young Lawyer Helps Chart Shift in Foreign Policy," *Wall Street Journal*, 12 September 2005, A1.

⚜ REVIEW QUESTIONS

1. How does Kaufman describe just war doctrine?
2. How does he use the term *assassination*?
3. Kaufman distinguishes between a punishment rationale, a self-defense rationale, and a consequentialist rationale for assassination. Why does he reject both the punishment rationale and the consequentialist rationale?
4. According to Kaufman, what is the formalist fallacy? Why does it mischaracterize just war theory?
5. According to Kaufman, what two questions must be answered in the affirmative to morally justify assassination?
6. Kaufman says there are serious concerns about the idea of assassination even if the target is a combatant. What are they?
7. State and explain Kaufman's conclusion.

⚜ DISCUSSION QUESTIONS

1. Does revenge or punishment justify the assassination of Osama bin Laden? What is your view? What if killing him had good consequences, such as stopping al-Qaeda attacks on the United States? Would that morally justify killing him? Why or why not?
2. Would the assassination of Hitler have been justified at the start of World War II? Explain your position.
3. Kaufman claims that an assassination order, or a bounty offered, for a target like bin Laden "dead or alive" is not morally permissible. Do you agree? Why or why not?

Targeted Killing

DANIEL STATMAN

Daniel Statman is professor of philosophy at the University of Haifa in Haifa, Israel. He is the author of *Moral Dilemmas* (1995) and *Religion and Morality* (1995) with Avi Sagi. He is also the author of more than thirty articles in ethics.

Statman argues that targeted killing is analogous to conventional war. If a conventional war such as the British attack on the Falkland Islands is morally justified, then so is the targeted killing of al-Qaeda or Hamas leaders. In Statman's view, targeted killing is morally preferable to conventional war because fewer civilians are killed. The gravity of the terrorist threat posed by al Qaeda and Hamas, and the lack of any other option for the community to defend itself from the threat, gives the community a moral license to kill in self-defense. In addition to self-defense, Statman endorses retribution as justifying targeted killing terrorists with blood on their hands.

Source: Targeted Killing by Daniel Statman from Philosophy 9/11: Thinking About the War on Terrorism by Timothy Shanahan. Copyright © 2005 by Carus Publishing Company. Peru, IL: Open Court Publishing Company.

INTRODUCTION

The threat of terror has found the West widely unprepared to deal with it. The standard means of waging war are irrelevant to contending with this threat; tanks, jets, and submarines are helpful when confronting other tanks, jets, and submarines, not hijackers carrying knives or terrorists wearing explosive belts. The standard means of fighting crime also seem unaccommodating in the face of this threat; the chances of Interpol capturing Bin Laden and his followers and bringing them to justice are remote, as are the chances of the Israeli police arresting and trying the leaders of the Hammas and Islamic Jihad. Hence, to effectively stop terror, a different model must be sought, not the model of conventional war with its machines and tools, nor that of the police and court activities conducted against ordinary criminals. Rather, the wars against terror must adopt methods that are less common, or altogether uncommon, in conventional wars. One such method, whose legitimacy I wish to defend here, is that of targeted killings.

In choosing the term "targeted killing" rather than "assassination," I have sought to avoid the negative moral connotation that is almost inherent in the latter. If the argument of this paper is sound, then not all acts of assassination are morally wrong or, alternatively, not all acts of targeted killing are assassinations. Prior to September 11, 2001, Israel was the only country openly employing this tactic in its fight against terror, and it was strongly condemned for doing so by most of the international community, including the U.S. But since the September 11th attacks, the U.S. itself has adopted this policy in its war against Al Qaeda. In November 2002, an American Predator UAV (Unmanned Aerial Vehicle) targeted and killed an Al Qaeda activist in Yemen[1] using a technique similar to that used by the Israeli army against Hammas or Islamic Jihad activists. Furthermore, in December 2002,

The New York Times reported that "[t]he CIA is authorized to kill individuals described as 'terrorist leaders' on a list approved by the White House."[2] However, some commentators continue to believe that there is a moral difference between the Israeli and the American positions, and I will address their argument later on.

The main thesis of this article is that acceptance of the legitimacy of the killing and destruction in a conventional war necessarily entails accepting the legitimacy of targeted killings in the war against terror. In other words, a principled objection to targeted killings necessarily entails a pacifist approach to conventional war. I present this thesis and defend it in Section I. In Section II, I explore the possibility of justifying targeted killings on the basis of retribution, which, I argue, might play a more significant role in this context than usually assumed. Section III rejects a sophisticated philosophical argument against targeted killings, namely, that based on the alleged problematic implications of "named killing" for war ethics. In Section IV, I turn to the effectiveness of targeted killings and, in Section V, analyze the moral status of targeted killings in the context of conventional war. The final section summarizes the conclusions of the discussion regarding the legitimacy of targeted killing.

I. MORALITY AND WAR

I mentioned at the outset two general models for dealing with threats to vital interests: the war model and the non-war (i.e., criminal law and individual self-defense) model. In war, goes the common wisdom, soldiers of all sides are permitted to kill any soldier of the adversary, unless the latter surrenders or in limited exceptional circumstances. This permission to kill is not contingent on establishing that the soldier being killed poses any significant threat to the other side or, even assuming that he does pose such a threat, that he is morally responsible for doing so. Moreover,

[1]Walter Pincus, *U.S. Strike Kills Six in Al Qaeda; Missile Fired by Predator Drone; Key Figure in Yemen Among Dead*, Wash. Post, Nov. 5, 2002, at A1.

[2]*C.I.A. Expands Authority To Kill Qaeda Leaders*, N.Y. Times, Dec. 15, 2002, at A2.

under the principle of *jus ad bellum*, states are not required to establish the imperativeness of the interests threatened in order to justify going to war. Usually a violation of territorial sovereignty will be considered a just cause for going to war, a *casus belli*, even if the consequences of that violation for human lives and dignity might be relatively insignificant. Many believe that the British attack on the Falkland Islands was not only legally justified but also morally justified, despite the fact that the Argentinean invasion most likely would not have led to the killing of British citizens or acts of oppression. Thus: (1) states can go to war for the sake of formal sovereignty with no need to show that, beyond that formal sovereignty, any vital interests are in clear and imminent danger, and (2) once they actually do wage war, they can kill any enemy soldier, regardless of the personal danger posed by or responsibility of those being killed. Following McMahan, I shall call this view the "Orthodox View."[3]

Things are, of course, totally different, both morally and legally, in the context of the relations between individuals under criminal law and accepted rules of self-defense. To kill in self-defense, one is required to verify that the perceived attacker poses a clear and imminent danger to one's vital interests and that the attacker bears responsibility for this danger. And, of course, with respect to punishment, it can be imposed only after establishing beyond reasonable doubt that the accused did commit the alleged crime with the required *mens rea*.

It is truly puzzling that most people who endorse the strongest restrictions on killing in self-defense and the most stringent procedures and application of criminal law, often including an objection to capital punishment, subscribe to the Orthodox View with regard to the morality and legality of killing in the context of war. What is puzzling is that not only do they accept this view, but they do so with almost no reservation and with no awareness of the tension that exists between the blanket license to kill (enemy soldiers)

in war and the strict limitations on killing in a non-war context. This seems another instance of the human ability to compartmentalize, a capacity that is probably advantageous from an evolutionary point of view, but still startling whenever we face it. I am referring to the cognitive ability to allocate different judgments to the different "compartments" within which we function: home, work, politics, etc. Thus, people generally fail to notice the moral problem with many instances of killings in war even when they are fierce objectors to the death penalty, because they view the situation of war as different from the non-war context. They see war as constituting a separate sphere with its own set of rules, which are, after all, almost universally accepted. Jurists are especially vulnerable to this kind of thinking, because since international law recognizes the legitimacy of large-scale killing in war (of soldiers), it fosters the line of thought that wars are simply different than regular conflicts between individuals and are governed by different rules.

Let me leave the psychology of these conflicting attitudes to others and focus instead on the relevant normative issues. The contention that war *qua* war is simply "different" and, hence, governed by a different set of rules is merely a sophisticated (albeit more moderate) version of the realist view, according to which "*Inter arma silent leges*" ("In time of war the laws are silent"). We need to understand why this is so, how it is that human life, held so sacred in domestic law, is held in such light regard by the laws of war. Killing in war can be justified only on the basis of the same fundamental principles that guide relations between individuals outside the sphere of war. If these principles fail to provide the justification for killing in war, then the Orthodox View can be maintained only at the cost of inconsistency and with the aid of psychological mechanisms such as compartmentalization and self-deception.

Discussing the tenability of the Orthodox View is far beyond the scope of the present paper. It is, however, crucial to note that most philosophers who have addressed this topic over the last two decades have taken for granted what may be called the unity of our moral and legal thought— i.e., that the same general justifications for killing

---

[3]Jeff McMahan, *Innocence, Self-Defense, and Killing in War*, 2 J. Pol. Phil. 193 (1994).

people in non-war situations must apply to war situations as well. This assumption has led some philosophers to call into question the validity of the Orthodox View and to suggest that some modifications are, in any event, warranted. I will offer two examples of such modifications, one relating to *jus ad bellum*, the other to *jus in bello*.

The first example is in the context of the previously mentioned Falkland Islands War. The common view holds that the Argentinean invasion of the Falkland Islands was a *casus belli*; hence the U.K. was morally and legally justified in going to war. Yet, according to Richard Norman, the war was unjustified as it was waged for the sake of formal sovereignty alone.[4] Just as in the case of individual self-defense, the mere formal violation of rights (for example, property rights) is not sufficient to justify killing another human being. Violation of territorial sovereignty can justify going to war only if it threatens substantive values such as life, dignity, or the survival of a culture and, of course, when there is no other way of protecting such values. Thus, the common view regarding the conditions that justify going to war tends to be overly lax.

The second example is the stance taken by Jeff McMahan. Arguing against the Orthodox View, he defends what he calls the "Moral View," under which a combatant's moral innocence or guilt is determined, in part, by whether or not he is fighting in a just war. If his war is unjust and if he is not forced to take part in it, he cannot claim a moral right to kill enemy soldiers on the basis of self-defense.[5] This conclusion, which makes a lot of moral sense, runs counter to a widespread convention of *jus in bello*, namely, that all combatants are "morally equal."

These two examples illustrate what happens to the ethics of war once one takes seriously the requirement to square the moral rules concerning war with those regulating relations in non-war situations. If the moral rationale for going to war is self-defense, then the same conditions that govern self-defense on the individual level must

do so at the level of nations too, in particular: (1) the rule that what is defended is either one's life or something close to it in value and (2) the rule that the attacker's responsibility is highly relevant in making him the object of killing in self-defense.

With this brief introduction in mind, we can now move to wars against terror.[6] Let me start by asking, What entitles the U.S. to define its campaign against Al Qaeda as war, with the loosening of various moral prohibitions implied by such a definition, rather than as a police enforcement action aimed at bringing a group of criminals to justice? The answer here—as with conventional war—lies in: (a) the gravity of the threat posed by Al Qaeda and (b) the impracticality of coping with this threat by conventional law-enforcing institutions and methods. The threat posed by Al Qaeda to the U.S. is enormous. It is not only a threat to the lives of thousands of people, Americans and others, but also the threat of the terrorizing results of such mass killing on the entire country in terms of the economy and the quality of day-to-day life. A war of terror does not mean that all citizens are under actual attack all the time, but that such attacks are frequent enough and devastating enough to make life unbearable. As Hobbes observed, being in a state of war does not mean that there are battles all the time, but, rather, a miserable condition in which

> there is no place for industry; because the fruit thereof is uncertain: and consequently no culture of the earth; no navigation, nor use of the commodities that might be imported by sea . . . no account of time; no arts; no letters; no society; and which is worst of all, continual fear, and danger of violent death; and the life of man, solitary, poor, nasty, brutish, and short.[7]

Clearly enough, condition (a) applies *a fortiori* to the situation to which Israel is subject in what the Palestinians call the *Alaqsa Intifada*, whose main characteristic is almost daily attempts

---

[4]Richard Norman, *Ethics, Killing and War*, 156–58 (1995).
[5]McMahan, *supra* note 3. *Cf.* Norman, *supra* note 4, at 172–73.

[6]I say "wars against terror" rather than "the war against terror" because I see no reason to regard the various actual or potential wars against terror as part of one big war against one defined enemy.
[7]Thomas Hobbes, *Leviathan*, pt. 1, ch. 13, at 84 (J.C.A. Gaskin ed., Oxford Univ. Press 1996) (1651).

at murdering Jews across Israel, in buses, restaurants, nightclubs, universities, wherever possible. If ever there could be a *casus belli* on grounds of self-defense, it is such a terror campaign launched against a country or some other collective. From a moral point of view, the values under threat in such cases are far more important than those involved in cases of a mere formal violation of sovereignty, which, under the common view, justify waging war. To make the point as clear as possible, if the United Kingdom was morally justified in waging war to regain control over the Falkland Islands when there was no threat to the lives of British citizens and no significant threat to their security or economy, then surely the U.S. is morally justified in going to war against Bin Laden to prevent another attack against it, an attack that could cause the loss of many innocent lives and have catastrophic effects on the life of the nation. And if the U.S. is justified in going to war after only one (awful) day of terror, Israel certainly has the right to do so after so many dark days of terror.

The second condition mentioned above for regarding a situation as war rather than as a law-enforcement operation, namely, the impracticality of coping with the threat by means of conventional law-enforcing institutions and methods, is met in the case of the U.S. campaign against Al Qaeda as well as in the case of the Israeli struggle with the Palestinian terror organizations. The proposition that Al Qaeda members could be prevented from carrying out further terror attacks by issuing an arrest order to the governments harboring them, is, at best, naïve, and the same is true with regard to the thousands of Palestinians involved in planning and executing murderous actions in Israel. Things might have been different had the Palestinian Authority and its police cooperated with Israel in capturing the criminals and bringing them to justice. But this, of course, is pure wishful thinking. The Palestinian Authority not only refrained from arresting terrorists and, in general, from taking action against terror; it actually supported it in various ways.[8]

If we are to accept that the struggle against Al Qaeda and, likewise, that against the Palestinian armed organizations can be described as war, it follows that just as the U.S. can use lethal means to kill Al Qaeda members, so Israel can do so to kill Hammas or Tanzim members—just like in conventional war. Yet, while in conventional wars, enemy combatants are identified by their uniform and are located in camps, bases, and bunkers separate from the civilian population, in wars of terror, the fighters hide amongst the civilian population, which shelters them and supports them by various means. Hence, the latter wars do not take the conventional form of soldiers from one side of the conflict fighting directly against soldiers from the other side in an open space—in trenches, in the air, or at sea, remote from civilian life. Indeed, they take a rather different form. If we are to continue to adhere to the fundamental idea of just war theory, namely, that wars are fought between combatants only and should avoid targeting non-combatants, we must conclude that in wars against terror, too, the combatants of the terrorized country may direct their weapons only at members and activists in the terror organizations against which they are fighting.

To complete the analogy between conventional wars and wars against terror, we can assume that just as all soldiers (but only soldiers) are legitimate targets in the former, regardless of their individual roles, the threat they pose as individuals, or their personal responsibility in the waging or conducting of the war, so in the latter all members of the relevant terror organizations are legitimate targets and can be killed by the terrorized side on the basis of the latter's right to self-defense. Moreover, members of terrorist organizations bear far greater moral responsibility for their actions than soldiers in conventional wars, because many of the latter are conscripts forced to participate in the war, whereas joining a terror organization is usually a more voluntary act.

The problem, of course, is that terrorists do not come out into the open to fight against the armed forces of the other side, but, rather, hide amongst the civilian population and use the homes of families and friends as bases in planning

---

[8]For the deep involvement of the Palestinian Authority in terror, see, e.g., Ronen Bergman, Authority Given (2002) (Hebrew).

and executing their attacks. But the fact that civilians are the shield behind which terrorists hide should not be grounds for granting the latter some sort of immunity from attack. If they use their homes as terror bases, they cannot claim that these bases must be regarded as innocent civilian buildings. If soldiers in a conventional war hide in a residential building and shoot through its windows at enemy soldiers, there is no dispute that the latter are justified in using snipers to target and kill the former. Thus, if in a war against terror, terrorists establish their base in a residential area from where they launch murderous attacks (dispatching suicide terrorists or firing artillery), the other side is justified in using snipers, helicopters, and other methods to target and kill the terrorists.

Targeted killing, then, emerges as the most natural manifestation of *jus in bello* in wars on terror, for under *jus in bello*, even if a war is unjust, it should be directed (to as great an extent as possible) only at combatants. This implies that wars against terror should be directed (to as great an extent as possible) only at terrorists. However, unlike enemy soldiers in conventional wars, terrorists are embedded amidst the civilian population and can be hit only (or mainly) in their homes, cars, and so forth. Thus, targeted killing is the most natural application of the principles of *jus in bello* in wars against terror.[9]

The moral legitimacy of targeted killing becomes even clearer when compared to the

alternative means of fighting terror—that is, the massive invasion of the community that shelters and supports the terrorists in an attempt to catch or kill the terrorists and destroy their infrastructure. This mode of operation was adopted, for example, by the U.S. and Britain in Afghanistan and by Israel in its "Operation Defensive Shield" carried out after the terrorist Passover massacre in March 2002. While many claim this method to be morally preferable to targeted killing—likely because it bears more of a resemblance to "real" war—I believe the opposite to be true. First, invading a civilian area inevitably leads to the deaths and injury of far more people, mostly innocent people, than careful use of targeted killing. Second, such actions bring death, misery, and destruction to people who are only minimally involved (if at all) in, or responsible for, terror or military attacks, whereas with targeted killing, collateral damage is significantly reduced (though not prevented altogether). Hence, targeted killing is the preferable method not only because, on a utilitarian calculation, it saves lives—a very weighty moral consideration—but also because it is more commensurate with a fundamental condition of justified self-defense, namely, that those killed are responsible for the threat posed. Members of the Hammas in Gaza are far more responsible for the threat of terror to Israel than their non-activist neighbors are; hence it is preferable from a moral standpoint to target the former directly rather than invade Gaza and inevitably cause great injury to the latter and to the general population.

Let me press this last point a bit further. Suppose that Arafat were to call a special meeting of the Palestinian government and formally declare war on Israel by all means available. Suppose further that in the wake of this declaration, Israel were to face a wave of terror identical to that it faced in the months preceding Operation Defensive Shield. Surely no one would question Israel's right to wage war in return, that is, to invade the Gaza Strip and the West Bank and fight against its enemy, though such an operation would claim the lives of many people bearing no, or only minimal, responsibility for the terror wreaked on Israel. How could such an operation be considered

[9]Some critics totally deny the fundamental distinction made by just war theory and international law between combatants and non-combatants and, hence, see nothing wrong in principle with acts of terrorism. A notorious example is Ted Honderich, *After the Terror* 151 (2002), who explicitly states that "the Palestinians have exercised a moral right in their terrorism against the Israelis . . . those who have killed themselves in the cause of their people have indeed sanctified themselves." Obviously, if indiscriminate killing of children is a legitimate means of achieving political aims, then targeting killing is even more so. Hence, targeted killing cannot be morally objected to on the ground of constituting an illegitimate means of warfare. Views such as Honderich's thus *reduce* the arguments available to opponents of targeted killing. For a critical analysis of his view, see Tamar Meisels, *The Trouble With Terror* (2003) (unpublished manuscript, on file with author).

morally justified, yet the measure of killing fewer people and only those more active in and responsible for the terror (namely, targeted killing) be less justified or even unjustified?

To conclude, it is my claim that there is a profound inconsistency in, on the one hand, accepting the legitimacy of killing in conventional war but, on the other, making a moral objection to targeted killing in wars against terror. If, as Georg Nolte emphasizes, "the right to life must be protected most strictly,"[10] it is, indeed, understandable that he would have qualms with regard to the killing of terrorist leaders or activists. However, it is then puzzling how he can accept large-scale killing in a war of human beings, i.e., soldiers (e.g., in Afghanistan[11]), whose personal responsibility for the waging of the war and whose direct threat to the other side are, at best, uncertain.

II. TARGETED KILLING AND RETRIBUTION

In a recent article on targeted killing, Steven David argues that the best moral justification for Israel's policy of targeted killing is retribution.[12] The argument is a simple and straightforward one: Those people targeted committed terrible crimes. Evildoers deserve to suffer in response and in a way suited to their crimes. Palestinian terrorists with blood on their hands therefore deserve death, the ultimate punishment for their crimes. Hence, the targeted killing of these terrorists is justified.

One could object to this argument by claiming that acts of retribution can be imposed only by a court of justice, within whose authority it is to punish and only after establishing the relevant facts of the case and the blameworthiness of the defendant. Retribution cannot be imposed by private individuals, nor by governments, but only by legal institutions.

But this objection must be wrong. First, for those who accept the idea of retribution,[13] the legal institution of punishment is the best means of achieving it, but not a necessary condition for its possibility. For retribution to apply, evildoers need to suffer, and this can be imposed by God, by Nature—or by some human being. No doubt there are powerful social and moral reasons for making the courts the only body that administers retribution in society, but these reasons bear no relevance on the justification of retribution per se, which, in principle, can be achieved outside the courtroom too. In the case of terrorists, the problem that arises is that retribution through the legal system is not an option with regard to most of them, because the countries that harbor them hardly ever bring them to trial within their territories, nor do they extradite them to be tried in a foreign domestic or international court. Since in such cases, retribution through the legal system is unfeasible, and if we take seriously the idea that evildoers deserve punishment, the inevitable conclusion is that retribution can, or must,[14] be imposed by some other entity, such as the army of the injured country.

Second, the role of courts in establishing the facts of the matter and the blameworthiness of the alleged criminal seems less significant in the context of terrorists because many of them are only too happy to admit their participation in the

---

[10]Georg Nolte, *Preventive Use of Force and Preventive Killings: Moves into a Different Legal Order*, 5 Theoretical Inquiries L. 111 (2004).

[11]*Id.* at [9–10], where Nolte concedes that "Taliban and Al Qaeda fighters could be killed by U.S. and other troops in Afghanistan as long as the United States was exercising its right of self-defence against organized and identified resistance in Afghanistan." Yet that this was a case of exercising the right of self-defense is exactly what needs to be established, and in any case, it does not imply that each individual Taliban fighter was a legitimate target.

[12]Steven R. David, *Israel's Policy of Targeted Killing*, 17 J. Ethics & Int'l Aff. 111 (2003).

[13]Needless to say, not everybody does. *See, e.g.*, David Dolinko, *Three Mistakes of Retributivism*, 39 UCLA L. Rev. 1623 (1992).

[14]I wish to take a neutral stance between the "hard" and "soft" views of retributivism. Under the former view, we have a moral duty to impose upon evildoers what they deserve, while under the latter, we are merely allowed to do so. For the purpose of the present argument, the weaker version is sufficient, because my central aim is to show that targeted killing is morally acceptable, not that it is morally mandatory.

relevant crimes or their active membership and roles in the relevant organizations.

In conventional wars, when the enemy upholds the conventions of war, retribution is irrelevant with regard to individual soldiers, and hence self-defense provides the only framework for justifying killing them. In wars against terror, retribution offers a justificatory framework that complements and bolsters the self-defense justification. Thus, killing enemy combatants in wars on terror—namely, activists in the terror organizations—is, if anything, more, and not less, justified than killing enemy combatants in conventional wars. . . .

SUMMARY AND CONCLUSIONS

The purpose of this paper is to provide a philosophical defense of targeted killing in wars against terror. It argues that if one accepts the moral legitimacy of the large-scale killing of combatants in conventional wars, one cannot object on moral grounds to the targeted killing of members of terrorist organizations in wars against terror. If one rejects this legitimacy, one must object to all killing in war, targeted and non-targeted alike, and thus not support the view, which is criticized here, that targeted killing is particularly disturbing from a moral point of view.

Defining a conflict as war, with the moral license to kill entailed thereby, is not an arbitrary decision. It has to do with the gravity of the threat to the vital interests of a given community and the absence of any other option for this community to defend itself against this threat. Under this understanding, certain conventional wars, such as the Falkland Islands War, do not justify the above license to kill, whereas certain unconventional wars, such as that waged against Al Qaeda, do. Moreover, the perception of a conflict as war and the legitimacy of using lethal measures in that conflict do not depend on the nature of the aggressor's motivation, be it national, religious, or otherwise, unless that motivation happens to affect the severity of the threat or the availability of non-war methods for coping with it.

Regarding the effectiveness of targeted killing in wars against terror, here, too, we can draw an analogy to conventional wars. Fighting armies do their best to choose effective measures, i.e., measures that will contribute to the defeat of their enemy. But very rarely will they be criticized, prospectively or retrospectively, on the grounds that ineffective actions caused the unnecessary deaths of enemy soldiers. Applied to targeted killing, this means that its effectiveness should concern us morally no more than the effectiveness of methods used or actions taken in conventional wars. At any rate, in most cases and in the long run, there is no convincing evidence that targeted killing is an ineffective means in fighting terror.

Finally, objectors to targeted killing (and to other anti-terrorism methods) often warn of overestimating the danger posed by terror and of hastening to use violent solutions instead of seeking a peacefully diplomatic solution. They urge the attacked country or collective to "understand" the roots of terror, implying that once these roots are understood and dealt with in a peaceful and constructive manner, the terror will vanish with no need for war. There is something to be said for these warnings. Yet, just as there is a danger of overestimating threats of terror, there is also a danger of underestimating them. Just as there is a danger of overlooking possible peaceful solutions and rushing to use force, there is also a danger of over-delaying the use of force due to false hopes for peaceful avenues. The atrocities in the former Yugoslavia in the 1990s provide us with a painful reminder of the toll in innocent lives that hesitation to use force to counter aggression can take.[15] The argument developed in this paper contends that with organizations such as Al Qaeda and the Hammas, the danger of over-delaying the use of force is more alarming than the prospect of missing out on peaceful solutions. Those who hold the opposite view and are more optimistic about human nature than I am are, of course, to be respected. But—one last time—I think their view applies, *a fortiori*, to conventional wars too.

---

[15]See, for example, Jonathan Glover, *Humanity: A Moral History of the 20th Century* at ch. 16, at 133–40 (2001), who argues that "the UN would have been more effective from the start if it had come closer to wielding Leviathan's power." *Id.* at 140.

⚜ REVIEW QUESTIONS

1. Statman distinguishes between two models for dealing with threats. What are they?
2. According to Statman, what is the Orthodox View of war? Why does he find this view puzzling?
3. How do Richard Norman and Jeff McMahan modify the Orthodox View?
4. Why does Statman think that the U.S. campaign against al Qaeda and Israel's attacks on Hamas are justified wars rather than police actions?
5. In what ways are conventional wars and wars against terror analogous, according to Statman? How are they not analogous?
6. Why does Statman think that targeted killing is morally legitimate? Why does he think it is morally preferable to conventional war?
7. What is Steven David's moral justification for targeted killing? Why does he accept it?

⚜ DISCUSSION QUESTIONS

1. Statman says that the threat posed by al Qaeda to the United States is enormous. Do you agree? If so, then why have there been no attacks on the United States since 2001?
2. Are wars against terror analogous to conventional wars? Why or why not?
3. Statman claims that targeted killing is morally preferable to conventional war. Do you agree? Why or why not?
4. Does retribution justify the targeted killing of Palestinian terrorists? Why or why not?

PROBLEM CASES

1. Osama bin Laden

In 1998 the CIA identified bin Laden as the leader of the al-Qaeda terrorist organization responsible for suicide bombing attacks on the U.S. embassies in Tanzania and Kenya. There were hundreds of casualties. A few days after the attacks, the CIA learned that bin Laden was scheduled to visit a terrorist training camp in Afghanistan. President Clinton ordered missile strikes to assassinate bin Laden and other leaders in retaliation. On August 20, 1998, about seventy-five cruise missiles hit four terrorist training camps in or near Khost, a city in eastern Afghanistan. The Khost camp, Zawhar Kili, was believed to be a meeting place for terrorist leaders, including bin Laden. After the attack, the CIA found out that bin Laden had indeed been at the Zawhar Kili camp, but had left an hour or so before the missiles hit. According to Pakistani journalist Ahmed Rashid, the air strikes killed twenty Afghans, seven Pakistanis, and seven others.

Ten years later, on August 20, 2008, newly declassified government documents were posted on the National Security Archive (www.nsarchive.org), which suggest that the 1998 air strikes not only failed to kill bin Laden but also helped al Qaeda and the Taliban in some ways. In particular, it is claimed that the attacks "provoked a new round of terrorist bombing plots," added to bin Laden's reputation "as an underdog standing firm in the face of bullying aggression," and resulted in the United States losing the moral high ground by imitating bin Laden's strategy of bombing in retaliation for grievances. Also, the attacks did not destroy or disrupt al Qaeda or the Taliban; they became even stronger and more effective after the attacks. Nevertheless, the attacks demonstrated U.S. military might and resolve to fight against terrorism. Also, the attacks may have deterred some terrorists and nations harboring terrorists.

All things considered, were these air strikes morally justified? Why or why not?

For the sake of argument, suppose the missile strikes had killed bin Laden. Three years later, maybe the attacks of 9/11 would not have happened. Bin Laden was central in planning the attacks. He came up with the plan to use commercial planes. He chose Muhammad Atta to be the leader of the terrorist attack team. He selected the targets, and he micromanaged the timing. However, if bin Laden had been killed in 1998, Ayman al-Zawahiri, his second-in-command, might have taken over the planning with the result that the 9/11 attacks would still have happened. We cannot be sure about the consequences of bin Laden's death.

If bin Laden had been killed in 1998 by the missile strikes, would those attacks have been morally acceptable? What is your view?

2. Ahmed Yassin

In 2004, Israeli helicopters killed Ahmed Yassin (age sixty-seven) with a missile strike. Yassin was leaving a mosque in Gaza city in his wheelchair when he was hit. The first missile hit him directly, leaving his body severely disfigured. Seven other people were killed in the attack, and another seventeen were injured, including two of Yassin's sons.

Yassin was a founder and leader of Hamas, the Palestinian organization that rules the Gaza portion of the Palestinian Territories. (In 2007, it won a large majority in the Palestinian parliament, and it has popular support in the Gaza Strip.) Hamas was created in 1987 by Yassin and two others at the beginning of the First Intifada, the popular uprising against Israeli rule in the Palestinian Territories. At the time of the assassination of Yassin, the United States and other countries classified Hamas as a terrorist organization because of its responsibility for numerous suicide bombings against Israelis.

The assassination of Yassin was condemned by Yasser Arafat, the Palestinian leader, as a "barbaric crime." In London, prime minister Tony Blair also condemned the killing. Hamas and other militant groups warned of more violence in retaliation. An estimated 200,000 mourners turned out for Yassin's funeral procession in Gaza.

Was Yassin's assassination by Israel morally justified? Why or why not?

3. Fidel Castro

(See Fabian Escalante, *Executive Action: 638 Ways to Kill Castro* [New York: Ocean Press, 2006].) Fabian Escalante was the head of the Cuban secret service. In his book he describes more than 600 ways in which the CIA tried to assassinate Fidel Castro, the Cuban dictator. The assassination attempts began in 1959 after the Cuban revolution and continued for nearly half a century. Perhaps the most famous was the loaded-cigar plot, in which the CIA planned to treat a box of cigars with a chemical that would explode when the cigar was lit. Another scheme was to give Castro a skin-diving suit dusted with a fungus that would produce a disabling skin disease and to contaminate the breathing apparatus with the bacterium that causes tuberculosis. Another idea was to booby-trap a seashell that would explode when the seashell was lifted; it was to be planted in an area where Castro was known to frequently skin-dive. Still another plot was to have poison pills delivered to a restaurant where Castro liked to eat. This plot involved Mafia figures Sam Giancani, Santos Trafficante, and Jonny Rosseli, who had contacts in Havana from the pre-Castro days.

These assassination attempts became public knowledge in 1975 when Senator Frank Church conducted hearings on "Alleged Assassination Plots Involving Foreign Leaders." In addition to the attempts to assassinate Castro, the hearings revealed attempts to assassinate other foreign leaders, including Patrice Lumumba of the Congo, Rafael Trujillo of the Dominican Republic, and Rene Schneider of Chile. As chair of the commission, Church famously described the CIA as a "rogue elephant rampaging out of control."

The assassination attempts on Castro were illegal. Were they morally justified? Explain your answer.

4. Salah Shehada

Hamas leader Salah Shehada (age forty) was killed in July 2002 when an Israeli F-16 jet dropped a one-ton bomb on an apartment building in the Gaza Strip where Shehada was living. The explosion caused the building to collapse and damaged several buildings nearby. Shehada was killed, along with fourteen other Palestinians, including several children. Palestinian doctors claimed that 154 civilians were injured as well.

Shehada was on Israel's most-wanted list at the time of his assassination. Israel claimed that he was directly responsible for hundreds of attacks on Israeli citizens and security forces. He was one of the founders of Hamas (along with Ahmed Yassin) and had spent some fifteen years as a Palestinian military leader.

Hamas reacted to the attack by calling it a massacre and vowing to take revenge against Israeli targets. President George W. Bush denounced the hit as "heavy-handed." Human rights organizations around the world criticized the attack, saying that intentionally dropping a one-ton bomb in the middle of the night on a crowded civilian neighborhood amounted to a war crime.

In 2005, a lawsuit was filed by the Center for Constitutional Rights. It alleged that Avraham Dichter, the military commander in charge of the operation against Shehada, had planned the assassinations of more than 300 Palestinian leaders and caused the deaths or injuries of hundreds of innocent bystanders. The lawsuit noted that assassination is illegal under international law.

In 2008, an Israeli commission said that the attack on Shehada did not involve the premeditated intention to kill civilians, and that the commanders did not know innocent people were in the building that was hit. If this is true, was the attack morally justified? Explain your answer.

It seems unlikely that the building occupied by Shehada in the middle of the night housed no one else. It seems safe to assume that there were innocent people in the building, and that the commanders of the attack knew this. Was the dropping of a one-ton bomb on the apartment building still morally justified? Why or why not?

SUGGESTED READINGS

Storming Media (www.stormingmedia.us) has abstracts of Pentagon reports on targeted killing defending it as legitimate military action against unlawful enemy combatants. The Federation of American Scientists (www.fas.org) has reports on assassinations and defenses of targeted killing by members of the military. The Brookings website (www.brookings.edu) has reports and articles on assassination and targeted killing. The Hoover Institute (www.hoover.org) has reports on assassination and targeted killing. The CIA website (www.cia.gov) has information on drones, missiles, and terrorists. Amnesty International (www.amnesty.org) has reports on assassinations by Israel and others; they are condemned as illegal and immoral. Assassinology (www.assassinology.org) examines assassination in detail—facts, people killed, conspiracies, and news. The *Stanford Encyclopedia of Philosophy* (http://plato.stanford.edu) has an interesting article on "The Problem of Dirty Hands" by Tony Coady.

Mark Bowden, *Killing Pablo* (New York: Atlantic Monthly Press, 2001), describes the assassination of cocaine trafficker Pablo Escobar on December 2, 1993, by a Delta Force sniper. The Delta Force is an elite Department of Defense group engaged in covert missions.

Stephen de Wijze, "Targeted Killing: A 'Dirty Hands' Analysis,'" *Contemporary Politics* 15, no. 3 (September 2009): 305–320, argues that targeted killing is neither entirely morally justified nor completely wrong. Rather, those who do it have "dirty hands," that is, they have done something wrong in order to do right.

Steven de Wijze, "Tragic Remorse—The Anguish of Dirty Hands," *Ethical Theory and Moral Practice* 7, no. 5 (January 2005): 453–471, explains and defends the moral emotion of tragic remorse that results from unavoidable wrongdoing.

Peter M. Cullen, "The Role of Targeted Killing in the Campaign against Terror," *Joint Force Quarterly* 48 (2008, 1st Quarter): 22–29, gives a careful discussion of the legality and morality of targeted killing of terrorists. He concludes that it is an effective tactic in the campaign against terror.

Ward Thomas, "Norms and Security," *International Security* 25, no. 1 (Summer 2000): 105–133, makes a case against international assassination, especially when the target is a national leader.

Jane Mayer, "The Predator War," *New Yorker* 85, no. 34 (October 26, 2009): 36–45, discusses the risks of the CIA covert drone program, noting that the program has carried out targeted assassinations without arousing controversy.

Scott Shane, "CIA Expanding Drone Assaults Inside Pakistan," *The New York Times*, December 4, 2009, reports on the increased CIA drone or Predator attacks inside Pakistan's tribal areas. Included are quotes from the CIA defending the covert program, which is described as one of Washington's "worst-kept secrets."

Harold Zeller, ed., *Assassination* (Cambridge, MA: Schenkman Publishing, 1974). This is a collection of articles on assassination by well-known philosophers. James Rachels defends the hypothetical assassination of Hitler, while Douglas Lackey argues that it would not have been morally justified because we cannot be sure of the consequences.

Michael L. Gross, "Assassination and Targeted Killing," *Journal of Applied Philosophy* 23, no. 3 (2006): 323–335, discusses the attempt to justify targeted killing by appealing to self-defense and law enforcement. He argues that the only possible way to justify named killing is self-defense.

Paul McGeough, *Kill Khalid* (New York: New Press, 2009), describes the attempted assassination of Hamas leader Kalid Mishal by Mossad, the Israeli secret service. They tried to poison him in 1997 when he was taking his sons for a haircut. Mishal became a Hamas hero, the martyr who did not die.

David Kretzmer, "Targeted Killing of Suspected Terrorists," *European Journal of International Law* 16, no. 2 (2005): 171–212, discusses the legality of targeted killing of suspected terrorists under international human rights law and international humanitarian law. Under the former system, such killings are lawful only if done to prevent an imminent attack. Under the latter system, the killings may be lawful if the suspected terrorists are viewed as combatants.

Steven R. David, "Israel's Policy of Targeted Killing," *Ethics and International Affairs* 17, no. 1 (Spring 2003): 111–126, argues that Israel's policy of hunting down and killing alleged Palestinian terrorists is legal, but raises doubts about its effectiveness because it exacerbated murderous retaliation against Israeli civilians, unmasked several informers, diverted intelligence resources, and drew international condemnation. The benefits include deterring some attacks and satisfying the desire for revenge and retribution.

Yael Stein, "By Any Name Illegal and Immoral: Response to 'Israel's Policy of Targeted Killing,'" *Ethics and International Affairs* 17, no. 1 (Spring 2003): 127–137, argues that the Israeli policy of killing suspected terrorists is illegal and immoral. The targets are civilians, not combatants. Revenge and retribution can serve to justify acts that are both illegal and immoral.

Steven R. David, "If Not Combatants, Certainly Not Civilians," *Ethics and International Affairs* 17, no. 1 (Spring 2003): 138–140, replies to Stein. Stein sees Palestinian terrorists as civilian noncombatants not engaged in war. David thinks they are combatants who seek to kill as many Israeli civilians as possible, and that Israel has the right and obligation to defend itself.

INDEX